SHAKESPEAREAN CONCEPTS

Also by Simon Trussler

THEATRE AT WORK
with Charles Marowitz

BURLESQUE PLAYS OF THE EIGHTEENTH CENTURY

EIGHTEENTH CENTURY COMEDY

JOHN OSBORNE
Writers and Their Work

THE PLAYS OF JOHN OSBORNE: AN ASSESSMENT

THE PLAYS OF ARNOLD WESKER: AN ASSESSMENT
with Glenda Leeming

THE PLAYS OF JOHN WHITING: AN ASSESSMENT

THE PLAYS OF HAROLD PINTER: AN ASSESSMENT

JOHN ARDEN
Columbia Essays on Modern Writers

A CLASSIFICATION FOR THE PERFORMING ARTS

EDWARD BOND
Writers and Their Work

ROYAL SHAKESPEARE COMPANY
An Annual Record of the Year's Work
1978 to 1985

NEW THEATRE VOICES OF THE SEVENTIES

Shakespearean Concepts

a dictionary of
terms and conventions
influences and institutions
themes, ideas, and genres
in the Elizabethan and Jacobean drama

SIMON TRUSSLER

METHUEN

A Methuen Dramabook

First published in Great Britain in 1989
by Methuen Drama
Michelin House, 81 Fulham Road, London SW3 6RB
and distributed in the United States of America
by HEB Inc., 70 Court Street, Portsmouth
New Hampshire 03801, USA

Typeset in 10 on 11 pt Times
by L. Anderson Typesetting
Woodchurch, Kent TN26 3TB

Printed in Great Britain
by Richard Clay Ltd, Bungay, Suffolk

To Laverne
with love and gratitude

British Library Cataloguing in Publication Data

Trussler, Simon
Shakespearean Concepts
1. Drama in English
Shakespeare, William, 1564-1616, Critical Studies
I. Title
822.3'3
ISBN 0-413-15940-X cased
ISBN 0-413-61980-X paperback

Introduction

Let me begin at the beginning, by explaining my title: *Shakespearean Concepts.* 'Shakespearean' is intended to denote not a person but a period — which is, very roughly, that of Shakespeare's working life and some little way beyond, from the late 1580s to the slow drift of the Elizabethan and Jacobean drama into the Caroline twilight of the 1630s. But perhaps the concept of 'concepts' might best be approached, with due caution, by suggesting what it is *not* meant to embrace.

In my childhood I possessed an encyclopedia which divided its subject matter neatly into four volumes, called *People*, *Places*, *Things*, and *Ideas*. Let me recycle those convenient facets: my little dictionary does *not* generally include entries for the people of the Elizabethan and Jacobean theatre, nor for the places in which they acted, nor yet for the 'things' — the plays — they performed. Instead, it attempts to deal with the ideas (and all those influences upon and products of ideas within the catchment-area of my sub-title) which shaped the world in which Shakespeare and his contemporaries lived. So a few people *will* be found included — from Aristotle and Seneca to Calvin and Montaigne — not as the subjects of mini-biographies, but as the propagators of influential ideas or modes of behaviour. So will a few places, whether countries like Italy or resorts in London such as the Inns of Court or Whitehall — not primarily as subjects for geographical or even historical location, but in an attempt to suggest what their importance and their associations would have been for the playwright or theatregoer of the day. As for things . . . well, not plays or playhouses, but a few seminal works of literature or polemic, and some of the nooks and crannies and conventions of the theatres, when these affected the way the Elizabethans and their successors perceived the plays they saw, and the way they were performed.

While my emphases in these entries on 'people', 'places', and 'things' may sometimes be new, other reference works covering the period do deal with such aspects of Shakespeare's theatre and his world: but very few deal even perfunctorily with *ideas,* and it is in this area that I hope this dictionary reaches the parts that others have ignored. Certainly, I first felt the lack of a book along these lines way back in my own student days in the early 'sixties, when, after a first-year lecture on Marlowe, I searched in vain — first among the literary reference works, then in the revered columns of the great *Oxford English Dictionary* — for the sense in which the lecturer had just used the word 'virtue'. If he had pronounced it in a way that suggested an alternative spelling, my ear did not catch the subtlety, any more than my eye was caught by the one reference in the *OED* which would have solved my problem: indeed, I could only have spotted the definition I needed if I had known it already. Appropriately, *Catch 22* was very much in fashion at the time.

When, after a good many years as a sort of free-lance theatrologue, I found myself teaching in a university, I had somehow got to know what 'virtù' meant, but I well recognized my own students' puzzlement when told that Tamburlaine displayed it. And still it didn't seem to be in the works of reference. Then I began noting just how many of the words used in the learned books and articles to which we were hopefully directing our students' attention were, in truth, part of the jargon of the theatrical or critical trades, and would either merely mystify the average first-year undergraduate, or be understood in a sense other than that intended. I began to pounce upon such words when I found myself using them in seminars, and to underline them in my reading. Soon, I had so far systematized myself as to jot them all down on separate sheets of paper, scribbling notes and definitions and clarifications as they occurred to me, then shuffling everything first into some sort of subject order, so as to fill a few of the obvious gaps, and finally into an alphabetic sequence. Then the real work began — of trying to give balance and some sort of stylistic consistency to what it was now clear had stretched beyond my early vision of a handy little booklet of a few dozen pages, and which my publisher encouraged me to think might have a wider use. However, I readily acknowledge the somewhat pragmatic and *ad hoc* way in which the book has come about, and know that in consequence gaps are sure to remain. Suggestions for filling them in any second edition will be most welcome.

It became clear quite early on that, although my original intention had been to clarify terms which related specifically to the Elizabethan and Jacobean world, it would be needful also to include some of the vocabulary of contemporary critical theory, if writing *about* the period was to be adequately understood. From the perspective of a Department of Drama rather than of English Literature, I also had to confess that I was often myself mystified by some to the terminology of the movements that had sprung up — or rather begun belatedly to lap these shores — since my own student days. What *was* 'deconstruction', anyway? Apparently, I was actually putting it into practice. So I found myself having to get to grips with terms like 'structuralism' and 'semiotics', which, although they *were* in some of the reference books, again too often seemed to have been defined for people who already knew what they meant. To those who already do know what they mean, my definitions will no doubt seem reductive and inadequate. I can only say that I often feel that way myself.

So I make no claim to originality of scholarship in this work, but only to having found a new way of assembling, conspectively and synthetically, the fruits of the scholarship of others. This is not to say I have been able (or would have wished) entirely to exclude my personal opinions from my definitions: what I *have* tried to do is to make clear which is which. And, of course, the coverage of this volume does overlap with other titles in the field, to some of which I have been particularly indebted. Clearly, such earlier guides to the world of the Shakespearean theatre as F. E. Halliday's *A Shakespeare Companion* (1964) and Stanley Wells's *Shakespeare: an Illustrated Dictionary* (1978) will not only amplify my own definitions in certain areas, but provide valuable guides to the plays, playwrights, actors, and theatre companies which I have deliberately excluded. A standby of my own undergraduate days, Joseph T. Shipley's *A Dictionary of World Literature* (1960) remains helpful in its own area of literary terms and genres, and has been admirably complemented by *Modern Critical Terms*, edited by Roger Fowler (1987), while J. A. Cuddon's *A Dictionary of Literary Terms* (1982) combines less discursively the virtues of both. I have found few works which attempt to analyze *ideas* within the format of an alphabetical reference work: but Raymond Williams's *Keywords: a Vocabulary of Culture and Society* (1976) is an obvious and valuable exception, though its contemporary emphasis limits its usefulness for the student of the Shakespearean period. Other reference works which do concern themselves primarily with the Elizabethan and Jacobean age include, for biographical data, *Who's Who in Shakespeare's England* by Alan and Veronica Palmer, *Lives of the Tudor Age*, compiled by Ann Hoffmann, and *Lives of the Stuart Age*, edited by Edwin Riddell (1976), while on place-names and localities Fran C. Chalfont's *Ben Jonson's London: a Jacobean Place-Name Dictionary* (1978) may be recommended. A work much wider in scope, but packed with concisely-presented information, is *The Renaissance: an Illustrated Encyclopedia*, by Ilan Rachum (1979).

Many of the foregoing works include guides to further reading, and there is no lack of bibliographies for most aspects of the study of the period. With some reluctance, therefore, I have decided not to include guidance to further reading, in part to keep the size of the volume such that it could be priced for the student pocket — but mainly because I conceive the book being used alongside, not instead of, other works of reference and criticism. Indeed, I hope that the main use of this dictionary will precisely be its readiness to hand when an obscure term is encountered in the student's reading, or some other kind of quick conceptual guidance is sought. While I am a great believer in the serendipitous value of browsing, this book is *not* intended for consecutive reading: reviewers, you have been warned. . . .

To acknowledge the assistance I have received other than from the reference works mentioned would, in effect, have necessitated the bibliography I wished to avoid: but where I have come across writers who,

Introduction

refreshingly, have not assumed that all their readers share their own erudition, and so have offered definitions of some of the terms they employ, it seemed more sensible to quote and acknowledge these than attempt a secondhand paraphrase of my own.

I would only add that, because this work is intended for the intelligent but non-specialist reader, I have not hesitated to use 'difficult' words or ideas where necessary, so long as these may be regarded as part of the intellectual baggage of our times, such as the average sixth-former might be expected to bring along to university. The words and ideas I have tried hardest to clarify are, precisely, those that would have formed part of the intellectual baggage of the young man entering the Inns of Court in the Elizabethan or Jacobean age, but which mean little — or even more confusingly, something different — in our own.

I have been most fortunate in enjoying the advice of Stanley Wells, Director of the Shakespeare Institute in the University of Birmingham, and of my colleague Bill Naismith in the Drama Department at Goldsmiths' College, University of London, both of whom read an early draft of this volume and made many helpful suggestions. And I have been happy, too, in my editors at Methuen London — successively, Nick Hern, who encouraged this book into existence from a first tentative suggestion over a pint of Marston's bitter in the Cheshire Cheese (whose proximity to the residence of Samuel Johnson was properly chastening), and Pamela Edwardes, who has seen the project through to fruition.

SIMON TRUSSLER
Goldsmiths' College, University of London
January 1989

Author's Note

The order of the entries in this dictionary is alphabetical by the *first word* of the entry: thus, 'Bad Quarto' precedes 'Badge', and 'Civil Law' comes (as it so frequently does in real life) before 'Civility'. Cross-references are indicated by the use of SMALL CAPITALS, like these, but appear in a form appropriate to their context, and so do not invariably follow the precise form of the main entry: thus, COMEDIES refers to the main entry 'Comedy', APPRENTICESHIP to 'Apprentice', NOVELLE to 'Novella', PATRON to 'Patronage', and the like. Some terms which occur very frequently — such as 'Elizabethan', or 'Greek' and 'Latin' in etymological contexts — are only put into small capitals where cross-referencing would be helpful to the understanding of the relevant entry.

To save space and avoid repetition, Shakespeare's plays are not normally attributed to him, and while the authors of other plays are generally credited, *dates* of plays are only provided when it is important to the understanding of the entry concerned to suggest a work's chronological position within 'our period'. I have to apologise for the frequency with which this latter term occurs, and explain why. 'Our period' means, very roughly, from the late 1580s to the early 1630s: neither 'Elizabethan' (unless used in a most inexact sense) nor even 'Elizabethan and Jacobean' would thus suffice, while 'late-Elizabethan to early-Caroline' would be cumbersome — and even more irritating to the reader than 'our period'. Writers quoted within the entries are of 'our period' in this sense, unless 'modern' or 'twentieth-century' or the like indicates an author or critic of more recent date. The spelling of quotations from sources in 'our period' has been modernized throughout.

A

Ab Ovo.   Latin phrase, literally meaning 'from the egg', used by HORACE to distinguish a narrative which begins at the beginning from one which plunges into the middle of the action, and so starts IN MEDIA RES.

Abecedarius.   See USHER.

Abuses of Players, An Act to Restrain.   Parliamentary statute of 1606 prohibiting the speaking of the name of God, Jesus, the Holy Ghost, or the Trinity except 'with fear and reverence'. In practice, few plays of our period since Marlowe's *Doctor Faustus* (*c*. 1588) had dealt directly with serious theological issues, but casual oaths were common in the drama before this act, and the revision of some earlier works thus became necessary after 1606 in order to avoid BLASPHEMY. This process may be examined by comparing the QUARTO editions of Shakespeare's *Henry I V* (Part One, 1598; Part Two, 1600) with the FOLIO text of 1623. *The Anatomy of Abuses* was also the title of a PURITAN tract of 1583 by Thomas Stubbes, which included a denunciation of the stage.

Academic Drama.   Term used to describe the plays performed by members of the UNIVERSITIES and INNS OF COURT — thus usefully (though not invariably) distinguishing these from the SCHOOL DRAMA associated with younger students. Of the works performed in LATIN, some were CLASSICAL in origin — the first such recorded performance being of a comedy by PLAUTUS in 1519 — and some newly-conceived, such as Edward Halliwell's *Dido*, which was performed at Cambridge before the Queen in 1564. Of those academic dramas written in the VERNACULAR, *Gammer Gurton's Needle* (1566), conjecturally by William Stevenson, is among the earliest of English COMEDIES. Although these plays did not feature directly in the popular repertoire, they had a significant influence on the reshaping of style and content consolidated in the 1580s by the UNIVERSITY WITS, while the later Cambridge PARNASSUS PLAYS provide important evidence about theatrical conditions and rivalries.

Accolade.   The symbolic gesture used in the making of a KNIGHT. This might take the form of an embrace or a placing of the hand on the neck, as well as the better-remembered touch of sword on shoulder.

Act and **Scene.**   Terms for the constituent parts or episodes of a play. Act

11

and scene divisions were scarcely used in the original QUARTO editions of Shakespeare's works, and inconsistently even in the FOLIO, those now generally employed being based on the divisions first adopted by Rowe in his collected edition of 1709 (in which locations — 'scenes' in the Restoration sense — are also first specified). Such divisions are, of course, useful in facilitating quick reference to a passage, but lack any real authority, and may be positively misleading. Although in practice 'scenes' may appear to be self-determined by a complete clearance of the stage (the indication generally followed by Shakespeare's editors), it should be noted that the dramatist who attended most closely to the printing of his plays, Ben Jonson, preferred the NEOCLASSICAL convention (as formulated by the French scholar Scaliger) of starting a new scene when a change occurred in the composition of the major participating characters. Jonson, like the French dramatists of the RENAISSANCE, also consistently divided his plays into five acts (following the precedent both of the choral movements in Greek TRAGEDY and of SENECA), as also did writers for the PRIVATE THEATRES, to designate the musical INTERVALS which were customary in these playhouses. But the frequency and nature of intervals in the PUBLIC THEATRES is uncertain, and it is questionable whether Shakespeare (at least until his final plays) and the POPULAR SCHOOL of dramatists thought in terms of acts at all. Thus, in theatrical IMAGERY, the use of the word 'act' tended for Shakespeare to mean 'action', while 'scene' generally denoted a performing space or stage. See under SCENE for this sense of the word, and see also ENTRANCES AND EXITS.

Acting. Term employed during the earlier part of our period to describe the *gestic* component in RHETORIC. The art of performing on stage was more generally described as PLAYING. Although the word 'acting' had acquired its present theatrical sense by the early seventeenth century, the term PERSONATION (a recent NEOLOGISM, used by Marston in 1599) appears to have been preferred to describe the more psychologically-recognizable style of Burbage, 'acting' thus suggesting the portrayal of CHARACTER in its distinctively JACOBEAN, typological sense.

Acting Edition. A text of a play specially prepared for purposes of performance, rather than for reading or study. In this sense, the so-called BAD QUARTOS of some of Shakespeare's plays, if printed from ASSEMBLED or REPORTED TEXTS, may, ironically, more accurately reflect how the plays were originally performed than the 'good' QUARTO or FOLIO versions — and the modern scholar Hardin Craig even argued that the 'bad' *Hamlet* was a touring version prepared by Shakespeare himself. Acting editions intended as such are, however, to be distinguished from any such accidents of PIRACY, as also from the various attempts to 'improve' Shakespeare by adaptation and revision from the Restoration onwards:

rather, acting editions are texts — sometimes published, but often surviving (if at all) only in prompt-book form — which reflect distinctively *theatrical* requirements, whether in the interests of shorter playing-time, for the fuller exploitation of a popular actor's skills, or (through the rearrangement of scenes) facilitating the elaborate changes of scenery increasingly required during the nineteenth century. Many of the plays which were included in the multi-volume anthologies of the late-eighteenth and early-nineteenth centuries, such as Bell's and Mrs. Inchbald's, include acting texts of the plays as then performed at Covent Garden or Drury Lane, and, indeed, actors rather than editors, from Garrick to Kemble to Macready, have generally been responsible for such pragmatic revisions. In the mid-nineteenth century, Samuel Phelps began the long process of restoring to the stage Shakespeare's original texts, which now — even in uncut form — tend to be regarded as sacrosanct, and so probably followed much more faithfully than in Shakespeare's own time.

Action. Of the six elements of the drama identified by ARISTOTLE, he believed that PLOT was the 'most important', since TRAGEDY was 'the imitation not of persons but of action and life, of happiness and misery'. Aristotle held that, although 'we have certain qualities in accordance with CHARACTER', it was 'in our actions that we are happy or the reverse'. NEOCLASSICAL critics usually agreed with this relative emphasis, and although most English dramatists of our period were not concerned with such 'authorities', ancient or modern, it is often helpful to view the work particularly of the JACOBEAN tragic writers in a light that is almost EXISTENTIAL as well as Aristotelian, if 'character' in the modern sense is perceived not as a matter of what people 'essentially' *are*, but as being formed by what they *do* — in short, by action.

Actor. Although the term came during our period to take on its present meaning of a stage player, its earlier sense of a steward, factor, or personal representative (that is, someone who *acts for* a client or superior) still survived, and (particularly when used as an IMAGE) might be compounded with or even overlay the theatrical meaning.

Africa. Until the fifteenth century, European knowledge of Africa was limited to the northern coastline, which for long had been under islamic rule. Portuguese exploration then brought contact with the western coast, a trade developing in spices, ivory, precious metals — and, of course, slaves. The Cape of Good Hope was finally, accidentally rounded in 1488, and by our period English, French, Spanish, and Dutch sailors were competing in the exploitation of the continent and its peoples. Although Elizabeth received an embassy from the King of Morocco in 1600, popular knowledge of Africa was, however, still very limited, and BLACK people were described almost indiscriminately as 'Negroes', 'Moors', or 'Ethiopes' — though Techelles's speech in Part Two of Marlowe's *Tamburlaine* (I, vi, 59-78) displays the greater if limited knowledge to be expected of its educated author. George Peele's *The Battle of Alcazar* (*c*. 1588) is the first known play to feature an African as its PROTAGONIST, although several lost MASQUES from the mid-century reflect in their titles an evident dramatic interest in Moors and other supposedly exotic races.

Agon. Greek term meaning 'contest', used to describe the confrontation between the PROTAGONIST and the ANTAGONIST in a TRAGEDY. Hence, used critically to denote any formalized dramatic CONFLICT of this kind — for example, between Othello and Iago in Shakespeare's play.

Air. A simple form of MADRIGAL, in which the uppermost 'voice' or 'part' was most prominent, and the words were arranged in repeated verses rather than in continuous sequence. Hence, the term also came to be applied to a solo SONG with LUTE accompaniment or to a tune or melody to which one's own words might be added. Collections of airs, by John Dowland among others, became increasingly popular from the late Elizabethan period onwards.

Alchemy. The scientific pursuit of the 'philosopher's stone', for the transmutation of base metals into gold. Just as no hard-and-fast distinction can be drawn between the study of ASTROLOGY and astronomy in our period — and even mathematical signs were viewed with caution, as probably concealing magical formulae — so alchemy was still virtually synonymous with the science of chemistry. It also embraced the quest for a universal solvent, and for the 'panacea', or remedy for all ills. Many Elizabethan alchemists were undoubtedly fraudulent (like those in Ben Jonson's play *The Alchemist*), but some, such as Dr. John Dee, commanded widespread respect, and alchemy, like astrology, was still widely accepted as a serious subject of study.

Alehouse. Not simply, as now, suggestive of any public drinking house, but the humblest variety, often situated in a private dwelling, as distinct from the TAVERN and the INN — which were also distinct from each other.

Alexandrine. An IAMBIC HEXAMETER, or verse line of six iambic feet. The name was conjecturally derived from a French romance on the deeds of Alexander of Macedon which utilized the measure. It became the standard meter of HEROIC VERSE in France, where it was known as the *tétramètre*, but was uncommon in England, though irregular instances occur, especially in Shakespeare's later plays.

Allegory. A term derived from the Greek for 'speaking otherwise', and first employed in RHETORIC to describe any literary narrative in which the characters and events may be understood as conveying a meaning beyond that of the ostensible action. Allegory may either deal with universal human attributes, as in the MORALITY PLAYS, or relate to a specific secondary situation, as in Spenser's idealized vision of Queen Elizabeth I as GLORIANA in his EPIC poem, *The Faerie Queen* (1589-96). In theatrical terms, allegory during our period became a distinctive characteristic of the MASQUE, while the TOURNAMENT had also assumed a largely allegoric form.

Alliteration. The repeated use of the same letter (usually but not invariably the initial letter) or sound for dramatic or poetic effect. Alliteration was employed by Shakespeare most frequently in his earlier plays, and also for satirical effect, as in the BURLESQUE tragedy during the last act of *A Midsummer Night's Dream* or in such lines of Ancient Pistol's in *Henry V* as 'The grave doth gape, and doting death is near'. Often, as here (but less intentionally), the effect is little more than mechanical, though it may be heightened by pertinent ONOMATOPOEIA, as in Berowne's 'This wimpled, whining, purblind, wayward boy' in *Love's Labour's Lost*.

Allowance. Term for the permission given by the Master of the REVELS to an acting company to perform a play, following the submission of the BOOK for his approval by the BOOK-KEEPER.

Allusion. As used in modern criticism, this word denotes either a reference (direct or indirect) to a contemporary person or event, or a borrowing from some other literary or artistic work. Allusions may provide a key to dating a play, suggest evidence for its source, or at least give an indication of its author's reading.

Altercatio. Latin term, legal in origin, denoting a rapid succession of questions and answers. Such dramatic dialogue in alternating lines, as in the BLANK VERSE of our period, is known as STICHOMYTHIA.

Anabasis. Greek term, literally meaning a 'rising up': in the drama, used critically to describe the action immediately preceding the DÉNOUEMENT.

Anachronism. Literally, from the Greek, this word means 'backwards time', and thus denotes an error in chronology attributing to an earlier age something not invented, discovered, or discussed until a later date. Shakespeare's anachronisms include Cleopatra playing at billiards, Gloucester needing spectacles in the Ancient Britain of *King Lear*, and a striking clock in the Ancient Rome of *Julius Caesar*. Although such 'errors' may produce an effect of comic BATHOS, they tell us as much about our own 'unhistorical' expectations of the Elizabethan perception of HISTORY as about any supposed 'ignorance' on Shakespeare's part.

Anagnorisis. See DISCOVERY.

Analogue. In critical usage, some feature or aspect of the plot, theme, or characterization of a play (or other literary work) for which a parallel may be found in other literatures or periods.

Analogy. The evoking or elaboration of similarity between objects or conditions whose resemblance may not be immediately (or literally) apparent. An example is the likeness which is frequently drawn in the Elizabethan period between the human body and the STATE — the concept of the BODY POLITIC.

Anapest. A verse MEASURE of three syllables, stressed di-di-*dum*, used by Shakespeare (with increasing freedom in his later plays) to vary the RHYTHM of the IAMBIC PENTAMETER.

Anaphora. A term used in RHETORIC, in the original Greek meaning 'carrying upwards', and so describing a repetition of the same word or similar words, 'carried upwards' from one clause or phrase to the next. A well-known example is John of Gaunt's speech with its nineteen phrases beginning with 'this', culminating in 'this England', in *Richard II*.

Anastrophe. In RHETORIC, a calculated inversion of the expected order of words. In the best BLANK VERSE drama, this will strikingly reinforce the sense, but it may otherwise merely reflect the dramatist's need to observe the metrical requirement for a particular stress.

Ancients. A term sometimes found in critical usage to describe the CLASSICAL writers in Ancient GREEK and in LATIN. The great controversy between the supporters of the superior authority of these 'ancients' as opposed to contemporary writers, or 'moderns', is a development of the later seventeenth century, though its origins can be traced to our period in the preference for NEOCLASSICAL precepts to be found in such writings as Sidney's APOLOGY FOR POETRY, and in much of the theory (though less of the practice) of Ben Jonson.

Antagonist. The opponent to the hero or PROTAGONIST of a play. He may be open in his opposition, or an ostensible friend to the hero, as is Iago to Othello. However, the critical assertion that such a CONFLICT of strong central CHARACTERS is central to a play, though true of much drama from the nineteenth century onwards, is arguably a product of the ROMANTIC (and late-capitalist) stress on individualism: such simple oppositions of character are less predictably to be found in the drama of our period.

Anthology.   From the Greek, literally meaning a 'collection of flowers', and so a term used to describe any collection of poems, EPIGRAMS, or other literary material assembled into a book from various sources. Such collections were very popular in the earlier part of our period, from the first publication of *Tottel's Miscellany* in 1557 to *England's Parnassus* and *England's Helicon*, which both appeared in 1600.

Anti-Masque.   An element of the MASQUE introduced (or borrowed from continental models) by Ben Jonson, in which an anarchic, farcical, or BURLESQUE interlude was introduced into the main action — which it often preceded, leading some dramatists to interpret the term as 'ante-masque'. Others, from its ingredient of buffoonery, assumed an 'antic masque' to be intended. Jonson's own purpose (though it provided cause for both forms of misunderstanding) was to provide a foil to the main action: this might ostensibly serve to emphasize by juxtaposition its wonder and beauty, but could also imply a comic criticism of the idealized nature of the masque proper, and so, whether intentionally or otherwise, be said, in a manner akin to CARNIVAL, to subvert it. The anti-masque was generally performed by professional actors, whereas the masque itself was the preserve of amateur players of the COURT.

Apocrypha.   This term, derived from the Greek word meaning 'hidden', is used to describe writings of doubtful or spurious authorship — most familiarly, the collection of those books excluded from the BIBLE as lacking in divine inspiration. It is also applied to those plays attributed by some authorities to Shakespeare, but now considered to be outside the acknowledged CANON of his work. A *Shakespeare Apocrypha* was edited by C. F. Tucker Brooke in 1908.

Apology.   Term frequently to be found in tracts and other polemical writings of our period, as in the titles of Sidney's APOLOGY FOR POETRY, or of Thomas Heywood's *Apology for Actors* (1612). It indicates not (as now) an expression of regret, but a reasoned defence or explanation.

Apology for Poetry.   A critical treatise written *c*. 1580-83 by Sir Philip Sidney, though not published (posthumously) until 1595 (when an alternative edition also appeared, entitled *The Defence of Poesy*). The first systematic examination of 'poetry' (a term used by Sidney and his contemporaries to embrace all imaginative writing) in the English language, it was strongly influenced by the NEOCLASSICAL reconstruction of ARISTOTLE, and was in part designed to answer PURITAN attacks against poetry on moral grounds, just as Aristotle had in part been concerned to respond to PLATO. Sidney's rigid rule-making for both TRAGEDY and COMEDY was largely ignored by the professional dramatists of our period, as were his strictures against any mixing of the GENRES: but the *Apology* remains important for its statement of a RENAISSANCE ideal of which many of the better-read members of an Elizabethan audience would have been aware, whether or not they endorsed it in every detail. It is also, of course, important to note that the *Apology* was written well *before* the great flowering of the drama in the late 1580s.

Apostrophe.   From the Greek for 'turning away', and so a term used in RHETORIC to describe the interruption of a train of thought in order that a direct appeal or declaration may be made, whether addressed to a person present at the time, a deity, a dead person, or even an abstract quality.

Apparel.   See COSTUME.

Apprentice.   In the GUILD system, a person serving, under irrevocable INDENTURES, a period of training under a MASTER CRAFTSMAN, generally lasting from seven to twelve years. Intake of apprentices was restricted according to local requirements and the supposed need to preserve a craft's MONOPOLY. Apprentices, who were unpaid, were regarded as members of the household of their masters, who were expected to provide both formal and moral education as well as training in their craft. An apprentice subsequently became a JOURNEYMAN and later, in theory, his own master; but the breakdown of such old certainties (despite such measures as the Statute of ARTIFICERS) was a frequent topic of COMPLAINT and SATIRE, as in CITIZEN COMEDY. Gatherings of apprentices on HOLIDAYS (particularly Shrovetide) were regarded as potentially riotous, though apprentice riots were generally in pursuit of such 'moral' causes as abusing prostitutes or shaming adulterers rather than expressions of desire for social change. In 1617 an apprentice mob wrecked the newly-converted Phoenix Theatre in Drury Lane. Some BOY PLAYERS in our period were described as being 'apprenticed' to adult actors for two or three years, but this could not have been in any legal or binding sense.

Apron Stage.   This term is sometimes used as if synonymous with the projecting platform stage of the Elizabethan PUBLIC THEATRES: but it is more helpfully reserved to distinguish that part of the stage which projected beyond the proscenium arch in the Restoration theatre (that is, after 1660), when it was the main acting area. In the twentieth century, this style of apron stage has often found favour in attempts to make conventional modern theatres (including the Royal Shakespeare Theatre at Stratford-upon-Avon) supposedly more suitable for Shakespearean productions.

Aptronym. A name suited to the CHARACTER or trade of a person or of a character in a play. See also CHARACTONYM and LABEL NAME.

Arete. Greek term used to describe the distinctive qualities of individual excellence held, in RENAISSANCE thinking, to raise one man above another, as distinct from the dominant belief of the medieval period in forms of corporate expression, whether in the creation of cathedrals or the writing and acting of MYSTERY PLAYS. *Arete,* like VIRTU, could distinguish evil genius as well as HUMANISTIC achievement.

Aretino, Pietro (1492-1556). Italian playwright, poet, and satirist, whose supposedly amoral and blasphemous wit both fascinated and repelled his English readers, for whom, with MACHIAVELLI, he came to embody their equivocal feelings about ITALY.

Ariosto, Lodovico (1474-1533). Italian poet, whose greatest achievement was the long epic poem *Orlando Furioso* (*Mad Orlando*, 1516), translated into English in 1591. However, his COMEDY *I suppositi*, translated into English by George Gascoigne as *Supposes* (performed 1566, published 1573), had more influence upon the Elizabethan theatre, and was reputedly the first prose comedy of the period.

Aristocracy. In our period, this term denoted a form of GOVERNMENT by those privileged by birth and fortune (as distinct from monarchic or democratic rule), rather than describing, as today, the higher ranks of the NOBILITY.

Aristotle (384-322 BC). GREEK philosopher, whose *Poetics* deals primarily with the nature of TRAGEDY as exemplified in the works of the major Greek dramatic poets of the preceding century — Aeschylus, Sophocles, and to a lesser extent Euripides. Understanding of Aristotle in the earlier RENAISSANCE was largely filtered through the work of HORACE, since the *Poetics* was not translated into the more accessible LATIN until 1548. Thus, although Aristotle himself was largely a descriptive rather than a prescriptive critic, his NEOCLASSICAL interpreters (among whom Castelvetro was probably the most influential, following the publication of his commentary in 1570) reconstructed and extended his beliefs into a rigid set of rules — perhaps most misleadingly in the case of the supposed UNITIES. Scant regard was paid to these rules by the professional dramatists of our period (even Ben Jonson honouring them as often in the breach as the observance), although they were an important influence upon Sidney in his APOLOGY FOR POETRY. The *Poetics* also deals, fragmentarily but illuminatingly, with EPIC: however, the modern tendency to regard epic not as an alternative mode of performance but as a kind of narrative poetry which has now been displaced by the novel, has combined with the persistence of neoclassical misconceptions to create the belief that Aristotle was somehow trying to legislate against such discursive or EPISODIC modes of performance. In fact, he distinguishes between tragedy and epic simply as being appropriate to different purposes and occasions. (Thus, neither the German twentieth-century playwright Brecht nor the Elizabethan dramatists whose 'epic' approach Brecht in part imitated were as 'anti-Aristotelian' as Brecht himself believed.) Aristotle was also first in the long line of critics whose approach was in part determined by the need to defend the drama on moral grounds (in this case from the disapproval of PLATO), a need which may in part explain his belief in the CATHARTIC effects of tragedy.

Arms. The heraldic symbols on a shield or elsewhere, which supposedly originated in the need to distinguish medieval KNIGHTS in battle, and which were subsequently adopted by their families as of hereditary right. By the Elizabethan period, the granting of a 'coat of arms' by the College of Heralds was (as for Shakespeare) considered the mark of a GENTLEMAN. A display of coats of arms no doubt conveyed considerable EMBLEMATIC significance for the audiences of Shakespeare's times — not only in scenes of battle or confrontation, but, for example, in Hieronimo's explication of three 'escutcheons' (arm-bearing shields) in Kyd's *The Spanish Tragedy*. Members of acting companies wore the 'badge' and LIVERY of their noble PATRON.

Ars Poetica. See HORACE.

Art. Not, as in current usage, either a term specifically denoting painting, or intended to distinguish 'aesthetic' creation generally from scientific studies. For the Elizabethans, 'art' suggested, in Leo Salingar's helpful definition, 'any acquired and purposeful knowledge or skill, without distinguishing between aesthetic and utilitarian applications, and without carrying any necessary approval signal'. Any book claiming in its title to teach an 'art' thus dealt in practical and systematized instruction — as in Puttenham's *Art of English Poesy* (1589), where the author defines art as 'a certain order of rules prescribed by reason, and gathered by experience'. 'Art' could also be contrasted unfavourably (as it was by MONTAIGNE) with 'nature' — its continuing sense in 'artificial'. However, Italian writers such as Vasari had already made greater claims for its powers, notably asserting that sculpture, painting, and architecture should not, as formerly, be regarded as 'mechanical' arts, but should stand alongside poetry (as a branch of GRAMMAR and RHETORIC) and MUSIC (conceived as an aspect of mathematics), among the SEVEN LIBERAL ARTS.

Artificers, Statute of.   An Act of Parliament of 1563, which attempted to regulate employment and sustain the GUILD system, stipulating that all males between the ages of twelve and sixty were to become farm labourers unless they had served a seven-year APPRENTICESHIP to enter a traditional craft.

As From.   A STAGE DIRECTION, often to be found in the plays of our period, which, as a recent study by Alan Dessen suggests, raises many interesting questions as to CONVENTIONS of behaviour, gesture, COSTUME, MUSIC, and sound effects. Thus, entrances 'as from hunting' were probably signalled by distinctive apparel or weaponry, by the offstage sounding of a hunting horn, or even (as in the Second Part of *Henry VI*) by a hawk perched on the wrist, while 'as from dinner' may have been indicated simply by a napkin over the shoulder or a trencher in the hand. More tantalizing examples include entrances 'as newly landed and half naked' in Thomas Heywood's *The Four Prentices of London*, 'as out of a cave's mouth' in Marston's *Sophonisba*, and 'as out of a bush' in *The Two Noble Kinsmen*.

Aside.   A remark intended to be overheard only by one or a few of the other characters on stage, or by the audience alone. It is normally spoken not only in company but *in response to* another character's words, and is thus to be distinguished from the SOLILOQUY, which is usually more self-referential and reflective in nature. Asides were not only acceptable as a CONVENTION to the audiences of our period, but were facilitated in practice by the large stage area of the PUBLIC THEATRES. Although rarely found as a STAGE DIRECTION in the early texts of Shakespeare's plays, its requirement is usually clear from the context.

Assembled Text.   Term employed in modern BIBLIOGRAPHICAL CRITICISM to describe the theory put forward by Edmond Malone in the eighteenth century (and most widely propagated by John Dover Wilson in the inter-war period of our own) that certain plays included in the First FOLIO of Shakespeare's works, for which no PROMPT BOOK is thought to have existed, were 'assembled' for the press by putting together actors' PARTS with the PLOT of the play.

Astrology.   The 'science' of determining earthly fortunes from the movements of the stars and planets. Although very ancient in origin, astrology — still regarded in our period as synonymous with astronomy

21

Auto-da-Fé

— was particularly influential for the Elizabethans, with their belief in the theory of CORRESPONDENCES and their sense of the MUTABILITY or decay of the earth in contrast with the perfect harmony of the heavenly SPHERES. Astrological assistance was sought not only through the casting of personal horoscopes, but in such matters as the planting or gathering of crops. As with ALCHEMY, some of the practitioners of astrology were serious students of their subject, some fraudulent exploiters of the credulous — and some (probably including the notorious Simon Forman) a combination of the two. See also MAGIC.

Auto-da-Fé. Spanish term, literally meaning 'act of faith', describing the public exhibition of penitence and acceptance which followed a trial by the INQUISITION. The most extreme punishment on such occasions (which usually coincided with a public HOLIDAY) was burning at the stake.

Ayre. See AIR.

B

Baconian Theory. The belief that the plays of Shakespeare were in fact the work of Sir Francis Bacon (1561-1626). This theory, which dates only from the mid-nineteenth century, attempts to reconcile Shakespeare's relative lack of formal education with the erudition of his plays by attributing them instead to a known scholar and philosopher, basing its 'proof' on an assortment of outdated scholarship and cryptographic ingenuity.

Bad Quarto. Term used in BIBLIOGRAPHICAL CRITICISM to describe the four to six among Shakespeare's plays which show evidence in their first QUARTO editions of omissions, paraphrases of the original, metrical confusion, and other defects now thought to signify unauthoritative derivation — that is, not directly from the author's manuscript or PROMPT-BOOK, as in a REPORTED TEXT.

Badge. The sign or EMBLEM distinctive to a particular family, and worn by those belonging to it or owing it allegiance. The red rose of the House of Lancaster and the white rose of the House of York are probably the best-known examples. Compare ARMS.

Ballad. Any simple and straightforward SONG for a solo voice (as distinct from the many-parted MADRIGAL), usually narrative in form and often concerned with specific events of a topical, heroic, or sentimental nature. As in *The Winter's Tale* or Jonson's *Bartholomew Fair*, ballads were frequently sold by itinerant peddlers in BROADSIDE form, embellished with an appropriate WOODCUT. Ballad singers were supposed to be licensed by the Master of the REVELS.

Baronet. See KNIGHT.

Barriers. Originally the fences separating the combatants from the spectators at a medieval TOURNAMENT, and by our period synonymous with the tournament itself. Entertainments were a normal part of such proceedings, and Jonson, for example, provided speeches for the 'barriers' held in 1610 to celebrate the investiture of James's eldest son, Henry, as Prince of Wales.

Bathos. Greek term for 'sublimity', or 'the sublime', and as such the title of a work attributed to the Greek critic of the early Christian era,

Longinus. The concept of 'the sublime' has been influential in supporting inspirational or ROMANTIC as opposed to CLASSICAL concepts of art, but the English sense of the word 'bathos' was ironically inverted in an eighteenth-century mock-critical treatise by the poet Pope, and now describes a ludicrous and usually sudden descent *from* the sublime to the absurd, or, simply, any anti-climactic effect, whether unintentional or for the deliberate purposes of BURLESQUE.

Bawdy-Basket.   Loose-living female member of a VAGRANT group, or urban female peddler, who made part of her living from the basket of trinkets she attempted to sell or to barter advantageously. Many 'bawdy-baskets' also sold their own bodies, 'in lewd, loathsome lechery', or were accomplices in the duping of GULLS. The male equivalent of a 'bawdy-basket' was a CONY-CATCHER.

Bear-Baiting.   A 'sport', in which four or five dogs were pitted against a bear chained to a stake until one or other of the combatants was exhausted. Bets could be laid on the number of dogs killed or maimed. Bear-baiting seems to have reached its height of popularity during our period, though the first royal 'Master of All Our Bears' had been appointed in the reign of Richard III. Most townships had their 'official' bears, carefully tended by bearwards, while ownership of a good fighting dog was a matter of civic pride. No local FAIR was complete without its bear-baiting, which was also a frequent element of a royal PROGRESS or ambassadorial visit. The Bear Garden on Bankside was built *c.* 1526, and during Elizabeth's reign came under PURITAN attack along with the theatres, with which it became closely and sometimes competitively linked (thus, the PRIVY COUNCIL in 1591 prohibited the playhouses from opening on Thursdays, the day reserved for bear-baiting). The impresario Philip Henslowe and the actor Edward Alleyn procured the mastership of the bears in 1594, and when the Bear Garden was demolished in 1613 it was replaced by the Hope Theatre, which could be used both for baiting and for stage plays. Bear- and BULL-BAITING were not legally banned in Britain until 1835.

Bed Trick.   Term used in modern criticism to describe the stage CON-VENTION whereby one female character in a play is substituted for another, under cover of darkness, usually to effect a desired union, without the knowledge of the male participant — who, however, may then be converted or persuaded to the charms and virtues of the substituted lady, to whom he usually has an existing but neglected obligation. Thus, in *Measure for Measure*, Mariana is substituted for Isabella in the bed of Angelo, who is then 'sentenced' to marry her by the 'returned' Duke; while in *All's Well That Ends Well*, Helena, already wife to Bertram but unloved by him, substitutes herself in his bed in place of the desired

Diana, and by simultaneously getting herself pregnant fulfils the conditions on which her enforced husband has said he will come to love her. In Middleton and Rowley's *The Changeling*, Diaphanta manages to sustain a deceptive dalliance (intended to conceal her mistress's earlier loss of her own virginity) for so long that the chimney has to be set on fire to smoke her out.

Bible.   Literally, and simply, 'the book'. The Holy Bible thus assembles the CANON of writings regarded as of inspired origin and so sacred to the Christian faith. Until the REFORMATION, the LATIN translation of the Bible known as the Vulgate was in general use. Two translations of this version into the VERNACULAR were made at the instigation of the reformer John Wyclif in the fourteenth century, but the Church forbade their use, and the first printed English translation of the New Testament (by William Tyndale in 1526) was also outlawed. In 1535, however, the new emphasis on scriptural authority under the REFORMATION saw a complete translation by Miles Coverdale, which included the APOCRYPHA, receive official sanction, and a revision of this, known from its size as the Great Bible, became in 1540 'appointed to the use for the churches' — though the common people were forbidden by law to read it in private until the reign of Edward VI (1547-53). The Geneva Bible (so called from the place of its translators' exile under the Catholic Mary) appeared in its complete form in 1560, and remained influential among the general public, especially in PURITAN circles, although a revision known as the Bishops' Bible was made the 'appointed' version in 1568. These two translations would have been best known to Shakespeare, who often echoes their phraseology and imagery — though he makes direct biblical references very rarely indeed. The 'Authorised Version', which was prepared by a committee of churchmen under James I and published in 1611, went back to the original Hebrew and GREEK sources, but was also a recasting and refining of previous translations. Its long supremacy was, as the scholar Craig R. Thompson aptly puts it, 'one of style, not of scholarship', and in its keen feeling for speech rhythms and the art of practical RHETORIC it is clearly a product of the age of Shakespeare.

Bibliographical Criticism.   Term used to describe the new approach to the study of the early QUARTO and FOLIO editions of Shakespeare's plays, instigated by such scholars as Pollard, Greg, and McKerrow. Bibliographical criticism is based on a scientific understanding of Elizabethan printing-house practices, and their probable relationship to original sources such as FOUL PAPERS and (in the case of plays) PROMPT-BOOK copies.

Bills of Mortality.   The lists of deaths and their causes issued weekly from the sixteenth century onwards. The fact that they were published by the Company of Parish Clerks, representing 109 parishes in and around LONDON, provides some indication of how 'greater London' beyond the CITY boundaries was understood during our period, when 'within the Bills' was a colloquialism for 'within the metropolitan area'.

Black. In its lengthy entry for this word, the *Oxford English Dictionary* offers a variety of definitions relating to black as a colour, and to its neutral use as a racial description. It then notes meanings which include 'having dark or deadly purposes, malignant . . . disastrous, sinister', 'clouded with sorrow or melancholy', and 'indicating disgrace, censure, liability to punishment'. That such associations today may have racialist overtones does not mean that this was always so: indeed, the average Englishman of Shakespeare's time would have had little or no experience of meeting black people, and, given the opportunity, would probably have regarded them with simple curiosity rather than prejudice — which was rather more likely to be shown, for example, towards a JEW. Black was thus EMBLEMATIC of evil for the Elizabethans simply by contrast with the colour white, as representing respectively darkness and light, and so the forces of the Devil and the Lord. This association was *transferred to* people with black skins, rather than *deriving from* any inherent racialist feeling, and was an aspect of TYPOLOGY (similar to that which, for example, made any dramatic representation of a bastard presumptive of evil intent). However, as the modern scholar Gary Taylor notes, the three major non-European characters in Shakespeare's plays — Aaron in *Titus Andronicus*, Othello, and Caliban in *The Tempest* — all 'murder or attempt to murder whites; two plot rapes, and all three are sexually obsessed'. Despite early explorations, 'knowledge' of the continent of Africa still derived largely from popular mythology, and even the most basic geographical distinctions were largely ignored — as in the virtually interchangeable use of 'Moor' and 'Ethiopian' for 'African' (although the Prince of Morocco in *The Merchant of Venice* and, perhaps surprisingly, Cleopatra, are both described as 'tawny', indicating tanned rather than black complexions).

Blank Verse. Strictly, any unrhymed verse, but the term is now generally used to denote the IAMBIC PENTAMETER, the verse MEASURE which came to characterize the plays of our period. It is first to be found in the Earl of Surrey's translation of Virgil, published in 1557, and its theatrical use was pioneered by Sackville and Norton, authors of *Gorboduc*, often described as the first English TRAGEDY. Here, a strict iambic pattern — of five feet with a regular *di-dum* stress, and with each line END-STOPPED — was employed. In the PUBLIC THEATRES, Kyd's *Spanish Tragedy* may or not have preceded Marlowe's *Tamburlaine* in its use of the measure in the late 1580s, but it was Marlowe's so-called MIGHTY LINE in his early plays, the increasing communicative vigour achieved in his later work, and the diffusion of blank verse by the UNIVERSITY WITS, which established it as a distinctive theatrical medium. Shakespeare's works reflect the increasing flexibility with which the measure came to be used, and the various technical means — including ENJAMBMENT (the use of lines which are not end-stopped), changes in the expected emphasis, deliberate irregularities of metre (such as FEMININE ENDINGS), subtle manipulation of the CAESURA, and a variety of other devices — through which the expressive, rhetorical, and ironic potential of the medium came to be exploited. See also STRESS.

Blasphemy. Profane references to God or to other sacred matters, forbidden during our period, but prohibited by statute only from 1606, when the Act to Restrain ABUSES OF PLAYERS was passed by Parliament. G. E. Bentley cites the deletion by the Master of the REVELS from an extant manuscript play of such 'oaths' as 'Troth', ' 'Slife' (that is, 'by God's life'), 'by the lord', and even 'faith' as evidence of the effectiveness of the Act; and over fifty oaths appear in the QUARTO edition of *Othello* that are deleted in the FOLIO.

Boccaccio, Giovanni (*c.* 1313-75). Italian scholar, poet, and author of the *Decameron*, a collection of a hundred NOVELLE, which include folk tales, fairy stories, and FABLIAUX. Assembled in its final form between 1349 and 1351, for dramatists of our period it became a valuable SOURCE of plots, including elements of Shakespeare's *The Merchant of Venice* and *All's Well That Ends Well*.

Body Politic. The state, interpreted by way of ANALOGY, and in accordance with the theory of CORRESPONDENCES, to a human being, with the sovereign as its 'head', his laws its medicine, and his wars its blood-letting or purgation. Shakespeare's best-known use of such a MICROCOSM, in *Coriolanus*, portrays the politicians of Rome, with nice ambiguity, as the 'belly'.

Book. Not, in the theatrical usage of our period, the printed text of a play, but the final manuscript version, prepared by the BOOK-KEEPER, as submitted for the approval of the Master of the REVELS. The 'book' may have been the author's original manuscript, or FOUL PAPERS, as amended for playing, or a transcript incorporating additional STAGE DIRECTIONS and reminders about stage props and other technical requirements, in which case it would also have served as the PROMPT-BOOK for the play in performance.

Book-Keeper. The member of an acting company who prepared the

Bowdlerizing

BOOK of the play, obtained a licence for its performance, and prepared the PART for each actor, together with the PLOT for posting backstage. He was also responsible for the safe custody of all the PROMPT-BOOKS belonging to his troupe, and may or may not also have served as prompter during a performance.

Bowdlerizing.   A relatively modern term for the now unfashionable practice of deleting supposedly offensive passages from a play, to make it suitable for 'family reading'. Deriving from the efforts of Thomas Bowdler in his *Family Shakespeare*, published in 1818 (based on his sister's earlier attempt in 1807), the 'bowdlerizing' of Shakespeare's plays, usually in editions intended for use in schools (for example, those prepared by A.W. Verity), continued well into the post-war period of the present century. Bowdlerized editions are to be distinguished from ACTING EDITIONS, in which the deletions have generally been made on theatrical rather than moralistic grounds.

Boy Players.   Term most helpfully reserved for those two or three child APPRENTICES in each adult acting company who, in the absence of actresses, played the female characters (or possibly only the younger women: it is a matter of scholarly debate as to whether older, 'character' female roles were played by boys or adult males). Boy players may thus be distinguished from members of the CHILDREN'S COMPANIES, which were entirely composed of boys. No longer able to play women once their voices broke, some boy players proceeded into membership of an adult company.

Broadside.   A large sheet of paper (or broadsheet), printed on one side only. Thus, the term is often used to describe the BALLADS hawked in this format, which was also employed for the printing of FABLIAUX. A second, sometimes confused meaning derives from the naval sense of 'broadside', and denotes the simultaneous discharge of a ship's artillery — hence, any all-out polemical attack on an opponent.

Bull-Baiting.   The 'sport' of setting bulldogs and mastiffs against a bull in an improvised or specially-constructed ring. One such arena is shown on contemporary maps of Elizabethan London as close to the BEAR-BAITING on Bankside. Unlike the baited bear, the bull was generally un-chained, but whereas bears were specially trained to survive their ordeals, and often achieved a place in the public's affections, bulls were unpre-pared for their torture, and almost invariably killed. In some towns, butchers were actually forbidden to slaughter bulls until they had first been baited. Like bear-baiting, with which it often shared a programme, this 'sport' was not made illegal in Britain until 1835.

Burlesque. Term used to describe a distinctive GENRE of dramatic writing (or self-contained episode within a play), which parodies other artistic or theatrical forms. It is thus usefully distinguished from SATIRE, which is generally concerned with ridiculing real-life characters or foibles — or, at least, with content rather than form. Few full-length or self-contained burlesques were written during our period — Beaumont's *Knight of the Burning Pestle* (*c.* 1607) being the most notable — but many plays contain elements of burlesque, including the 'Nine Worthies' MASQUE in *Love's Labour's Lost* and the mock-tragedy of Pyramus and Thisbe in *A Midsummer Night's Dream*. INDUCTIONS often contain mixtures of burlesque and satire.

C

Caesura. In PROSODY, literally (from the Latin) the 'cutting' of a line of verse, or the point at which it naturally falls into two parts, obligatorily stressed in the HEROIC VERSE of the GREEK and LATIN poets. The term is also used, somewhat less precisely, to describe a 'felt pause' or 'silent beat' in a line of BLANK VERSE, where the early tendency for the caesura to fall after the second foot soon gave way to its placement becoming a matter of artistic judgement rather than formal compulsion. As the run-on line or ENJAMBMENT became commoner, even greater flexibility was possible in the placing of the caesura within a line.

Calvin, John (1509-64). Theologian and leader of the REFORMATION in Switzerland, where Calvin was forced to flee from his native France in 1535, having been imprisoned following his espousal of the PROTESTANT cause two years earlier. He published the original edition of his *Institutes of the Christian Religion* from Basle in 1536 (enlarged editions appearing in 1541 and 1560), and was thereafter based mainly in Geneva, where he succeeded in imposing a strict code of behaviour in private as well as in public life, prosecuting those who offended against his teaching. The distinguishing doctrine of Calvin's theology was his denial of man's free-will after the Fall, and his consequent stress on PREDESTINATION as well as JUSTIFICATION BY FAITH. These beliefs were strongly influential on the PURITANS in England, as also in SCOTLAND, where the church was reformed on Calvinist lines under the leadership of John KNOX — and, of course, in colonial North America, where they provided a religio-economic underpinning to the so-called 'protestant work ethic', in which the Calvinist reversal of the traditional Christian condemnation of USURY was also an important element.

Cancel. Term used in printing practice, and also in the BIBLIOGRAPHICAL CRITICISM of plays of our period, to describe a leaf inserted into a printed volume to replace one on which a serious error has occurred.

Canon. Originally, those books of the BIBLE regarded as genuinely sacred and inspired, and thus excluding the APOCRYPHA. Hence, any collection of writings held to be genuine, and specifically all those of Shakespeare's plays regarded as being his own work — according to current belief, all 36 included in the first FOLIO, with the probable addition of the conjecturally collaborative *Pericles* and *The Two Noble Kinsmen*.

Canzonet. A short MADRIGAL for solo voice.

Carnival. The concept of 'carnival' has been much utilized in recent Shakespearean and other criticism. The term derives from the Italian 'carne levare', the 'putting away of flesh', and thus originated as a description of the festivities which traditionally preceded the privations of Lent. The carnival season might be limited to the immediate SHROVETIDE period, or extend from the Epiphany (Twelfth Night) to Ash Wednesday or even later: thus, the association of carnival with topsy-turvydom possibly derives from customs associated with making the transition in the church calendar from the fixed celebration of Christmas to the moveable, lunar-regulated period leading up to Easter. Carnival now tends to have a more generalized meaning, suggesting all those HOLIDAY occasions when celebratory feasting was combined with some temporary inversion of the social order, for which, prior to the REFORMATION, the feast of CORPUS CHRISTI provided the other most notable opportunity. Carnival might be presided over by a Lord of Misrule, as in the classical Saturnalia, by the brief authority of a Boy Bishop, or be celebrated in sacred travesty, as during the Feast of Fools — while on the Continent, there were actually 'battles' at Shrovetide between Carnival and the personified privations of Lent. These were less common in England, but even the GRAMMAR SCHOOLS — only recently instituted in our period — had not been slow to evolve their own carnival ritual of 'barring out' their masters once a year. Some modern writers believe that Elizabethan COMEDY, in particular, reflects the world of carnival in the implicit opposition it creates between order and disorder (on occasion directly expressed, as in Jonson's *Bartholomew Fair*), and through its expression of the paradox of well-regulated riot. This belief attractively suggests an 'unofficial' or folk tradition far from the requirements of DECORUM and CIVILITY: and while in Shakespeare's case it appears to sit uneasily with the fear of anarchy and disorder which is a recurrent preoccupation of his work, it is arguably present in Falstaff, as in many of his CLOWNS and FOOLS.

Caroline. Concerning the reign of King Charles I (1625-49). The term is derived — as is JACOBEAN — from the Latin form of the king's name, in this case Carolus.

Castiglione, Baldassare (1478-1529).   Italian HUMANIST, author of THE COURTIER (which see).

Catastrophe. Literally, from the Greek, an 'overturning', and in Elizabethan usage synonymous with DÉNOUEMENT. The term is seldom so used in recent criticism, in order to avoid confusion with the modern, generalized sense.

Catch. A ROUND, usually with comic or punning words, for three or more voices — as, for example, sung by Sir Toby, Sir Andrew, and Feste in *Twelfth Night*. The SONG was probably so-called because the participants 'catch up' the words from one another.

Cathartic. Having the effect of *catharsis*, which ARISTOTLE believed to be the power of TRAGEDY 'through pity and fear to effect the purgation of such emotions'. Scholars continue to debate the precise meaning and implications of this definition, as of the term itself.

Cavalier Drama. Term denoting the kind of plays written by amateur dramatists at the COURT of Charles I, which tended to reflect the NEO-PLATONISM then fashionable under the influence of the Queen, Henrietta Maria.

Censorship. This was exerted after 1581 largely through the LICENSING powers vested in the Master of the REVELS. It was directed not only against BLASPHEMY, as reinforced after 1606 through the Act to Restrain ABUSES OF PLAYERS, but also against any supposedly subversive political content in plays. Thus, in a proclamation as early as 1559, Elizabeth ordered JUSTICES OF THE PEACE to examine plays and forbid those 'wherein either matters of religion or of the governance of the estate of the common weal shall be handled or treated', unless before an audience 'of grave and discreet persons'. Later, the performance of the lost SATIRE, *The Isle of Dogs*, conjecturally by Nashe, caused the closure of the theatres in 1597, while in 1601 Shakespeare's company, the Chamberlain's Men, came under suspicion for accepting a commission to present *Richard II*, including its deposition scene, on the eve of the Earl of Essex's rebellion. In 1604, the collaborative *Eastward Ho!* landed its authors in trouble with James I for a mere handful of anti-Scottish references, and twenty years later Middleton's *A Game at Chess* caused the temporary closure of the Globe on account of the play's anti-Spanish satire.

Chain of Being, The. Term borrowed from the poet Pope (though arguably having its origins in HOMER's allegory of Zeus letting down a golden chain from heaven), and applied by modern critics to the Elizabethan doctrine, influenced by NEOPLATONISM, of an ordered universe of strict hierarchy and degrees. This 'great chain' stretched, in E.M.W. Tillyard's words, 'from the foot of God's throne to the meanest of inanimate objects'. These latter were perceived as constituting the lowest order of existence, followed by the vegetative and then the sensitive creation: but there were differences also *within* each class: three ranks of 'sensitive' existence were thus defined as lower than man, who combined all the faculties of the other orders with the addition of understanding, and so was a 'little world' or MICROCOSM in himself. Each class of being was said to have its 'primate' — the whale or the dolphin among the fishes, usually the eagle among the birds, the lion or the elephant among the animals, even God among the angels. Tillyard's influential book, *The Elizabethan World Picture* (1943), in explicating this supposed world-view, was rather too successful in correcting what he believed to have been the earlier, over-secular perception of Elizabethan society: thus, when Tillyard, for example, quotes Ulysses's speech on 'degree, priority, and place' in *Troilus and Cressida* (I, iii) as a simple statement of the Elizabethan (indeed, of Shakespeare's personal) view of a hierarchical 'chain of being', this is to ignore both the dramatic context of the speech and its function in characterizing Ulysses by juxtaposing what he says with the way he proceeds to act. The Elizabethan world was in a transitional state of great ideological ferment, and cannot be assessed by any official rule-book of beliefs, though the concept of the 'chain of being' certainly provided a common frame of reference, frequently but not uncritically utilized for literary and theatrical purposes.

Chaos. Not simply disorder and confusion, as today, but the condition of the universe before the divine order created in the CHAIN OF BEING, or, in Tillyard's words, 'the cosmic anarchy before creation and the wholesale dissolution that would result if the pressure of Providence relaxed and allowed the law of NATURE to cease functioning'. Hence the conception of chaos as a distinct 'period' of sacred HISTORY, as in Othello's despairing cry, 'chaos is come again'.

Chapbook. General description for any cheap and popular book hawked by a peddler, as distinct from the larger, single-sided BROADSIDE. Political polemics, religious tracts, children's stories, BALLADS, and old ROMANCES or new CONY-CATCHING tales could all appear in the form of chapbooks, which were often decorated with WOODCUTS.

Chapel Royal. Physically situated within the COURT of the Palace of ST. JAMES'S, 'the Chapel' could also refer to the body of clergy and musicians which formed its staff: thus, on occasion, 'the Chapel' of the royal household became itinerant, accompanying the monarch on PROGRESSES around the country. The Chapel Royal was of crucial importance to the development of English church MUSIC under Elizabeth, and also provided recruits for one of the best-known companies of BOY PLAYERS, the Children of the Chapel, who played in both the first and second of the PRIVATE THEATRES at Blackfriars, where their connection with the Chapel was eventually severed.

Character. Although 'characters' of living people, in our sense of 'biographies', were beginning to be written during our period, in theatrical usage 'character' did not mean, as it does today, the outward expression of one's individual psychology or 'inner nature', but, on the contrary, conformity to a certain type, as required by DECORUM — and, indeed, by the belief that each man was a reflection or MICROCOSM of the universal. Thus, one of the exponents of the vogue for CHARACTER WRITING, Sir Thomas Overbury, explained that 'To square out a character by our English level, it is a picture . . . quaintly drawn in various colours, all of them heightened by one shadowing'. Despite Shakespeare's greater interest in individual motivation, his contemporaries — for example, through Jonson's concept of the HUMOURS in COMEDY, and in the embryonic EXISTENTIALISM of Webster's tragic figures — largely drew character in terms of such TYPOLOGY. Not only was this in accordance with NEOCLASSICAL precepts, and a reflection of contemporary medical thinking, but also, pragmatically, because of the dramatist's need to write in accordance with the LINES followed by particular actors. Even Shakespeare's most complex characters cannot be fully understood if it is not realized that they are also types — Hamlet, for example, a MALCONTENT, whose behaviour is only fully explicable within the CONVENTIONS of the REVENGE PLAY. The use of the word 'character' to describe a PART in a play does not occur until the eighteenth century.

Character Writing.   Collections of sketches of types of CHARACTERS in the sense described above, influenced by the original *Characters* of the Athenian philosopher Theophrastus. The first such collection of note was Joseph Hall's *Characters of Virtues and Vices* (1608). Sir Thomas Overbury's *Characters*, first published in 1614, was supplemented in its later editions by Donne, Webster, and Dekker, while John Earle's *Microcosmography* (1628) was perhaps the best work in this GENRE.

Charactonym.   The naming of a character in a play after the qualities he displays or embodies — such as Shakespeare's Aguecheek and Mistress Overdone, Marston's Malevole, or Jonson's Littlewit. See also APTRONYM and LABEL NAME.

Children's Companies.   Term used to distinguish the acting troupes entirely composed of male children from the BOY PLAYERS who performed with the adult companies. Nominally they comprised pupils from the various choir schools, such as the CHAPEL ROYAL, such children's companies being highly popular at COURT before 1576 (where they had given 46 performances since Elizabeth's accession, compared with only 32 by the adult players). Their activities lapsed between 1584 and 1600, when they again became fashionable, playing exclusively in PRIVATE THEATRES like the Blackfriars. During the early JACOBEAN period, the children's companies flourished in SATIRE, and participated in the WAR OF THE THEATRES, but after Burbage moved his adult players to the Blackfriars in 1608 they rapidly declined in public favour.

Chivalry. Originally, this term signified the qualifications, qualities, and customs of KNIGHTHOOD, as derived from the French *chevalier*, a knight or horseman. Hence, the conventionalized behaviour appropriate to knighthood, such as COURTESY and readiness to engage in COMBAT and to take part in TOURNAMENTS on chivalric terms. Hotspur in Shakespeare's *Henry IV* combines (rather to excess) the love of horses and HONOUR appropriate to chivalry, but his somewhat brusque attitude to women scarcely exemplifies the associated code of COURTLY LOVE. By our period, chivalry was in decline, but arguably it had always been rooted in aspirations to recapture the values of an entirely imaginary, idealized past. The French poet Molinet thus described St. Michael's mythical slaying of the dragon as the 'first deed of knighthood and chivalrous prowess'. The historian Huizinga aptly summed up chivalry as 'pride aspiring to honour'.

Chorus. Originally, a group of celebrants in the religious rituals from which developed the TRAGEDY and COMEDY of Ancient Greece. Their role, although on occasion participatory, was more usually that of distanced commentators on the action. Hence, the name was adopted in our period for an individual character in a play whose function was to introduce the action, often in the form of a PROLOGUE, or to bridge its episodes by means of a linking narrative. A Chorus was most integrally employed by Shakespeare in *Henry V*, in which the character also has a dramatic function as a high-sounding patriot whose attitudes juxtapose ironically with those of the low-life realists: but also of structural importance is the Chorus in *The Winter's Tale*, where it is necessary to link two acts that are sixteen years apart in time, and in *Pericles*, where the role is given to the poet Gower.

Chronicle. A form of historical writing, recording events in their proper chronological sequence, which had its origins in the attempt of the fourth-century theologian Eusebius to list the main incidents of GREEK, Hebrew, Persian, and Roman history in parallel columns — suggesting in this use of ANALOGY a perception of HISTORY (earlier exemplified in the *Parallel Lives* of PLUTARCH) which was to become characteristic of the medieval mind. Shakespeare used not only Plutarch's *Lives* for his Roman plays, but the near-contemporary chronicles of HALL and HOLINSHED for the English histories he wrote in the 1590s — a decade which saw the height of the vogue for such chronicle plays, though some critics trace the GENRE back to Bale's *King John, c.* 1534, while Ford's *Perkin Warbeck* was written as late as *c.* 1630. The term 'chronicle play' is used by most modern critics as synonymous with 'history play', though it is sometimes reserved for the more loosely-knit and EPISODIC among them, and so in Shakespeare's case to distinguish the first from the second TETRALOGY .

Cinquecento. Italian term, literally meaning 'the five hundreds', designating specifically the sixteenth century, or more generally the high RENAISSANCE in Italy — the age of Raphael, da Vinci, and Michelangelo in art, and of ARIOSTO, CASTIGLIONE, and MACHIAVELLI in the realms of literature and ideas.

Citizen. The inhabitant of a CITY, as distinct from a countryman. The designation is also used in our period to describe the class of MERCHANTS and tradesmen who lived in the City of LONDON rather than in WEST-MINSTER, which was now more fashionable because of its proximity to the COURT. The social status of a citizen was regarded as between that of a GENTLEMAN and a YEOMAN.

Citizen Comedy, City Comedy. Interchangeable terms current in modern criticism to describe those plays, particularly prevalent in the early JACOBEAN period, which dealt with the contemporary life of LONDON, largely in terms of SATIRE. This definition would exclude such an earlier work as Dekker's *The Shoemakers' Holiday* (1599), which was not only set in an earlier historical period, but was also altogether more benevolent in tone. Chapman's *An Humorous Day's Mirth* (1597) was arguably the first 'city comedy', though a truly astringent satirical tone is not to be found until the *Eastward Ho!* of Chapman, Jonson, and Marston (1605). Apart from these three writers, some of whose later work also 'fits' into the GENRE, its chief exponent was Thomas Middleton, with such plays as *A Mad World, My Masters* (1606) and *A Chaste Maid in Cheapside* (1611).

Cittern. A four-stringed musical instrument, similar to a LUTE, but with a flat back, and more circular as viewed from the front.

City. In theatrical terms, 'the city', together with the COURT and the COUNTRY, was one of the three available types of location for COMEDY. More specifically, and especially in CITIZEN COMEDY, 'the city' was always the City of LONDON — the self-governing area contained within the walls, as distinct from WESTMINSTER (already becoming more fashionable in our period, though not yet distinguished in conventional usage as 'the town').

Civil Law. This term derives from the Latin *jus civile*, or the 'law for the citizens' (and so sometimes still called 'Roman law'), signifying that it regulated the lives of ordinary people — as distinct, originally, from 'canon' or 'ecclesiastical law', which, however, had been made redundant

37

by the REFORMATION. By our period, therefore, 'civil law', comprising the body of statutory enactments as taught in the UNIVERSITIES, was instead to be distinguished from the COMMON LAW, based on custom and precedent, and studied in the INNS OF COURT.

Civility.   The graceful and cultivated behaviour supposedly required of a GENTLEMAN. Civility was said by the HUMANIST Gabriel Harvey to be, together with 'eloquence in speech', 'the goodliest graces of the most noble Commonwealth upon Earth'. 'Civility' assumed a rejection of old, barbarous influences, and in this sense the theatre, with its roots in popular tradition and its retention of such elements as the CLOWN and the JIG, often failed the test. Compare COURTESY.

Classical.   This term, now used in a confusing variety of senses, derives from the LATIN *scriptor classicus*, and so originally distinguished a 'writer for the superior classes' from one who pleased a proletarian audience. However, 'classical' gradually came to describe any writer of high quality, and during our period the term thus embraced the whole body of writings and their authors which had come down from Ancient Greece and Rome. More generally, it denoted the whole 'classical' period, when the HUMANISTS believed a balanced perfection to have been achieved which the modern age should emulate. The later opposition between 'classic' and ROMANTIC has confused this sense of the term, since it attributes 'classical' qualities to those authors who formed part of what may more properly be called the NEOCLASSICAL tradition. This was not fully expressed in English culture until the later-seventeenth and early-eighteenth centuries, although during our period both Sidney and Jonson advocated (rather more than they practised) certain 'neoclassical' doctrines. Today, even more confusingly, 'classical' is often used merely to distinguish any work of music, literature, or other art which has come to form part of the established or 'accepted' repertoire — though arguably the distinction now commonplace between so-called 'classical' and 'popular' music takes the term back to its original Latin associations with the social class for which a work is intended, as distinct from suggesting its intrinsic quality.

Clerk.   In our period, synonymous with 'cleric', and so denoting membership of the clergy of the Church of England. Members of the UNIVERSITIES were 'clerks' in status, and hence the term's gradual extension of meaning to include any scholarly or learned person.

Climax.   In popular usage, simply the culmination of any event, or in the theatre of a play or episode thereof. However, in RHETORIC, the term (which means literally a 'ladder') denotes a sequence of ideas (or, in the theatre, of events) presented in an increasingly impressive manner.

Closure. A modern critical term for the perceived wholeness of a play (or other work of art), as marked by the satisfaction achieved in its resolution or ending. The concept may or may not displace such earlier areas of critical debate as CATHARSIS, DÉNOUEMENT, or CATASTROPHE, through its apparent avoidance of the prescriptive or moral assumptions implicit in these.

Clown. A term which is often used synonymously with FOOL, but which contributes to the latter's complex ancestry the more specific attributes of the countryman — a rustic simpleton, honest yokel, and crafty servant in varying proportions. In Elizabethan drama it is perhaps helpful to distinguish 'clowns', as characters employing a broad, often seemingly unconscious humour, from 'fools', as professionals living by their wits, whether in or out of the play — what distinguishes, say, the supposedly 'clownish' Launce, Dromio, Costard, Young Gobbo, or Dogberry, from a Touchstone, Feste, or Lavatch. In the theatre there would also have been some differentiation by means of COSTUME, between the homespun of the clown and the MOTLEY of the fool. But neither Elizabethans nor modern critics (or actors) have been consistent in making such distinctions, and at the time more depended upon the personality of a company's resident clown than could be defined by any set of rules — as when, in 1599, the reputedly more sophisticated Robert Armin replaced Will Kempe, better known for his JIGS, in Shakespeare's company, the Chamberlain's Men.

Cock-Fighting. Kind of 'sport' popular in England since the thirteenth century, in which two specially-bred and trained gamecocks were set against each other, usually in a cockpit attached to a local TAVERN or other public place. Larger towns would have purpose-built venues, such as the Cockpit in London's Drury Lane, which in 1616 was converted into the PRIVATE THEATRE also known as the Phoenix. Plays were also performed on occasion in the Cockpit-at-Court in the Palace of WHITEHALL.

Collaboration. The writing of plays jointly by two or more dramatists. *Gorboduc* (1565), by Sackville and Norton, is one of the earliest known collaborative works (though many of the MYSTERY PLAYS were assuredly so), while no less than eight authors were credited with a share in another early TRAGEDY, *The Misfortunes of Arthur* (1588). G. E. Bentley has calculated that of the fifteen-hundred or so plays which we know at least by name between 1590 and 1642, some 370 were of unknown authorship, while of the remainder nearly 250 were collaborations. The actual proportion was probably higher, since in HENSLOWE'S DIARY only a third of the plays mentioned were the work of a single author, and Henslowe records payments for up to five writers for a single play. Some dramatists seem to have worked more frequently in collaboration than others — indeed,

Colloquia

Beaumont and Fletcher were so inseparably (even posthumously) yoked as to become subject to numerous misattributions. Shakespeare and Jonson were notable among those who usually (but not invariably) preferred to work alone (and some recent analysis proposes a greater involvement of other authors in the Shakespearean CANON than tradition has allowed). It is not generally possible to attribute portions of collaborative plays to particular authors other than on stylistic (and so conjectural) grounds, though some authors tend to be recognizable because of the distinctive nature of their contributions — William Rowley, for example, who specialized in episodes involving CLOWNS and broad comic action.

Colloquia, or Colloquies.   Short collections of DIALOGUES in LATIN, an instrument of teaching employed in the GRAMMAR SCHOOLS.

Combat.   A form of armed encounter between two combatants, subject to the rules of CHIVALRY, but to be distinguished from the TOURNAMENT in that its cause generally originated in a real individual grievance or matter of national dispute The intended single combat over a matter of personal HONOUR between Mowbray and Bolingbroke in *Richard II* is prepared with due medieval ceremony, and it was part of the King's PREROGATIVE to forbid its coming to issue; while political realities usually prevented the settlement of wider disputes by such means, as in the case of Prince Hal's thwarted offer of single combat with Hotspur before the Battle of Shrewsbury in the First Part of *Henry IV*.

Comedy.   A dramatic GENRE which, since ARISTOTLE, has been conventionally contrasted with TRAGEDY, in part because it generally deals with characters of a lower social class. In Sidney's statement of the NEOCLASSICAL view in his APOLOGY FOR POETRY, comedy is also said to be 'an imitation of the common errors of our life', which the poet 'representeth in the most ridiculous and scornful sort that may be, so as it is impossible that any beholder can be content to be such a one'. This largely moral definition (although useful against PURITAN attacks on the theatre) stresses that comedy should be concerned with arousing 'delight' rather than laughter, which Sidney dismisses as 'only a scornful tickling', more suited to the despised and usually undiscussed form of FARCE. Many Elizabethan playwrights, ignoring such theoretical precepts, undoubtedly did intend their comedy to be funny — Jonson among them, though in his critical writings he also argued for the moral function of the form. But Shakespearean comedy is perhaps better distinguished by its ability to 'delight' than for provoking sustained laughter. Its (usually) happy endings in marriage are, some critics argue, a reflection of the ancient origins of comedy in fertility ritual, celebrating the triumph of spring over winter, youth over age. Others have tried to distinguish between Shakespeare's

CLASSICAL and ROMANTIC comedies — the former regarded as deriving from Roman models in plotting and stagecraft, the latter as looser in construction and dependent on the CONVENTION of COURTLY LOVE — but the criteria employed seem too selective to be very helpful.

Commedia dell'Arte. A theatrical form originating in Italy in the mid-sixteenth century. Its literal meaning, the 'comedy of the professionals', distinguishes it from the *commedia erudita,* the term used to describe orthodox NEOCLASSICAL plays largely performed by courtly amateurs. *Commedia dell'arte* followed a scenario, as the basis for controlled improvisation, rather than a script, and was largely performed in masks representing a range of stock characters. These included rascally servants such as Harlequin and Brighella, the braggart soldier or Capitano, and the aged and perennially-outwitted Pantalone. Although its popularity spread westwards as far as France, it does not appear to have had much influence upon the Elizabethan theatre, and no certain visits by *commedia* companies are recorded later than 1568. However, Shakespeare employed mask-names from *commedia* such as Braggart and Pedant in *Love's Labour's Lost*, while his Parolles in *All's Well That Ends Well* is a direct descendant of (and Falstaff in the second Henrician TRILOGY a strongly individualized variant on) the Capitano — himself a descendant of the MILES GLORIOSUS of PLAUTUS. Later, *commedia* types contributed to the complex genealogy of English pantomime.

Common Law. As distinct from CIVIL LAW, which was based on statutory enactments (and also from 'canon' or 'ecclesiastical law', which had become redundant following the REFORMATION), the 'common law' was derived from traditional usage (that is, it was 'common' to the whole nation rather than derived from local customs) and the precedents of earlier judicial decisions which supposedly reflected such usage. This branch of the LAW was studied in the INNS OF COURT, whereas instruction in civil law was the concern of the UNIVERSITIES. Our period sees the growth of parliamentary opposition to laws, common or PREROGATIVE, made without its consent.

Commonplace Book. A collection of striking or morally apt quotations noted down from one's personal reading, or as heard in SERMONS, DISPUTATIONS, and the like. Commonplace books were sometimes arranged according to subjects or in other groupings — for which the martyrologist John FOXE put into print a notebook with appropriate headings already provided. Often first used as instruments of learning in the GRAMMAR SCHOOLS, commonplace books were no less part of the equipment of every POET or dramatist, and were no doubt especially useful in the working up of TAGS and SENTENTIAE. The word 'commonplace' in this context has the sense of a 'universal truth' rather than its present-day associations of triteness.

Complaint.   In poetry, often a monologue in which the writer laments an unrequited love, seeks relief from personal misery, or bemoans the unhappy state of the world. In modern criticism of the drama, references to the 'complaint tradition' sum up the tendency for dramatized invectives against moral or social ills to be couched in a heightened style and an often deliberately dissonant 'tone of voice'. Such 'complaints' usually presume a decline from the superior standards of an idealized past, and so tend to be conservative in their distrust of change, which is assumed to be for the worse. See also SATIRE.

Conceit.   Deriving from the Latin *conceptus*, the term in our period thus signifies most straightforwardly any 'concept', idea, or thought, but was already coming to suggest a particularly witty or poetically fanciful elaboration of an idea. The first QUARTO of *Romeo and Juliet* thus describes the play as 'an excellent conceited tragedy'. In modern criticism, the term usually denotes any skilfully-wrought poetic or literary device. See also WIT.

Conduct Book.   A kind of instructional work, often by a clergyman, offering guidance on the proper conduct of family and personal relationships. Conduct books became popular from around the middle of the sixteenth century.

Conflict.   In relation to the drama, this term usually denotes a struggle between opposing characters, or the ideas they represent, and since the early nineteenth century has been widely regarded almost as the essence of what is 'dramatic'. Modern plays tend to justify such an emphasis, reflecting as they do the combined influence of the capitalist concern with personal enterprise and success, the ROMANTIC stress on the uniqueness of the individual, and the 'scientific' respectability lent to both of these by the Darwinian theory of natural selection through the 'survival of the fittest'. It is certainly true that 'conflict' can generate considerable theatrical excitement, but the temptation to impose assumptions moulded by nineteenth- and twentieth-century socio-economic conditions upon the drama of the Elizabethans, whose beliefs about the individual and society were quite different, should be avoided.

Consort.   Elizabethan form of 'concert', often used in the modern sense of 'orchestra', or ensemble of players. In a 'whole consort' all the instruments were of one kind (wind instruments, strings, etc.), while a 'broken consort' featured a mixture of different kinds. A consort of VIOLS included all the instruments of that family.

Constable. The most immediate representative of authority for ordinary people in rural England. The constable was not a policeman in the modern sense, but generally a tradesman or YEOMAN farmer who worked under the local JUSTICES OF THE PEACE, assisting in the maintenance of order in the PARISH, and performing such duties as searching out VAGRANTS and overseeing the conduct of APPRENTICES.

Contemptus Mundi, or *de contemptu mundi*. Latin phrase, literally meaning 'contempt of the world', from the belief that this world is but a bridge to the next.

Convention. Any shorthand form of communication between a play-wright or acting company and an audience. Thus, different 'conventional' expectations are aroused by the anticipation of a COMEDY rather than a TRAGEDY, and, in our period, the theatrical presentation of a theme such as REVENGE would be no less dependent upon shared expectations between actors and audience than the recognition of a CHARACTER type such as the MALCONTENT. Some conventions require what Coleridge called a 'willing suspension of disbelief' on the audience's part, in what would otherwise appear artificial or even mechanical — for example, the handling of DIALOGUE for the better understanding of the audience (as in the EXPO-SITION, the ASIDE, or the SOLILOQUY), or matters of plot convenience such as the almost invariable readiness of characters in Elizabethan plays to believe SLANDER and be fooled by the slightest DISGUISE. Other con-ventions involve the acceptance of a sort of moral sleight of hand, such as is involved in the BED TRICK or the sudden conversions of fathers to the virtues of previously undesired sons-in-law. These conventions of the Elizabethan theatre may require some adjustment from a modern audience — whose members are probably not consciously aware of the different but no less 'conventional' kinds of shorthand employed by playwrights of their own times.

Conveyance. In Elizabethan critical terminology, the use of figures of speech or other stylistic devices to convey meaning in a work of literature (though the present legal meaning of the term, as a transfer of property ownership, was also current).

Cony-Catching. The art of swindling and outwitting the credulous, especially at cards. The term derives from the identification (popularized by Greene in the 1590s) of conies (rabbits) with GULLS and simpletons. A cony-catcher was thus a cheat, thief, or, as he would be described today, a confidence-trickster. His female counterpart was often a BAWDY-BASKET.

Cony-Catching Pamphlets. Description of the sub-GENRE of prose literature which was ostensibly designed to thwart CONY-CATCHING by offering cautionary tales illustrating its techniques — rather as today's tabloid press asserts moral high-mindedness in its graphic descriptions of the sexual or other misdemeanours of the famous.

Copyhold.   An ancient form of tenure, whereby LAND was held 'at the will of the Lord according to the custom of the manor'. It was so-called since the tenant held a 'copy' or transcript of the manorial COURT-ROLL which recorded the admissions of tenants to their holding. Many copyholders were among the victims of ENCLOSURE, or of pressure to convert to leasehold tenancies at a higher rent.

Coranto.   Elizabethan three-in-a-measure DANCE, often written for the VIRGINAL, and usually for aristocratic occasions rather than popular performance. The coranto was also the name given (from the French word for a 'runner') after *c.* 1620 to an early form of newsletter, containing dispatches from foreign correspondents.

Corpus Christi, Feast of.   Annual festival of the Catholic Church, instituted in 1264 to celebrate the transubstantiation of the body and blood of Christ into the bread and wine of the Eucharist. It was celebrated on the Thursday after Trinity Sunday, which usually fell in early June: the occasion thus became a near-equivalent to the pagan festivities associated with Midsummer's Day, just as Yuletide had already been taken over by the Church as Christmas, and the fertility rites associated with Easter had been absorbed into the Christian commemoration of the Resurrection. The expunging of the feast of Corpus Christi from the PROTESTANT calendar was one of the various reasons for the decline of the MYSTERY PLAYS associated with its celebration, which had also been an occasion for CARNIVAL.

Correspondences, Theory of.   The belief in a relationship between the larger world of the MACROCOSM and its reflection at the level of the MICROCOSM. Thus, in making the assertion that war is preferable to 'luxurious idleness', Shakespeare's neighbour Dudley Digges likened the capacity of a poison to purge and cleanse the human system to the function of war in ridding the BODY POLITIC of its diseases. Conversely, he claimed, just as 'idleness ministers each active HUMOUR fit occasion of working, to the endangering of most healthful bodies', so 'quiet security gives busy heads leisure to divide the commonwealth into contentious factions'. Queen Elizabeth, according to the same principle, corresponded to the PRIMUM MOBILE of the physical universe, governing the motions of the SPHERES, conceived as the other ranks of the social order. The passion for such 'correspondences' was particularly strong in the medieval mind, and led, for example, to the formulation of the 'seven cardinal VIRTUES' to set against the 'seven deadly sins'. It can be seen, too, in the recurring patterns of sacred HISTORY traced by theological writers obsessed with the pursuit of ANALOGY.

Costume. Generally known as 'apparel', costume in the Elizabethan theatre was elaborately and extensively employed, in contrast to the relative lack (outside the MASQUE) of scenic decoration. The use of costume was intended, often in highly conventionalized and possibly inaccurate forms, to convey social rank, to designate historical or foreign characters, or to signify the supernatural and the abnormal. It was also EMBLEMATIC, in that gaudy and exotic clothing conveyed foolishness, while a plain, honest man wore plain, honest apparel, and the CLOWN and FOOL were also distinguished (even from each other) by their respective costumes. It was a recognized perquisite of the servants of the NOBILITY to sell-off to the players the wardrobe of their deceased employers, and royal gifts to enhance a theatre's stock of apparel were sometimes made following performances at COURT.

Coterie. Modern term used to describe the select, mutually-admiring, and self-knowing audiences thought by some critics to have attended the PRIVATE THEATRES, especially in the early JACOBEAN period, by contrast with the supposedly more heterogeneous audiences at the PUBLIC THEATRES. The balance between 'elite' and 'popular' audiences in the theatre of our period is currently a matter of sustained and unresolved scholarly debate, the once-orthodox belief of such scholars as Alfred Harbage in the socially diverse audiences of the public Elizabethan playhouses having been challenged by scholars claiming that only the relatively well-to-do were able to attend. It may be that this less 'democratic' view reflects the changing temper of the times in which it is being asserted as much as it does any new evidence being put forward. See also RIVAL TRADITIONS.

Couplet. See HEROIC COUPLET.

Court. By our period, this term (which derives simply from the name given to the quadrangular open space enclosed by a large castle or manor house), had come to denote not only a specific residence of the sovereign, but his surroundings and entourage wherever he travelled. Royal residences in or around London included not only WHITEHALL Palace and ST. JAMES'S, but Greenwich Palace, Hampton Court, Richmond, and Windsor. Theatrical performances 'at court', especially MASQUES, could have been in the great hall of any of these places, or wherever the sovereign was staying during a royal PROGRESS, though Whitehall was most convenient both geographically and in terms of the facilities of its Banqueting House and, on a smaller-scale, of the Cockpit-at-Court, which were both used for theatrical purposes.

Court-Roll.   Records kept by a manorial court, detailing the entitlements of the tenants and of those whose tenure of their LAND was by COPYHOLD.

Courtesy.   Not merely politeness and CIVILITY, but the gracious behaviour, derived from the medieval code of CHIVALRY and the training of those ESQUIRES aspiring to become KNIGHTS, now to be expected of the COURTIER, and for which COURTESY-BOOKS set out a course of instruction.

Courtesy-Book.   Term denoting a book containing advice on the attitudes and actions thought appropriate to the NOBILITY and GENTRY. Though such advice might, of course, be included in various kinds of literary work, the 'courtesy-book' became a distinct GENRE during the sixteenth century, though some authorities cite examples as early as the thirteenth. Castiglione's THE COURTIER, discussed in the article following, was probably the best known of the courtesy-books which originated from ITALY, while the ideals of the HUMANISTS remained influential in English examples from Sir Thomas Elyot's *The Book of the Governor* (1531) to Henry Peacham's *The Complete Gentleman* (1622).

Courtier.   A person of culture, COURTESY, and CIVILITY, conversant especially in music and poetry, whose behaviour might suitably have been modelled on the influential COURTESY-BOOK by Castiglione, *The Courtier* (1528), which was translated into English in 1561. This work takes the form of four DIALOGUES at the court of Urbino, whose duchess presides over a discussion of the necessary qualifications of the courtier-intellectual. Alike in military, sporting, and moral respects, the behaviour of the courtier was to be displayed with an (apparently) unaffected SPREZZATURA. There are also discussions in *The Courtier* of the chastity of WOMEN and the ideal of PLATONIC LOVE.

Courtly Love.   A medieval concept first developed in France during the twelfth century, and derived largely from feudal relationships and fealties. It was based on the devoted service to be given to a noble lady by her faithful lover, despite all rebuffs, and the fact that their love cannot be consummated, or sometimes even declared — this very constraint inspiring the lover to deeds of high achievement, and ennobling his mind. The concept of courtly love (or *amour courtois*) remained influential in our period in the modified form advocated in such works as THE COURTIER, in some of the writings of Sidney and Spenser, and later in the cult of NEOPLATONISM which was briefly influential at the COURT of Charles I.

D

Dactyl. In PROSODY, a three-syllable verse FOOT, stressed *dum-di-di*. The dactylic foot occurs occasionally in Shakespeare's plays as a variation on the IAMBIC, the effect usually being to achieve a falling RHYTHM. The HEROIC VERSE of Ancient Greece and Rome was written in dactylic HEXA-METERS (lines of six feet), with an obligatory CAESURA.

Dance. An often neglected element of the drama of our period. Apart from the inclusion of dances within and (especially) at the conclusion of plays — usually in the contrasting forms of the GALLIARD and PAVAN — most performances at the PUBLIC THEATRES were followed by a JIG, while at the PRIVATE THEATRES the MUSIC played during the INTERVAL after each ACT would on occasion have accompanied a dance. The MASQUE form (and masques occurring within regular plays) made most organic use of dance within a dramatic action.

Dead March. See MARCH.

Death, Dance of.   A late-medieval form of MEMENTO MORI, thought to originate either in thirteenth-century French tales of three young noblemen who were accosted by three dead men of hideous appearance, or in the mimed accompaniment to SERMONS by mendicant preachers on the need for repentance, in which figures representing the various orders of society were dragged away by their own corpses. The personification of Death by a single, skeletal figure, rather than by worm-ridden bodies fresh from graveyards, is apparently a later development. Although dances of death are known on occasion to have been 'performed', and Death is often a character in the MORALITY PLAYS (as the 'mighty messenger' of God in *Everyman*, for example), the two forms appear to have developed independently. A 'dance of death' became widespread in other EMBLEMATIC forms of art, notably the ecclesiastical mural and the more humble WOODCUT. Thus, the fifteenth-century murals from the Church of the Innocents in Paris became the loose originals for a *Danse Macabre* of woodcuts published in 1485, and Hans Holbein combined such 'high' and popular art in his own series of woodcuts on the theme in 1538. Pictorial 'dances' were often accompanied by sets of verses, and John Lydgate so embellished the mural in the north cloisters of old St. Paul's Cathedral. Modern critics variously see the dance as an aspect of CONTEMPTUS MUNDI, or, less positively, as denying the redemptive quality of the true Christian

47

attitude. TRAGEDY of the JACOBEAN period, in particular, tends to display the levelling and purely corruptive effects of death, at the expense of any redemptive promise.

Débat. A debate conducted through a literary medium, usually concerned with questions of love or morality, of which early examples are to be found in the *Frogs* and *Clouds* of the Ancient GREEK comic writer Aristophanes. The *débat* was particularly popular in the poetry of the medieval era, and took dramatic form early in the Tudor period in Medwall's *Fulgens and Lucrece* (*c.* 1497), while as late as 1629 Jonson included a *débat* as a central episode in his comedy *The New Inn*. See also DIALOGUE.

Deconstruction. Term in modern currency, describing a body or tendency of thought which is broadly critical of (or, in a 'post-structuralist' context, consciously successive to) the tenets of STRUCTURALISM. In the most basic sense of the term, this dictionary is a work of 'deconstruction', not only in that it breaks down the 'cultural signature' of a period into its component parts without presuming that the sum of those parts is an ascertainable whole, but also in its awareness that the supposedly objective lexicographer is no less a product of a particular culture than those manifestations of a previous culture he is attempting to define. The 'deconstructive' critic typically takes himself less seriously than his immediate predecessors, and rather enjoys recognizing the paradox of utilizing words to deplore 'logocentrism', while acknowledging that, just as no judgement is final, nor is any critical technique or vocabulary. More specifically, 'deconstruction' has brought traditional concepts of CLOSURE into question, an emphasis which has a particular relevance to drama in general (in which one theatrical moment lasts on stage as long as any other), and to the drama of our period in particular, since we approach many of Shakespeare's plays (at least) as *already known* to us, yet eternally 'incomplete' without some critical or theatrical interpretation which is, by definition, only one among the infinite variety of ways in which meaning may be imposed upon a play.

Decorum. The principle of appropriateness, or propriety, and in particular, as the historian Michael Hawkins has succinctly put it, 'the virtues felt to be appropriate to particular types of men'. In literature and art, 'decorum' thus signified the matching of style to content. The supposed need for 'decorum' was not widely observed in England until later in the seventeenth century, when it was mainly understood as pertaining to the balanced, dignified style called for by ARISTOTLE in the *Rhetoric*. But it was advocated in the NEOCLASSICAL criticism of our period, as derived from the writings of HORACE, whose emphasis was on the use of language appropriate to a character's station in life — a concept refined by Castelvetro into almost a theatricalization of the class-structure. Frank Kermode defines 'decorum' as being more generally understood in our period as 'the propriety of what was said to the speaker, to his hearers, to the situation, to the speaker's purpose, and to the function of the passage in the play as a whole'. Although Kermode was there arguing for Shakespeare's increasing sense of decorum, as finally expressed through *The Tempest*, it was probably most practically influential during our period in helping to shape the form and content of Jonsonian COMEDY. The sense of 'decorum' as 'respectable social behaviour' did not emerge until the Victorian period.

Deer. The main object of hunting, or 'the chase', as pursued by the monarch and the NOBILITY. The red deer or stag was considered the noblest beast, but the smaller fallow deer and the elusive roebuck were also quarries — foxes and other vermin only being hunted as enemies to the deer, and hares by ordinary people for food. Hunting had long been a class issue, since the creation and maintenance of forests (in the sense of wide tracts of land suitable for the chase, rather than of densely-wooded areas) had encroached on traditional rights, and poachers continued to pit their wits against the local foresters, or 'verderers'. Ironically, even the deer-parks of the nobility did not escape from the drive for the more profitable use of LAND: thus, the eighteen owned by the Earl of Pembroke at the beginning of Elizabeth's reign were slowly given over to pasture or arable for rent. IMAGERY derived from the chase is frequently to be found in the plays of our period. See also HAWKING.

Defence of Poesy. See APOLOGY FOR POETRY.

Demonology. The study (as distinct from the practice) of demons. In 1597, before his accession to the English throne, King James had written a treatise entitled *Demonology* in DIALOGUE form, and continued to be interested in the subject — probably accounting for the increase in concern over WITCHCRAFT, and its more severe punishment, in the early seventeenth century.

Dénouement. Literally, from the French, an 'untying', and so employed in its Greek form by ARISTOTLE to signify the resolving of the complications of the action at the end of a play. It should properly be distinguished from a CLIMAX, which concerns a building-up of events at any stage of the action, and of which the *dénouement* is the consequence. The term was, however, synonymous in our period with CATASTROPHE.

Determinism. A term dating from the mid-nineteenth century in the sense defined by Raymond Williams as the assumption of 'pre-existing and commonly "external" conditions which fix the course of some process or event'. The concept of 'determinism' might thus be found in modern critical and historical writing concerning our period to describe, for example, the mental outlook behind the CALVINISTIC doctrine of PRE-DESTINATION, or more loosely the sense of 'fate' as predetermining the course of the action in a TRAGEDY. Today, social or economic factors tend rather to be regarded as 'deterministic' in their effects on people's lives — while EXISTENTIALISM offers a (generally) secular version of the opposing theological belief in free-will.

Deus ex Machina.   Literally, from the Latin, 'a god from the machine' — so called from the use of a mechanical device to propel a god into the performing area in Ancient Greek TRAGEDY. Since he was usually required to resolve complications beyond the capacity of the human characters, the term continues in critical use to describe any arbitrary device employed to tie up a play's problematic loose-ends.

Dialectic.   Strictly, a method of philosophical enquiry, as employed in the Socratic DIALOGUES of PLATO. More generally, the term suggests any careful and sustained process of reasoning, and often an internal or actual process of debate — as in the method of political reasoning employed in Marx's 'dialectical materialism'. Shakespeare's most 'dialectical' works would thus be those in which there is a sustained balance of internal argument between the characters, as in such PROBLEM PLAYS as *Troilus and Cressida* and *Measure for Measure*.

Dialogue.   In general usage, simply the direct, alternating speeches of characters in a play (or other literary work). The 'dialogue' was also, however, a distinct GENRE, first being employed in the so-called Socratic dialogues of PLATO, in which a philosophical DIALECTIC took the form of a stylized conversation between participants representing divergent points of view. Other 'dialogues', such as Plato's own *Symposium* or Lucian's *Dialogues of the Dead*, were intended rather for pleasurable reading. Although this form of 'dialogue' was not widely employed in our period, its techniques were employed in DISPUTATIONS and such other exercises in RHETORIC as the DÉBAT. A little later, Dryden utilized the form in his important work of NEOCLASSICAL criticism, the *Essay of Dramatic Poesy* (1668).

Dibrach.   See PYRRHIC FOOT.

Discovery.   In NEOCLASSICAL criticism and analysis, the moment of realization or revelation in a play (sometimes translated as 'recognition', which misleadingly restricts the sense). 'Discovery' (in the original Greek, *anagnorisis*) was defined by ARISTOTLE as 'a change from ignorance to knowledge' — as opposed to (but often suitably combined with) the 'reversal' or PERIPETEIA in a dramatic action. In the discussion of Elizabethan stage practice, however, the term more often denotes characters already present on the stage (and so, in stage directions, 'discovered') at the beginning of a scene, rather than entering in the usual way. This has encouraged widespread scholarly speculation about the 'discovery space' presumably involved, and the possible existence of an INNER-STAGE — a belief now generally discredited, it being pointed out that the double entry-doors shown in the wall of the TIRING-HOUSE in de Witt's sketch of the Swan Theatre, or a simple curtained alcove, would have been adequate for a 'discovery'.

Disguise. The donning of a new COSTUME to achieve concealment of a character's identity. In the broadest sense, of course, all drama is 'disguising', a term which had long been used to describe the mumming plays of the folk tradition, and sometimes for the earlier forms of MASQUE, while in the MORALITY PLAY tradition the VICES often had to disguise themselves as VIRTUES. By our period, it was an accepted CONVENTION that disguise, however minimal or EMBLEMATIC, should be entirely successful in its intended deception until the character involved wished to reveal himself — or, frequently, herself, since trans-sexual disguise, with all the theatrical and actual ambiguities involved in BOY PLAYERS taking the roles of WOMEN disguising themselves as men, was a popular device, not least in Shakespeare's plays. Disguise may be used to maintain watchful oversight, as by the Dukes both in Marston's *The Malcontent* and in *Measure for Measure* and by Justice Overdo in Jonson's *Bartholomew Fair*; for the greater security or authority supposed to lie in a male identity, as in *The Merchant of Venice* or *Twelfth Night*; or to explore the nature of sexual identity itself, as in *As You Like It*. It may be secured through supernatural intervention, as in *A Midsummer Night's Dream*, or be assumed for the pursuit of an amorous intention — perhaps to avoid paternal objections, as in the case of Lucentio in *The Taming of the Shrew*, or to woo someone of a different social status, or to test a loved one's fidelity, as in many of the older popular comedies.

Disintegrator. Term used in BIBLIOGRAPHICAL CRITICISM to describe a critic who believes that there are elements of other authors' COLLABORATION or intervention to be found in Shakespeare's plays, or holds that there were various stages of revision by Shakespeare himself. Such theories are not much in vogue at the present time.

Disputation. A formal debate, intended to test the resourcefulness of the participants in the use of RHETORIC and LOGIC, or in the discussion of PHILOSOPHY or theological issues. Participation was a requirement for the Bachelor's and higher degrees of both the UNIVERSITIES — but such disputations also formed part of the entertainment offered to Elizabeth and James on their visits to Oxford and Cambridge, a reminder of the appetite in our period for witnessing displays of oratorical as well as theatrical skill.

Dissociation of Sensibility.   Term coined by the twentieth-century poet and critic T.S. Eliot to describe the failure of a poet or other writer properly to 'feel' what he is describing, through the separation of emotional from intellectual responses. Eliot believed that such a 'dissociation' set in towards the end of the seventeenth century in English literature — but he did not entirely exempt Shakespeare from its symptoms, as in his suggestion that *Hamlet* is an 'artistic failure' because its hero's feelings lack an OBJECTIVE CORRELATIVE. His vision of our period as one when thought and feeling were perfectly sythesized is, in any case, a romantic simplification, in excess of the facts as they appear.

Divine Right of Kings, The.   The belief, originating in GERMANY and SPAIN during the fifteenth century, that the sovereign was vice-regent to God, and that rebellion against him was thus tantamount to rebellion against God. Although Shakespeare's HISTORY plays often appear to ascribe the doctrine to English medieval monarchs, their claims were primarily hereditary, and the propounding of 'divine right' was thus an aspect of the so-called TUDOR MYTH. Under the doctrine, a tyrannical as well as a just ruler had to be obeyed, since the latter might be serving as an instrument of divine punishment, or SCOURGE OF GOD.

Double-Ending.   See FEMININE ENDING.

Dramatic Irony.   The possession by an audience of knowledge of which a character or characters in the play are kept in ignorance, until the moment of *anagnorisis* or DISCOVERY, often leading to the PERIPETEIA or reversal. 'Dramatic irony' is thus to be distinguished from IRONY in its unqualified sense — which is actually more complex.

Dramatis Personae.   Latin term for 'the persons of the play'. It has been used, largely since the eighteenth century, to head the list of characters (sometimes with their original actors) found at the beginning of the printed text of a play. Occasionally, playtexts in the Elizabethan period would contain lists of 'The Actors' Names' or 'The Principal Comedians', but only the First FOLIO among contemporary printed editions of Shakespeare's plays contains such a list, and the names of the characters were added to only seven plays. Just one extant text from our period, that of Webster's *The Duchess of Malfi* (published in 1623), gives the actors' names alongside the parts they played.

Dubbing.   See ACCOLADE.

Dumb-Show.   A mimed or visualized episode in a play. Sometimes this might be for purely spectacular effect, as in the case of a procession PASSING OVER the stage — in which case, the STAGE DIRECTIONS in the text might be of the briefest, though the dumb-show itself might occupy considerable stage time. Frequently, however, a dumb-show conveyed vital information by visual and EMBLEMATIC means, as in the case of the murders in dumb-show of Isabella and Camillo in Webster's *The White Devil* (1612). Earlier in our period, dumb-shows, accompanied by MUSIC, had often been used as visual synopses of the action about to follow, as before each of the five acts of *Gorboduc* (1561) — and before the play-within-the-play in *Hamlet* (though here for Shakespeare's more complex dramaturgical purposes). Thomas Heywood was employing dumb-show in his *A Maidenhead Well Lost* as late as 1634.

E

Education. See PETTY SCHOOLS (for elementary education), GRAMMAR SCHOOLS (for secondary education), and UNIVERSITIES. See also INNS OF COURT and GRESHAM COLLEGE.

Elect, The. See PREDESTINATION.

Element. One of the simple ('elementary') substances of which all matter was thought to be constituted. According to ARISTOTLE, there were four — fire, air, water, and earth, in the descending order accorded to them in the CHAIN OF BEING. But medieval ALCHEMY added to these the *quinta essentia*, or 'quintessence', supposedly an ingredient common to (and unifying) the others. The capacity of the elements to change, one into another, was regarded as a clear instance of the MUTABILITY of earthly things.

Elizabethan. Strictly, that period covered by the reign of Queen Elizabeth I, from 1558 to 1603. However, in critical usage relating to the drama, the term is often used to denote only the later part of the period when theatrical activity flourished, from the 1580s onwards, or even, loosely, to embrace also the JACOBEAN and even CAROLINE periods, as continuing the 'golden age' of 'Elizabethan' drama.

Ellipsis. This term may be used in modern criticism either to denote the omission of a word or words in a literary work to achieve a more concise or colloquial style, or to describe the use of the typographical convention so named, whereby three full points (thus . . .) within a quoted passage indicate a deliberate omission.

Emblem Book. A collection of WOODCUTS illustrating moral subjects, each illustrated with a 'caption' or *explicatio*, either newly composed for the purpose or taken from a scriptural, proverbial, or other source. Many emblem books were embellished with verses in LATIN, on the model of the first, the *Emblematus Libellus* of Alciati (1522). But there were also emblem books in English, notably by Francis Quarles and George Wither, and in some of these even the printed verses were given an EMBLEMATIC shape through the typographical layout of the poem on the printed page. Among Spenser's earliest poetic endeavours were verses for an English edition of a Dutch emblem book, *A Theatre for Worldlings* (1569).

Emblematic. Although derived from the Elizabethan sense of EMBLEM, in its adjectival form, this term is much used (and sometimes abused) in modern criticism, to meet the need for an appropriate way of describing those elements in a play (or other work of art) which achieve their signification by visual rather than verbal means. The present critical stress on such non-verbal elements (partly a consequence of the recent interest in SEMIOLOGY), is in corrective recognition of the fact that Elizabethan audiences were not only highly alert to such clear visual signifiers as COSTUME or the DUMB-SHOW, but, through the 'visualization' of verbal IMAGERY, could be 'tuned-in' to the conventionalized 'picture-language' familiar to the popular imagination — through the ubiquitous pictorial street SIGNS, the WOODCUTS of EMBLEM BOOKS, and even such earlier, medieval 'emblematic' forms as the stained-glass window and the tapestry.

Emendation. The process of correcting supposedly misprinted or ambiguous words or passages, particularly in the editing of Shakespeare's plays. Emendations began to creep into the texts of Shakespeare's plays in the early eighteenth century, through the often misguided labours of such early editors as Rowe and Theobald. BIBLIOGRAPHICAL CRITICISM now enables some emendations to be made on relatively scientific grounds (as in the case of recurrent errors caused by likely ambiguities between one letter and another in an original manuscript, or in remedying the habitually faulty work of a certain compositor): but the practice is much more sparingly employed by modern editors, who will at least base their decisions on what they consider the most authoritative QUARTO, or upon the First FOLIO text of a play, and a reasoned consideration of the process by which the text may have been corrupted.

Empathy. Modern critical term, describing the attempt to induce as complete an identification as is possible on the spectator's or reader's part with the experiences and circumstances of a character in a play or other literary work. 'Empathy' is thus to be distinguished from the more detached readiness to understand implied by 'sympathy', or the deliberate critical detachment advocated by Brecht for his own style of EPIC theatre.

Enclosure. The practice of fencing-in LAND that had previously been farmed by the medieval strip-system or used as common pasture, and of taking back into larger estates small tenancies held in COPYHOLD, in the supposed interests of greater agricultural efficiency. Early in the sixteenth century, enclosures were often carried out in the belief that land so used for sheep farming (at first for wool, but subsequently for meat) could produce a return half as much again as from traditional, labour-intensive husbandry; but as grain prices increased, improved arable management increasingly became the object. Although undoubtedly the cause of hardship to poorer tenants, and one cause of the increase in VAGRANTS, the enclosure movement in our period was local and sporadic, and is not now thought by historians to have been comparable in its adverse effects to the more widespread enclosures which began in the mid-eighteenth century. Shakespeare's interests were affected by the projected enclosure of an open field near Stratford, but his attitude towards the proposal is uncertain.

End-Stopped Line. A line which reaches a simultaneous grammatical and metrical conclusion, distinctively found in the ALEXANDRINE and in the HEROIC COUPLET. The BLANK VERSE characteristic of Elizabethan drama permitted freer use of the run-on line or ENJAMBMENT, though as a general rule end-stopped lines predominate in the earlier years of the period — as in the so-called MIGHTY LINE of Marlowe.

Enjambment, *enjambement.* In verse, the carrying-over of sense from one line to the next, or in rhymed couplets from one couplet to the next. The part of the line carried over is known in PROSODY as *le rejet.* In critical discussion of the BLANK VERSE of our period, such an occurrence is more commonly and conveniently known as a run-on (as distinct from an END-STOPPED) line. It almost invariably occurs following a WEAK ENDING.

Entrance and **Exit.** Entrances and exits are often the only indication of a scenic unit in the original printed texts of Elizabethan plays. Entrances (presumably because they were of greater concern to the BOOK-KEEPER) were more regularly marked than exits, though a complete clearance of the stage at the end of a SCENE might be signified by an 'exeunt'. It was a generally-observed CONVENTION of stagecraft that characters who had just departed should not immediately re-enter at the start of a new scene, and where this does happen it may therefore indicate an INTERVAL occurring between one ACT and the next, as was usual in the PRIVATE THEATRES. See also AS FROM and PASSING OVER.

Epic. Originally, the form of the long and discursive HEROIC verse narratives, recounting stories of mythic and legendary heroes and their deeds, of which the *Iliad* and *Odyssey* of HOMER in GREEK and the consciously imitative *Aeneid* of Virgil in LATIN survived from the literature of the CLASSICAL world. ARISTOTLE pointed out the distinctive formal qualities of this kind of epic as being closer to HISTORY than is TRAGEDY, without 'limits as to length', and capable, though in narrative form, of conveying a variety of viewpoints and incidents. He advocated that the epic poet should say very little in his own person, but rather speak through his characters — a useful reminder that epic was originally a *performing* medium, as it was to remain until the end of the medieval period (some critics distinguish the epic poetry of later periods, intended to be read rather than performed, as 'secondary' or 'literary' epic). The term 'epic' is often employed in modern criticism in the sense utilized by Bertolt Brecht, to denote a style of EPISODIC theatre which appeals to reason rather than to emotion — a perception of the form which is, except in its political purposes, closer to Aristotle's than is usually recognized. Even Brecht's employment of 'alienation effects', or devices to 'distance' the audience from an emotional response, was to some extent paralleled in the original, generally bibulous circumstances of epic performance — far less formal occasions than those of the religious festivals during which Greek tragedy was enacted. And whereas tragedy, though also dealing with familiar stories, was performed only once, the audiences of the epic narrator might have several opportunities to see his performance, and so be necessarily more responsive to Brecht's concern that epic should deal with the 'how?' and 'why?' of events, rather than the mere suspense of 'what happens next?' Elizabethan plays, of course, also frequently deal with familiar themes or re-tell well-known stories, and perhaps come closest to 'epic' (in the Brechtian sense) in those HISTORY plays of Shakespeare's which were based on PLUTARCH or derived from the CHRONICLES of HALL and HOLINSHED.

Epicurianism.   See STOICISM.

Epigram.   This term derives from the GREEK word for an inscription, as originally added to a statue or public building: more generally, it was used to describe any such succinct and self-contained statement. In Ancient Greece and Rome, the writing of epigrams developed into a distinct GENRE, and a long-popular ANTHOLOGY of some four thousand epigrams of CLASSICAL origin was compiled during the tenth century. The epigram became a popular poetic medium in the seventeenth century (when one of Jonson's pushed the form to its limits by occupying almost two hundred lines), but the term is today more usually applied to a judgement or comparison tersely and wittily encapsulated in prose. The SENTENTIAE found in the plays of our period often take the form of epigrams.

Epilogue.   Originally, in RHETORIC, the peroration, or concluding, recapitulatory part of a speech. Hence the use of the term in the theatre of our period to describe a speech which marks the close of a play. It was normally delivered by one of the actors, sometimes simply 'coming forward' in or out of character, or by a CHORUS whose interventions may throughout have 'framed' the action. Sometimes an epilogue summed up the action, sometimes defended it, and often solicited applause. Although the use of an epilogue became more fashionable than the inclusion of a PROLOGUE, it remained an entirely optional ingredient at this time (it became almost compulsory during the Restoration), and is conspicuous for its absence from any of Shakespeare's tragedies.

Episodic. Term used to describe a play (or other literary work) characterized by a succession of short incidents, of a relatively self-contained nature. When ARISTOTLE condemned episodic plays, he was using the term in the different sense of a digression interpolated into the action, and not in the vaguer but pejorative sense used by many modern critics of 'loosely-knit' or 'poorly constructed'. EPIC drama is, indeed, deliberately episodic, as is much Elizabethan drama. *Antony and Cleopatra*, which contains some forty distinct SCENES, is probably most distinctively so among Shakespeare's plays.

Eponymous. From the Greek, meaning 'giving one's name to', and so used to describe a central character in a play or other work who gives his or her name to that work — as did the PROTAGONIST in much Shakespearean and other TRAGEDY of our period.

Esquire. This term derives from the Latin word for a shield, thus signifying the original duty of the 'esquire' of bearing the ARMS of the KNIGHT he served, and to whose status he aspired. During our period the esquire continued to rank immediately below the knight in the NOBILITY, but the word itself was undergoing the transition by which it eventually came to denote (usually in the abbreviated form of 'squire') an untitled member of the LAND-owning GENTRY. Shakespeare uses the word in both senses.

Essay. A short prose composition, usually devoted to the discursive consideration of a single topic — a definition which the classical CHARACTER WRITING of Theophrastus as well as much early epistolatory writing might be said to include. In our period, however, the term derives from its more self-aware use in French by MONTAIGNE, whose collection of *Essais* was published in 1580. Francis Bacon published his own *Essays* in 1597.

Estate. Term often used to indicate a person's social rank, deriving from the medieval belief that men were called to one of (usually three) estates — the clergy (in English terms, the Lords Spiritual), the NOBILITY (or Lords Temporal), and the common people, who are often thus referred to as 'the third estate'. The term is frequently used as if synonymous with 'order' or 'degree'. See also CHAIN OF BEING.

Euphuism. An ornate style of writing first popularized by John Lyly in his two-part prose ROMANCE *Euphues* (1578-80). Euphuism is marked by an elaborate maintenance of balance or antithesis, the self-conscious employment of ALLITERATION, the use of labyrinthine similes, wide-ranging ALLUSIONS, and complex figures of RHETORIC. The 'euphuistic' style, which to some extent was helpful in creating an awareness of the manipulative possibilities of language, remained influential for a decade or so, and is to be found employed in some of the verbal excesses of the males in *Love's Labour's Lost* — where its use is almost certainly a deliberate aspect of Shakespeare's characterization rather than due to any unconscious assimilation of the style by the young Shakespeare.

Exemplum.   A short story used to illustrate a moral point, common in SERMONS since the medieval period, and often assembled into collections of *exempla,* of which the medieval GESTA ROMANORUM remained influential in our period. The term is also sometimes used in modern criticism of the Elizabethan drama to describe an episode, perhaps only loosely connected to the plot, which has been included for a specific didactic or satiric purpose. Such a purpose will often be made clear at the close of the episode by means of a SENTENTIA.

Exeunt.   See ENTRANCE AND EXIT.

Existentialism.   A modern body of philosophical theory, originating in the nineteenth century, though most commonly associated with the (often contrasting) ideas of French writers of the period during and immediately after the Second World War, notably Sartre and Camus. To summarize the philosophy in the well-known aphorism 'existence precedes essence' is to over-simplify, but does conveniently suggest why the term 'existential' is sometimes to be found in modern criticism of Jacobean TRAGEDY, whose characters (arguably unlike Shakespeare's) often appear to have no 'essential' qualities, but rather to be shaped 'existentially' — that is, by the sum of their successive actions, or simply by what they *do*. Existentialism perceives human life as the sum total of such a succession of choices, each freely taken, and always open to the repudiation of accumulated past choices in favour of a new direction: and this is not dissimilar from the belief of ARISTOTLE that CHARACTER in a play is 'that which reveals moral purpose, showing what kinds of things a man chooses or avoids, where that is not obvious' — at moments, that is, of 'existential choice'.

Exit.   See ENTRANCE AND EXIT.

Exposition.   The conveying in a play, usually in the opening or early scenes, of such basic information about earlier events and the disposition and relationships of the characters as is necessary for an audience to be able to understand the situation as the action proceeds. While Elizabethan dramatists saw no need to disguise exposition, if a PROLOGUE, CHORUS, or DUMB-SHOW was the most convenient way of effecting it, they also employed a variety of less explicit means, combining these with the setting of an appropriate tone — as, for example, in the first act of Shakespeare's *Henry V*, in which, despite the presence of an introductory Chorus, the essential background is actually provided in the process of portraying ecclesiastical and courtly politicking. When, in *The Tempest*, Shakespeare uncharacteristically adhered to the UNITIES, including that of time, the first-act exposition avoids clumsiness only with difficulty, and the assistance of persuasive players.

Eyas. Term in HAWKING used to denote an unfledged or untrained falcon — and famously so employed by Shakespeare, when Rosencrantz in *Hamlet* describes the supposedly unskilled members of the CHILDREN'S COMPANIES as 'little eyases'.

F

Fabliau (plural *fabliaux*).   A short, comical tale in verse, usually concerning ordinary life. Women, priests, and dupes were the favourite targets for its sometimes cruel satire. Popular in FRANCE from the thirteenth century or earlier, it was, like the Italian NOVELLA, a useful SOURCE of plots for the Elizabethan drama. Some of Chaucer's *Canterbury Tales*, such as the Miller's, Friar's, and Summoner's, may appropriately be described as *fabliaux*.

Fair.   Probably originating as a gathering for worship in a sacred place, to which itinerant traders and entertainers quickly attached themselves, fairs became occasions for the sale of staple commodities and livestock, for the hiring of workers — and, increasingly, for entertainment. The possession of a royal charter, such as that granted by Henry I in 1133 for Bartholomew Fair in Smithfield, London, conferred the right to hold such occasions annually, and other notable 'charter fairs' included those at Stourbridge, Greenwich, and Southwark — as also the May Fair from which the now fashionable London district gets its name. Theatrical entertainments of various kinds were given at most fairs, including MOTIONS, or puppet-plays, as in Jonson's vivid dramatization of *Bartholomew Fair* (1614). See also CARNIVAL and HOLIDAY.

Faith, Justification by.   See JUSTIFICATION BY FAITH.

Falconry.   See HAWKING.

Falling Action.   Critical term sometimes used to describe that part of a play which follows the 'rising' of the action to the DÉNOUEMENT.

Farce.   This term, as applied to a short, broadly comical dramatic piece, derives from the French word for 'stuffing', which, it has been suggested, alludes to the insertion of a scene of 'low' comic action into a religious drama. The term was, however, also used in medieval France to describe a dramatic equivalent to the FABLIAU, which often dealt with battles of wit and strength between characters whose main concerns were, as the modern critic L. G. Salingar lists them, 'food, sex, money, and winning the last laugh'. Usually fast-moving in pace and of a cheerfully physical nature, farcical plays have formed part of the repertoire of popular performance since CLASSICAL times. NEOCLASSICAL criticism clearly distinguished

COMEDY from farce, Sidney in the APOLOGY FOR POETRY describing plays such as *Gammer Gurton's Needle* (1566) as farcical because they evoked laughter rather than 'delight' and attempted no serious criticism of morals. Such neat distinctions were, however, largely ignored by the writers of our period, who tended to strike a personal balance between laughter and delight, which reflected artistic preference rather than a conscious choice of GENRE. Even the formally self-aware Ben Jonson was among the most adept of playwrights in blending 'farcical' incident with 'comic' instruction. The opinion of some modern critics that *The Comedy of Errors* is Shakespeare's only farce derives from a more recent view of the form, which tends to stress its supposedly mechanistic nature — but if *The Comedy of Errors* is indeed a farce, it is both ironic and significant of the age's lack of concern with generic niceties that it is also the only one of Shakespeare's plays which, in its very title, declares, quite contrarily, its formal identity. Farce may arguably be seen as closer in some ways to TRAGEDY than to comedy, since it typically deals with humanity in extreme rather than everyday situations, threatens our most sacred taboos, and often deals in a comic variation upon the CATHARTIC effect rather than in the quieter, reconciliatory satisfactions of comedy.

Feminine Ending.   An additional, unstressed syllable at the end of an IAMBIC PENTAMETER, one of the various means of varying the regularity of BLANK VERSE. Also known as a 'double-ending'.

Field of the Cloth of Gold.   Name given to the week-long TOURNAMENT when Henry VIII of England met Francis I of France at Guisnes in 1520. The 'cloth of gold' itself decorated the trunk of a 'tree of NOBILITY', on which were hung the ARMS of the challenging and answering KNIGHTS.

Flaw, Tragic.   See HAMARTIA.

Florio, John (1553-1625).   English translator, and author of an Italian-English dictionary, *A World of Words* (1598), but chiefly renowned for his version of the *Essays* of MONTAIGNE (1603).

Flourish.   A fanfare of trumpets, used in the SOUNDINGS before a performance in the Elizabethan theatre, and within the play to announce the arrival of royalty, or alarms and retreats during battle scenes.

Flyting.   The term, which derives from the Old English word for 'striving' or 'struggling', describes in the literature of our period a sort of formalized contest of abuse, as in the argument between Hotspur and Glendower in the First Part of *Henry IV,* or in the quarrel between Zenocrate and Zabina in Marlowe's *Tamburlaine* (III, iii). The critic Neil

Rhodes's description of the pamphleteering wars conducted by Thomas Nashe in the 1590s as attempts 'to turn journalism into drama' aptly suggests the cultivated, self-aware quality of the art of 'flyting'.

Folio. Strictly, any book made up of sheets of paper folded only once (thus forming four printed pages), and so twice the size of a QUARTO. This was the format frequently used for longer or collected works of theology or philosophy, as also for the collection of 36 of Shakespeare's plays issued in 1623, some years after his death, and generally referred to as the First Folio (a Second appearing in 1632, a Third — including *Pericles* and much of the APOCRYPHA — in 1663, and a Fourth in 1685). The Shakespearean First Folio was only the second such collection of plays by a contemporary writer to appear, Ben Jonson having issued in 1616 a folio edition of his own *Works* — a term thought by many to be presumptuous for describing mere plays. Only Beaumont and Fletcher were similarly honoured during our period, with the publication of a folio collection of plays attributed to them in 1647. Unlike Jonson, Shakespeare took little or no interest in seeing his plays into print, and of the plays in the First Folio half had never before been published in any form.

Folly Literature. Modern critical term for those writings which gave a literary permanence to the tradition of the CLOWN and the FOOL. The best-remembered example of its HUMANIST manifestation is Erasmus's *Praise of Folly* (1509), but in popular form it is to be found in EMBLEM-BOOKS, JEST-BOOKS, and even in CONY-CATCHING PAMPHLETS. Dekker's *The Gull's Hornbook* (1609) is perhaps the best example from our period, but certain CHARACTER WRITING also catches the style, and it is often to be found as an element of the PICARESQUE.

Fool. In our period, a character in a play supposed to live professionally by his wits, such as Touchstone in *As You Like It*, Feste in *Twelfth Night*, or the Fool in *King Lear*. Although the term 'fool' is often used synonymously with CLOWN, both in Elizabethan usage and our own, that rustic simpleton (as separately discussed) is only one of the fool's many ancestors, which include the itinerant *mimus* of Ancient Rome, many of the wandering popular entertainers of the medieval period, the COURT jester, the VICE of the MORALITY PLAYS, and characters from the writings now described as FOLLY LITERATURE. A further complication is that actors playing the fool-roles as their LINE — most notable among whom were Richard Tarlton, Will Kempe, and Robert Armin — were often professionally identified with that role outside the theatre (and, as Hamlet complains, some were also given to improvising within it). An Elizabethan audience's sense of the fool thus became a complex blend of his ancestry, his function as a character within a particular play, and the personal attributes of the actor taking the part. The clown or fool normally took the leading part in the JIG which followed performances in the PUBLIC THEATRES. His distinctive dress was known as MOTLEY.

Foot. A unit of RHYTHM in verse, usually comprising either two or three syllables of distinctive STRESS, and generally further distinguished by the MEASURE, or total of such metrical feet constituting the full verse line. Among the possible combinations of long and short, stressed and unstressed syllables, the DACTYL was the distinctive rhythm of CLASSICAL verse, while the IAMBIC stress in PENTAMETER measure of BLANK VERSE was characteristic of the plays of the Elizabethan period. See also SCANSION.

Form. A term sometimes used in modern criticism as synonymous with GENRE — but more especially in contexts where 'form', signifying the style or tone of a work, is being contrasted with (or distinguished from) 'content' or substance.

Fortune. Often represented in EMBLEMATIC guise in our period, as she had been in CLASSICAL times as the goddess Fortuna — sometimes three-dimensionally, at the rudder of a ship, in her role as the pilot of destiny. By the medieval period, the 'wheel of fortune' was the more familiar image, on which PRINCES rose only to fall, along with their crowns and sceptres, as the wheel inevitably continued to turn. Lydgate's *Falls of Princes* (*c*. 1434) is notable among literary works based on the concept.

Foul Papers. Term used in BIBLIOGRAPHICAL CRITICISM to denote the author's heavily-corrected manuscript of a play (or other work) — that is, a working manuscript as opposed to a 'fair copy', the surviving term for the revised and more legible version, as submitted by some dramatists to the acting company. In the First FOLIO of Shakespeare's works, it is claimed that the plays are 'truly set forth according to their first original': but here the word 'original' means 'authoritative', and does not necessarily imply that the 'foul papers' were used as printing copy — though scholars believe that in fact they often were. Indeed, the tradition that Shakespeare, in Jonson's words, 'never blotted out line' supports the likelihood that his 'foul papers' were also in many cases the versions used for the PROMPT-BOOK.

Foxe, John (1517-87). English writer, whose *Acts and Monuments of These Latter Perilous Days*, popularly-called his *Book of Martyrs*, was first published in English in 1563. Augmented in 1570, it became, apart from the BIBLE itself, probably the most widely-owned and read work of popular theology in PROTESTANT households. Foxe also published a thematically-divided COMMONPLACE BOOK.

France. By the later fifteenth century, France had recovered from the Hundred Years War with England, her traditional enemy, as dramatized by Shakespeare from the CHRONICLES in the second Henrician TETRALOGY. Many of the internal dissensions which had contributed to her disastrous defeat at Agincourt in 1415 were already in process of healing before the final battle of the war, in 1453, deprived England of all her French possessions apart from Calais. However, during the sixteenth century France became embroiled in conflict with SPAIN and the essentially GERMAN Holy Roman Empire for political hegemony in ITALY: and no sooner had this struggle come to an end with her withdrawal in 1559 (a year which also saw the recapture of Calais, thanks to Mary's brief and ill-advised involvement), than the long religious conflict involving the Huguenot followers of CALVIN began. This ended with limited toleration being granted to the PROTESTANTS in 1598, but not before the infamous treatment of the Huguenots (at the instigation of the queen mother, Catherine de Medici) in the Massacre of St. Bartholomew of 1572 had led to a massive influx of refugees to England, and a resurgence of traditional English hostility towards France. This was tempered politically by the emergence of Spain as chief rival for naval supremacy, and artistically by admiration for the flowering of French literature led by Rabelais and the poet Marot, and sustained by Ronsard and the highly-influential MONTAIGNE.

Freehold. The entitlement to land or property in one's own right, as distinct from the less secure (in our period) form of tenancy known as COPYHOLD. In the English counties, those enfranchised to elect members to the House of Commons needed to possess freehold land of an annual rental value of forty shillings (and as such would also be considered YEOMEN). Since the value of land was generally expressed as equivalent to twenty years' annual rental, such 'forty-shilling freeholders' were said to be 'worth' forty pounds (twenty times forty shillings).

G

Galliard.   A popular Elizabethan DANCE of three-in-a-measure time and rapid, quite complicated steps. The dance, which was of Italian origin, is generally associated with the PAVAN in the development by composers of the instrumental suite from such forms.

Gatherer.   One of those who took the money at the entrances to Elizabethan playhouses. The gatherers are thought to have been appointed by the HOUSEKEEPER, who took half the receipts from the galleries as rent.

Genre.   Critical term, derived from the French word for 'kind', and thus used both to distinguish drama from (say) the novel or (in modern usage) poetry, and also to describe the distinctive formal modes into which drama itself falls — TRAGEDY, COMEDY, FARCE, and so on. 'Bastard genres' are those such as TRAGI-COMEDY which combine the attributes of two or more forms. The Elizabethan period was more conscious of such generic distinctions than our own, as is suggested by the title-page description of the first FOLIO of Shakespeare's plays as his *Comedies, Histories, and Tragedies*, and the division of the work accordingly. Despite Polonius's famous catalogue in *Hamlet* of 'tragedy, comedy, history, pastoral-comical, historical-pastoral, tragical-historical, tragical-comical-historical-pastoral', such a mode as PASTORAL, or indeed SATIRE, is less a distinctive genre than a mood or 'tone of dramatic voice', which may be realized through various formal associations.

Gentility.   The attributes supposedly shared in our period by all those with claims to belong to the NOBILITY and GENTRY. The COURTESY-BOOKS constituted guides to the behaviour appropriate to THE COURTIER — which was also the title of the best-known of them, by Castiglione.

Gentleman.   Strictly, a gentleman was distinguished by his possession (like Shakespeare) of a coat of ARMS, and was entitled to the designation MASTER. Below the NOBILITY, he stood above the CITIZEN and the YEOMAN among those commoners who took a share in GOVERNMENT. However, by the Elizabethan period the title no longer invariably designated a member of a particular social class, but was coming to be used to describe any person who enjoyed a leisured and cultivated life-style — though an appropriate ancestry naturally helped. The ranks of gentlemen were now even allowed to include professional men such as lawyers and doctors, who would have attended the UNIVERSITIES and the INNS OF COURT. Compare ESQUIRE.

Gentry.   Though in the common usage of our period this term described the quality and rank of a GENTLEMAN, it could also be used to designate all superior classes of society — the sovereign and the NOBILITY (or ARISTO-CRACY) being the 'greater gentry', while KNIGHTS, ESQUIRES, and gentlemen constituted the 'minor gentry'.

Germany.   The far-flung and fragmented territories of Germany were by our period all that remained of the ideal of a Holy Roman Empire, which had been proclaimed by Charlemagne in 800. Despite the securing of the previously-elective imperial crown by the Hapsburg dynasty in 1438, political power remained distributed among over three hundred separate PRINCES, prelates, and municipalities. But by the fifteenth century the strength of the HANSA had made this trading alliance into a powerful political as well as economic force, and the material prosperity of the period is also evident from factors as diverse as the building of cathedrals and the German domination of the newly-emerging craft of printing — while, under HUMANIST influence, no less than twelve new universities were created between the foundation of Leipzig in 1409 and that of Wittenberg in 1502. Paradoxically, the fact that LUTHER was able virtually to lead the REFORMATION from Wittenberg reflected both the intellectual ferment within the nation at this time, and the potential for its further disintegration in the period of struggle which ensued. In 1555 the Peace of Augsburg provided a limited basis for religious tolerance, but by this time Germany had been reduced to a state of passive exhaustion, out of which the Catholics slowly regathered their strength for the renewed religious hostilities which led eventually to the outbreak of the Thirty Years War in 1618. At the cost of the near-devastation of the nation, these finally brought tolerance for the followers of CALVIN, as well as for Lutherans and Catholics, but did nothing to resolve the continuing political divisions. Before (and even during) the war, acting companies of 'English comedians' were touring regularly in Germany — ironically, returning the Faust legend to its origins *via* Marlowe's play, which eventually, in a puppet version, became virtually the German equivalent to the English Punch and Judy. *Doctor Faustus* is, of course, set in Wittenberg, and it is no accident that this is also where Hamlet was a student — its combination of intellectual excitement and theological danger representing also the impressionistic English view of the nation as a whole, which at this time was capable of offering little in the way of political threat or friendship.

Gest, Gestus.   Modern critical term, employed by the German dramatist Bertolt Brecht, and perhaps best translated, by John Willett, as 'showing an attitude'. A 'gestus' is intended to indicate the way in which the actor should not *show feeling*, as in his conventional training, but *display behaviour*, or externalize the essentials of an attitude or relationship within a specific social context. The 'gestus' is a difficult concept, but it has been used increasingly in recent years in attempts to describe the probable style of Elizabethan acting — which, in its understanding of the presentational techniques of RHETORIC, as in its use of EPISODIC material frequently on an EPIC scale, may, it is suggested, have more nearly approximated to the Brechtian approach than to the Stanislavskian method evolved essentially in response to the requirements of modern NATURALISM.

Gesta.   From the Latin word for 'deeds', this term described collections of stories recounting deeds of CHIVALRY, saints' lives, or other popular legends. As in the GESTA ROMANORUM, the moral attached to each story encouraged its use as an EXEMPLUM.

Gesta Romanorum.   Collection of stories or GESTA in LATIN, literally meaning *The Deeds of the Romans*. Dating from around 1400, it was printed in an English translation *c*. 1510, and eventually included some 200 tales, derived, despite its title, as much from CHIVALRY, the lives of the saints, and popular legend as from CLASSICAL Rome. The *Gesta Romanorum* was a much-used SOURCE for the Elizabethan drama — including, for example, the episode of the caskets in Shakespeare's *The Merchant of Venice*.

Ghosts.   There was a widespread popular belief during our period in the existence of supernatural spirits, though these were probably viewed with some scepticism by the better-educated. Since PROTESTANT theology had no place for PURGATORY, to which ghosts were previously thought to be condemned while they purged their sins, they could only come from Hell, and so had to be of malign intent. For an Elizabethan audience of *Hamlet* this was a crucial point, from which derives Horatio's extreme caution and Hamlet's own concern for further proof of the Ghost's claims — though the folkloric belief that the spirits of the dead wandered their earthly surroundings for a year after interment also persisted. Elizabethan drama had the authority of SENECA for the dramatic use of ghosts, particularly in the REVENGE PLAY.

Gild, Gild Merchant.   See GUILD, GUILD MERCHANT.

Gloriana.   A name frequently given to Queen Elizabeth, especially in ALLEGORY, from its first such usage in Spenser's *Faerie Queen* (1589-96).

Gossip.   A familiar acquaintance, or person of reputed good-fellowship.

Government

More specifically, one of the women invited to be present at a birth, or to serve as god-parent (from *god-sib*, or relative through God). The meaning has only more recently been extended to include the idle talk which the TYPOLOGY of WOMEN insists should characterize such gatherings.

Government. Sir Thomas Smith's *De Republica Anglorum* defined three forms of government — monarchy, ARISTOCRACY, and democracy. England was, of course, a monarchy, ruled by forms of PREROGATIVE which were reinforced by the cultivation of the TUDOR MYTH. Elizabeth herself could and did reign absolutely in certain areas such as the creation of foreign POLICY, while the active members of the PRIVY COUNCIL, who were generally either commoners or peers of Elizabeth's own creation, largely directed national affairs. Parliament was not at this time an essential instrument of government, and was generally summoned only when its consent was necessary for levying taxation. The House of Commons comprised roughly four-fifths of members elected by the boroughs, the remainder being chosen by those of requisite FREEHOLD within the counties. Local government was largely in the hands of the minor GENTRY, from whose ranks were generally drawn the JUSTICES OF THE PEACE (numbering around fifteen hundred, all unpaid, by contrast with some five hundred salaried civil servants), who served under the executive authority of the sheriff of the county. Some authorities distinguish GENTLEMEN, CITIZENS, and YEOMEN, as participants in government, from ARTIFICERS and labourers, who were not. There was, however, mobility within these social classes, both upwards and (owing in particular to the impoverishing effects of PRIMOGENITURE on younger brothers) downwards as well. The relative stability of the later Elizabethan period, despite the severe economic difficulties associated with the PRICE REVOLUTION, was largely thanks to the Queen's skill in keeping all these forces of government in equilibrium — a skill at which neither James I nor his son proved so adept.

Grammar School. The form of free school, of which there were around 350 by the end of the Elizabethan period, attended by boys aged between seven or eight and fourteen or fifteen, after leaving their PETTY SCHOOL. Sons of the NOBILITY were in the main still instructed by private tutors, for whose guidance the widely influential work *The Schoolmaster* was written by the HUMANIST Roger Ascham in 1570. But the GENTRY were already sending their sons to the grammar schools, although most of these had been endowed (particularly after the REFORMATION) for the benefit of the poor children of their neighbourhood, despite the inability of many parents to spare them from work. The grammar schools were concerned with the teaching of 'grammar' in its medieval sense of 'the art of interpreting poets and writers of HISTORY, and of writing and speaking correctly', but in practice this large aim was generally narrowed down to mere rote learning of the LATIN language, through the ubiquitous *Lily's Grammar* (1540), the use of VULGARIA and COLLOQUIA, the method of 'double translation', and some original composition using Cicero and Pliny as models for IMITATION. GREEK and Old Testament Hebrew were sometimes also studied, and in later years RHETORIC, perhaps tested by means of DISPUTATIONS. But LOGIC, the third element of the medieval TRIVIUM, was increasingly becoming the preserve of the UNIVERSITIES, as were the apparently more practical subjects of the QUADRIVIUM. Teaching, usually in a single schoolroom under one master and his assistant or usher, must in practice have been less than systematic. There was no provision for physical recreation, while the working days were long and vacations brief. Some schools did, however, become known for the SCHOOL DRAMA they produced.

Great Chain of Being. See CHAIN OF BEING.

Greek. Medieval knowledge of Greek literature and thought — even of ARISTOTLE, despite his influence in shaping the SCHOLASTICISM of the period — was derived largely through LATIN translations. Inspiration for the revival of the study of the language itself during the RENAISSANCE is traditionally attributed to PLUTARCH — rather ironically, since he himself failed to master it. The influx of scholars from the east which followed the Fall of Constantinople in 1453 certainly played its part in the process, but the introduction of printing, and the wider dissemination of original texts which this permitted, was probably of more enduring importance. Thus, the works of HOMER were first put into print in 1488, and Aldus Manutius oversaw editions of Thucydides, Theophrastus, Aristophanes, Sophocles, and Euripides between 1494 and 1515. Largely under the influence of the itinerant HUMANIST Erasmus, interest in Greek began to spread to England in the early sixteenth century, and it was at the UNIVERSITY of Cambridge that Erasmus prepared the first Greek translation of the New Testament of the BIBLE in 1516. But although Greek had become a subject of study in the GRAMMAR SCHOOLS by our period, it could not challenge the predominance of Latin. If Shakespeare possessed, as Jonson claimed, 'small Latin and less Greek' — both, of course, relative to Jonson's sense of his own superior scholarship — he was probably representative in this of most men of grammar-school EDUCATION.

Gresham College. Founded in 1597, in Basinghall Street, London, under the will of Sir Thomas Gresham (d. 1579), this was the most influential of the experiments in providing educational facilities more in tune with true HUMANISTIC thinking than the UNIVERSITIES. Lectures in divinity, LAW, astronomy, MUSIC, geometry, RHETORIC, physics, and other subjects were given, both in English and in LATIN. Ben Jonson may have been among the lecturers in rhetoric here.

Groundlings. Familiar term for those members of the audience at a PUBLIC THEATRE who paid the lowest admission charge, one penny, to stand in the uncovered yard around and below the platform stage. They were thus sometimes said, with punning irony, to be the most 'understanding' members of the audience.

Guild, Gild. As distinct from the GUILD MERCHANT, below, a guild was one of the various exclusive organizations concerned with preserving both standards and their own MONOPOLY within a particular craft or trade — whose skills were its 'mystery', hence the term MYSTERY PLAYS for the dramatic cycles performed by many of these civic guilds during the later middle ages. Guilds were self-regulating, those who broke their statutes being subject to the jurisdiction of the mayor in the guildhall, or common meeting-place. Each APPRENTICE to a trade was enabled to become a JOURNEYMAN, and subsequently had the opportunity to become his own MASTER — but by our period the power of the guilds, and consequently the controlled social mobility they offered, had been considerably diminished, not only by statute, but through the increasing mobility of labour outside the towns where the strength of the guilds lay, and the emergence of an embryonic capitalism. The mutual dependence and stability they supposedly ensured is dramatized nostalgically in Dekker's *The Shoemakers' Holiday* (1599).

Guild Merchant, Gild Merchant. An association of all the traders or MERCHANTS in a medieval town. The right to form a guild merchant was normally conferred by royal charter, and, as its officers tended to be the same as those of the borough, often in course of time the two effectively merged to conduct municipal affairs. The guild merchant is to be distinguished from the craft and trade GUILDS, discussed above, which were often created because the smaller businessmen and craftsmen were squeezed out of the more powerful organization.

Gulls. Credulous persons — this sense probably deriving from one of the ornithological meanings of the word, as an 'unfledged bird'. Since human 'gulls' were also expected to be full of social pretension and ambition, and often possessed more money than sense, they could be the more easily imposed upon by CONY-CATCHERS and BAWDY-BASKETS. Dekker wrote his *Gull's Hornbook* in 1609 as an ironical guide to their behaviour — including behaviour at a theatre.

H

Hall (Halle), Edward (*c.* 1498-1547). English PROTESTANT historian, whose CHRONICLE of the Wars of the Roses, *The Union of the Two Noble and Illustrious Families of Lancaster and York* (1542, enlarged by Richard Grafton in 1548 and 1550), covers the period from 1399 to 1532. Interpreting its subject matter didactically as a warning against insurrection and civil war, the work, along with HOLINSHED's *Chronicles*, helped to establish the version of recent HISTORY now known as the TUDOR MYTH, which saw the accession of Henry VII as the reconciliatory climax to a long period of discord — itself regarded as divine retribution for the unlawful usurpation of Richard II. Hall's work was an important SOURCE for Shakespeare's history plays.

Hamartia. Term used in the *Poetics* of ARISTOTLE to describe the 'tragic flaw' which (rather than 'vice or depravity') he declared to be the cause of the misfortunes leading to the CATASTROPHE of the noble PROTAGONIST of a TRAGEDY. Whether this 'flaw' is due to a simple lack of knowledge, to an error of judgement, to HUBRIS, or to an inherent weakness of character, has long been a matter of debate, since examples of all these versions of *hamartia* can be found in the tragedies of Ancient Greece. The concept is still to be found in critical discussions of Shakespeare's tragic protagonists — how usefully may perhaps be judged by the fact that King Lear is arguably a good candidate for any or all the foregoing interpretations.

Hansa. Also known as the Hanseatic League, the Hansa was an association (or GUILD, the literal meaning of the word) of the leading merchants of northern GERMANY and Scandinavia. It first emerged in the twelfth century, and remained the dominant force in overseas trade — also wielding considerable political power inside Germany — until the challenge from Dutch and English seafarers gathered in strength during the sixteenth. The English company of 'Merchant Adventurers' succeeded in having the Hansa expelled from its LONDON headquarters in 1597.

Hautboy, Hoyboye. Elizabethan form of oboe, an 'upper' instrument (hence the corruption of the French *haut bois*, or 'high-wood'). It may have been used in the theatre as an alternative to the trumpet to signify the entrance or departure of a king.

Hawking, or Falconry. Field sport in which birds of prey, notably the falcon, are trained (by a skilled falconer) to capture birds and smaller animals. Along with the hunting of DEER, falconry was one of the two most popular pastimes of the COURT and NOBILITY. Although of comparatively recent origin, it had (perhaps for this reason) developed its own large vocabulary of specialist terms, whose IMAGERY is often utilized in the drama of our period, when hawking was enjoying its heyday and also had a large literature of its own.

Heavenly Spheres.   See SPHERES.

Heavens.   Term for the covering over the platform stage of the Elizabethan PUBLIC THEATRES, from which properties (and even players) could be lowered. 'The heavens' were supported by two pillars or 'stage-posts', and in de Witt's drawing of the Swan Theatre appear to be roofed with tiles, while the underside would normally have been painted or otherwise decorated with sun, moon, stars, and zodiacal signs. The theatrical and astronomical implications are METATHEATRICALLY juxtaposed in Hamlet's reference to 'this brave o'erhanging firmament' (II, ii). In the EMBLEMATIC tradition of the MYSTERY PLAYS, the space below the stage was conversely known as HELL.

Hell.   In EMBLEMATIC contrast with the HEAVENS, this was a description for the space below the stage in the PUBLIC THEATRES. There is even a record in HENSLOWE'S DIARY of a 'hell's mouth' — presumably a highly-decorated set of gaping diabolic jaws, as in the MYSTERY PLAYS, which could be placed over a TRAP. GHOSTS, as of Hamlet's Father, could appropriately speak or appear from below the stage, whence, more conjecturally, Doctor Faustus's limbs could have been cast up at the close of Marlowe's play.

Henslowe's Diary.   Term used, somewhat misleadingly, to describe the accounts and memoranda of the theatre manager Philip Henslowe (d. 1616). These are extant for the period from 1592 to 1603, and begin simply as lists of companies which used Henslowe's theatre (presumably the Rose), together with the plays they performed and receipts therefrom. But after 1597 the 'diary' notes advances made to playwrights, the purchase of costumes, properties, and so on. It is a unique piece of documentary evidence concerning the working and equipment of the Elizabethan theatre, though Henslowe's relationship as HOUSEKEEPER to visiting companies, and subsequently his role virtually as banker to (rather than SHARER in) the Admiral's Men did not typify the invariable practice.

Heroic Couplet.   In English poetry, rhymed verse in pairs of IAMBIC PENTAMETERS — the distinctive mode of Dryden, Pope, and other poets of the late-seventeenth and early-eighteenth century. Although also used in the verse of our period — for example, in Marlowe's *Hero and Leander* — heroic couplets are relatively rare in its drama (other than for emphatic purposes, as in SENTENTIAE or TAGS). Their frequent use in Shakespeare's *Love's Labour's Lost,* and marked occurrence in his *Richard II,* are, however, among the notable exceptions, while later in his career the couplet passages in *All's Well That Ends Well* strike a less than satisfactory balance between, in G.K. Hunter's words, 'the intellectual complexity of the antitheses' and the 'neatness of the structure' — always a danger in their dramatic use. 'Heroic drama' is also a term used to distinguish the content of those plays of the Restoration in which a strong central figure experiences a conflict between the claims of love and honour. The Restoration poet and dramatist John Dryden thus reconstructed *Antony and Cleopatra* into his own NEOCLASSICAL version, *All for Love*, exemplifying such a conflict, though here he abandoned the heroic couplets he had earlier been championing, and returned to BLANK VERSE. Interestingly, ARISTOTLE distinguished the iambic meter from the Greek heroic MEASURE, the DACTYLIC HEXAMETER, because the former was closer to the RHYTHM of everyday speech, and so more appropriate for satirical lampoons.

Heroic Verse, Heroics. Generally, the verse form distinctive to the EPIC poetry of a nation — in GREEK and LATIN, the DACTYLIC HEXAMETER, in France the iambic HEXAMETER, and in England the IAMBIC PENTAMETER, either unrhymed, as in BLANK VERSE, or rhymed, as in HEROIC COUPLETS (with which the term is sometimes, misleadingly, taken to be synonymous).

Hexameter. In PROSODY, a verse line comprising six feet — DACTYLIC in the HEROIC VERSE of the GREEK and LATIN poets.

Hireling. A member of an Elizabethan acting troupe who was paid by the week, as distinct from a SHARER in the company. Not only some of the actors but also the GATHERERS, musicians, BOOK-KEEPER, and TIREMAN were hirelings.

History. In the sense of a narrative rendering of past events, history had been widely written by the Ancient Greeks and Romans — notably, by Herodotus and Thucydides in the fifth century BC. It was not, however, concerned with an understanding of the past in its own terms, as is the modern academic discipline: rather, it aimed both to tell a 'story' (the word is of the same derivation as 'history' and was for long interchangeable with it — as in 'The Tragical History of Pyramus and Thisbe'), and to derive moral, patriotic, or philosophic conclusions from it.

Histrio-Mastix

In the medieval period, the chronological annals which constituted the CHRONICLES of the time in part reflected the Christian view that 'sacred' or 'universal' history had, in the BIBLE, already been written — including the 'future' history of the Apocalypse and Last Judgement. But the twelfth-century Benedictine monk Gervase of Canterbury suggested the possibility of shaping more recent, secular history to demonstrate the workings of providence — while other writers, such as the fourteenth-century French historian Froissart, portrayed events according to the ideals of CHIVALRY, even then in decline, and saw an arbitrary and often malevolent FORTUNE as controlling man's destiny. Just as PLUTARCH had looked for parallels between the great Greek and Roman figures, so history continued to work by ANALOGY rather than analysis, as in the cautionary MIRROR FOR MAGISTRATES: and such an approach was reinforced by the return during the RENAISSANCE to the CLASSICAL conception of the subject as a branch of RHETORIC, largely intended to provide a good supply of EXEMPLA. In Shakespeare's England, Froissart (in Berners's ornate translation, published in 1524-25) was read alongside more recent works, such as the influential *History of Italy* by the Florentine Francesco Guicciardini, in its English translation by Geoffrey Fenton; the *Anglica Historia* (1534) of Polydore Vergil; and the less 'literary' chronicles of HALL and HOLINSHED, with their emphasis on the clash of noble figures and their patriotic anticipation of the national harmony restored by the accession of Henry VII, so important to the making of the TUDOR MYTH. Sidney — echoing the assertion of ARISTOTLE that poetry was 'more philosophical' than history — declared in the APOLOGY FOR POETRY that 'the best of the historian is subject to the POET'. Thus Shakespeare, like many of his fellow dramatists, uses historical writing with only a little less freedom than other, fictional SOURCE material: and it is perhaps significant of the functional way in which history was viewed that none of his characters ever discusses it.

Histrio-Mastix. Literally, *The Players' Scourge*, which was also the sub-title of the PURITAN pamphlet of that name by William Prynne, published in 1633. A vituperative attack on the theatre, it caused the imprisonment of its author for attacking Charles I and Henrietta Maria for participating in theatrical activities. There was also a play of this title, probably by Marston, which formed part of the WAR OF THE THEATRES.

Holiday. Originally a 'holy day', since Sundays and other religious festivals were also those on which nobody was expected to work. Although the REFORMATION had seen the expulsion of numerous saints from the calendar of the Church of England, saints' days and festivals were still marked as 'red-letter days', on some of which, such as at SHROVETIDE (preceding Lent), CARNIVAL-like celebrations were tradition-ally held. The idea of a holiday as a single annual break lasting several consecutive weeks is relatively recent.

Holinshed, Raphael (*c.* 1530-*c.* 1580).   English historian, responsible for the sections on English HISTORY included in *The Chronicles of England, Scotland, and Ireland* (1577, second edition 1587). Collectively if misleadingly known as *Holinshed's* CHRONICLES, these largely helped to perpetuate HALL's view of the Wars of the Roses as a process of divine retribution for the usurpation of Richard II, culminating in the reconciliatory marriage of Henry VII to Elizabeth of York. The broader historical sweep of Holinshed's work made it a SOURCE not only for Shakespeare's English history plays, especially the later TETRALOGY, but also for *Macbeth*, *Cymbeline*, and possibly *King Lear*.

Holy Office.   See INQUISITION.

Holy Roman Empire.   See GERMANY.

Homer.   Unknown Greek author to whom the great EPIC poems of Ancient Greece — the *Iliad* and the *Odyssey* — are traditionally attributed. Derived from texts first edited in the sixth century BC, these works are now generally considered to have been by different authors, or even the cumulative creation of a succession of epic performers, the *Odyssey* being thought the later of the two. Shakespeare used a Homeric theme only once, in *Troilus and Cressida*, and although Homer speaks the PROLOGUE to three of Thomas Heywood's TETRALOGY of mythological *Ages* plays, the dramatist in fact derived his material from later writers.

Homily.   Religious discourse or SERMON, usually of a kind less devoted to theological niceties than to the practicalities of everyday living. Hence, any long (and in ironic usage tedious) moralizing speech or tract. Two *Books of Homilies* were published in 1547 and 1563, appointed to be read in churches.

Honour.   'What is honour? A word.' Such is Falstaff's ultimately reductive definition in the First Part of *Henry IV*. Perhaps more significantly, the apparently 'noble' figure of Prince Hal has earlier in the same play promised to accrete honour to himself by allowing Hotspur, as his 'factor', to 'engross up glorious deeds on my behalf', and then to 'call him to so strict account' as to 'tear the reckoning from his heart'. As David Margolies has pointed out, this interpretation of the concept of 'honour' in the insistent IMAGERY of a commercial transaction exemplifies the conflict in our period between 'honour' as, on the one hand, still popularly conceived — within the medieval tradition of CHIVALRY, based on service to others and the integrity of one's own behaviour — and, on the other, its increasingly individualized sense as the cultivation and preservation of a self-image resembling what might today be called 'machismo'. If one's 'honour', in this sense, was disputed or affronted, it demanded the 'satisfaction' of that newly-fashionable version of personal COMBAT, the duel.

Horace (Quintus Horace Flaccus, 65-8 BC). Roman poet, satirist, and critic, whose *Ars Poetica*, or *Art of Poetry*, originated as a verse epistle in LATIN, offering guidance to a would-be writer, perhaps of a play. Horace lays great stress on the ruling principle of DECORUM, advising against the mixing of GENRES, the display of violence on the stage, and any lack of VERISIMILITUDE. In all these and other respects he exerted a greater influence upon NEOCLASSICAL criticism than ARISTOTLE, from whose writings many of Horace's ideas are, however, ultimately derived.

Horn. Musical instrument of the brass family, used in the Elizabethan theatre to signal or accompany HUNTING scenes.

Hornbook. Educational aid used in the PETTY or elementary schools. A hornbook was a wooden tablet with a handle, covered with a sheet of paper or parchment, on which was printed the ABC, the Lord's Prayer, and sometimes the Roman numerals. The parchment was protected by a transparent sheet of horn. The term is used more generally in our period to describe any primer or elementary work — even one intended for adults, as was Dekker's ironically-titled *Gull's Hornbook* (1609).

Hospitality. The provision of food and shelter for wayfarers and of charitable succour for the poor, regarded throughout the later middle ages as an obligation both by monastic institutions and by the wealthier citizens of a community. The dissolution of the monasteries after 1539, together with the inflationary movement known as the PRICE REVOLUTION and other economic changes, was seen in COMPLAINT literature and dramatic SATIRE as having led to a decline in such provision, and a consequent increase in the number of VAGRANTS. Generally, 'hospitality' in our period is still associated with a moral and social *obligation* to strangers or inferiors, more than with the good-hearted entertainment of one's own friends and neighbours. Although the Elizabethans may have idealized its past observance, there is much truth in Michael Bristol's claim that, at least at the theoretical level, 'the image of an idyllic country hospitality' represented a unanimously-held social belief to a greater extent than 'the philosophical abstractions' of the CHAIN OF BEING. The Elizabethan POOR LAWS were in part enacted to remedy the destitution brought about by the decline in 'hospitality'.

Housekeeper. The actual owner of a theatre, who as a general rule was entitled to take as his rent half the takings from the galleries which had been paid to the GATHERERS, whom he appointed. At the Globe, and later at the second Blackfriars, the leading SHARERS in the resident company, the Chamberlain's (later King's) Men were their own housekeepers, but Philip Henslowe at the Rose and Francis Langley at the Swan preferred to hire out their theatres, though also becoming, in effect, bankers to the companies which occupied them.

Hubris. The GREEK term for 'pride' or 'insolence', and so used by ARISTOTLE to describe the quality which leads the hero of Ancient Greek TRAGEDY to pay no heed to the warnings of gods or men, and brings about his fall. It may or may not in itself constitute the HAMARTIA, or tragic flaw. Dramatists in our period paid little heed to the NEOCLASSICAL theory which attempted to give prescriptive force to Aristotle's primarily descriptive analysis, but 'hubris' remains a popular term among modern critics, sometimes where 'pride' would readily suffice.

Humanism. Even in its ambiguity, this term sums up conveniently the lively intellectual currents of the RENAISSANCE, as distinct from the increasingly stagnant waters of medieval SCHOLASTICISM. Humanism may thus be understood both as referring to the stress on the revival of interest in CLASSICAL writings in GREEK and LATIN (manifested in EDUCATION in the LITERAE HUMANIORES, or humane studies), and (in its more commonly-understood application) as defining the greater emphasis now placed on the study of man and the advance of the human condition, by contrast with the passive acceptance of the divine will associated with the medieval mind. Arguably, the first sense of the word connects inextricably with the second, since humanists believed that the literature of classical times was more important for the grounding it offered in HISTORY, moral philosophy, and political science, than for scholarly or purely antiquarian study of the classical world. Conventionally, the origins of the humanistic attitude are associated with PETRARCH, and certainly its characteristic 'mood' or strain of thinking was established well before the REFORMATION — the sectarian nature of which was in many ways contrary to the spirit of humanism, as the life (and death) of Sir Thomas More (1478-1535) bears witness. Other leading English humanists were John Colet (*c.* 1467-1519), Sir Thomas Elyot (1490-1546), and Roger Ascham (1515-68), while the visits to England of the Dutch scholar Erasmus (1466-1536) were also an important influence.

Humour. Derived from the Latin word for 'moisture', a 'humour' in the Middle Ages and later indicated one of the four fluids supposed to indicate, by their predominance in the human body, the disposition of each person — blood suggesting sanguinity, phlegm signifying balance (that is, a *phlegmatic* temperament), while yellow bile stood for choler and black bile for MELANCHOLY. Although practitioners of Hippocratic medicine still used the word 'humour' to denote such attributes, by our period the meaning of the word was also becoming more generalized, connoting any kind of dominant mood or affectation. Both so-called CHARACTER-WRITING and Ben Jonson's 'COMEDY of humours' are loosely based on this belief. Jonson's own 'theory' of humours is debated in the INDUCTION to his *Every Man out of His Humour* (1599), and the title of that play in effect also suggests Jonson's moral purpose in 'comedy of humours', of ridiculing or shocking 'everyman' out of his folly (though his work is much less rigorously tied to this 'theory' than is sometimes claimed). The word 'humour' did not acquire its present meaning, as the cause of laughter, until the eighteenth century: but see also WIT.

Hunting.   See DEER and also HAWKING.

Hyperbole.   From the GREEK for 'overcasting', this term denotes a figure of speech — employed in RHETORIC, in the drama, or in general use — in which exaggeration is utilized for calculated effect. In unskilled hands, however, there is always the danger of high-sounding hyperbole descending unintentionally into BATHOS, and ill-considered dramatic hyperbole is thus a common target for BURLESQUE.

Hypostatize.   To give a human attribute to a material object or abstract quality, often by way of direct address of evocation, as in the APOSTROPHE.

I

Iambic. In PROSODY, a verse FOOT stressed *di-dum*, which in the un-rhymed PENTAMETER line of BLANK VERSE became the distinctive MEASURE of Elizabethan drama. The word is derived from the GREEK *iambus*, 'invective', since it was first employed in verse SATIRE, in which ARISTOTLE claimed that it more closely resembled the natural RHYTHM of everyday speech than did the DACTYLIC HEXAMETERS of Greek HEROIC verse.

Ibid. Commonly abbreviated form of the Latin *ibidem*, meaning 'in the same place'. The abbreviation is often found in footnoted references in literary criticism, where it denotes that the passage cited is to be found 'in the same place' as the immediately preceding reference. See also OP. CIT.

Iconography. Term derived from the Greek *icon*, or 'image', and strictly denoting the study of the sacred images of the Orthodox Church. It may also be found in critical terminology, where in general usage it describes the study of the pictorial evidence concerning any subject and its signification, and more specifically denotes embellishments to literary material, as found, for example, in the WOODCUTS illustrating EMBLEM BOOKS. Compare EMBLEMATIC.

Ictus. Term derived from the Latin word for a 'stroke', and used to describe the accent mark sometimes placed over a letter in the written text of a verse play to denote where a syllable not normally stressed should, when spoken, be given the emphasis the MEASURE requires. See LIGHT STRESS.

Image. During our period, this term, used in its general sense to indicate a physical likeness or apparition, already had the more specialized meaning in RHETORIC of a figure of speech. It is in this sense, denoting a writer's intention to achieve the verbal equivalent of a physical actuality or the impression of an emotional state, that the term is to be found in modern critical usage, where the technique employed in a sustained and purposeful way is known as IMAGERY. An image may or may not take the form of a SYMBOL. Some modern critics also use the word 'image' to describe our shared but subjective perception of a cultural or other entity: thus, the 'image' of Shakespeare changes from generation to generation, according to each age's values and judgements. Arguably, recent critics have been more preoccupied with Shakespeare's 'image' in this sense than with his imagery.

Imagery. Relatively modern term in critical usage, denoting the use of a pattern, strain, or 'cluster' of IMAGES to achieve a particular effect in a play or other work of literature. The study of imagery in the plays of Shakespeare and his contemporaries became critically fashionable following the publication of Caroline Spurgeon's *Shakespeare's Imagery* in 1935, and can often be illuminating in its illustration and analysis of pervasive strains (images of blood, perhaps, or sound, or food, or disease, or wild animals) — cumulatively creating what Spurgeon called 'dominating pictures' — in particular plays or groups of plays. Such an approach is limited, however — both by the amateur psychologizing which creeps in when a particular strain of imagery seems to give clues to an author's state of mind, and by its usual underlying assumption that plays are to be treated as works of written literature, since the detection of 'image clusters' and suchlike demands the close study of a text on the printed page. The use of imagery in the theatre of our period was rather a matter of immediate communication with an audience visually attuned to 'translating' a SIGN into an imaginative equivalent and to giving it the appropriate EMBLEMATIC significance.

Imitation. Not, as today, perceived (in relation to the writer's or poet's craft) as close to plagiarism, or meant to suggest that an author is 'lacking in originality', but the proper and desirable technique of following approved models and precedents. The intention of *imitatio* — the Latin equivalent of the term — was, according to the HUMANIST scholar Roger Ascham, 'to express lively and perfectly that example which ye go about to follow'. Imitation was thus familiarly practised by POETS and dramatists of our period, when poetry was understood not as a form of highly personal reflection but as an aspect of RHETORIC, and its ART as much a matter of application and practice as any other. Moreover, 'imitation' of this kind was only the means towards the desired end of 'imitating' or finding an appropriate poetic likeness for NATURE itself.

In Media Res. A phrase first found in the *Ars Poetica* of HORACE, where its sense is 'into the midst of things'. Hence the term is employed to describe the narrative technique of any play or other imaginative work which plunges into the middle of its story, rather than 'beginning at the beginning', or AB OVO.

Indenture. This term was most commonly used in our period to describe the form of contract between an APPRENTICE and a MASTER CRAFTSMAN. However, it had originally been used to describe any form of contract of which the two parts were torn in such a way as to create irregular serrations — an assurance to both parties that only the genuine counterpart would exactly match the 'indentures' of their own. The term is thus frequently to be found in its plural form, as when an apprentice 'took back his indentures' on completion of his apprenticeship.

Independent. A member of the extreme PURITAN movement of 'independents', who believed in the local autonomy of each gathering of believers. The independents were persecuted during our period, but achieved brief political ascendancy under Cromwell, after 1648. They are ancestors of today's congregationalists.

Induction. This word is simply an earlier, alternative form of 'introduction', but is usefully retained to distinguish a particular kind of preliminary scene in a play, usually so-named, which is not directly connected to the main plot. In one of its two most characteristic forms, it introduces the play that follows to its audience by creating a kind of parallel or first-level play-world — the world of Christopher Sly in Shakespeare's *The Taming of the Shrew*, for example, to which the main action of the play then becomes subservient, or illustrative, or simply 'less real'. Alternatively, it takes the form of a dramatized 'statement of intent' or artistic APOLOGY, during which the actors (often in their own persons) and sometimes a figure representing the dramatist discuss the coming play or suggest its underlying intentions. This latter approach is more characteristic of the technique of Ben Jonson or John Marston — though the Induction to Marston's *The Malcontent*, which is particularly interesting for its illumination of the differing practices of the PUBLIC and PRIVATE playhouses, was almost certainly written by John Webster.

Inn. An inn during our period is to be distinguished not only from the humbler ALEHOUSE, but also from the TAVERN. The word 'inn' was originally synonymous with a 'house' or 'lodging' (as in INNS OF COURT, below), but was used more specifically to describe a building attached to a monastery for the provision of shelter and HOSPITALITY to passing travellers. Such buildings subsequently became separate and eventually secular hostelries, but their purpose was still primarily to offer residential accommodation to travellers, whereas taverns were intended to cater for their local communities. Inns could also provide entertainments for their guests, including gaming and plays (alike prohibited in taverns) — while the inn-yards, enclosed on three sides and tiered with galleries which formed the entrances to rooms, provided such appropriate settings for drama that companies of players often hired them for this purpose, and some scholars argue that it was on the model of this playing space that the first purpose-built theatres were created. Certainly, it was in part the attempts of the Corporation of the City of LONDON in 1574 to control such playing in inns that led James Burbage to build the Theatre in 1576, though dramatic performances in inns continued until 1596.

Inner Stage. Term used for the conjectural recessed alcove in the TIRING-HOUSE wall at the rear of the stage in the Elizabethan PUBLIC THEATRES, or (yet more conjecturally) for some kind of curtained structure projecting from it. Scenes requiring an 'inner' presentation (such as a cave or tomb) were thought to have been set on this inner stage, which could presumably have been curtained-off for this purpose, or when a DISCOVERY was being prepared. If any such space existed, it is now thought more probable that it was no more than a confined recess, from which CONVENTION permitted any 'discovery' scene to flow almost at once into the main playing area. Apart from the sight-line problems which would have been created by any more sustained use of an 'inner stage', the one surviving drawing of an Elizabethan public theatre (by de Witt) does not even show a middle door into the tiring-house — which may in any case only have led to a corridor shared with the other doors used for ENTRANCES AND EXITS.

Inns of Chancery. Since the fifteenth century, the collective name for the colleges-cum-residences in London of younger students of the LAW, before they proceeded to the more advanced legal training offered by the INNS OF COURT, to which the Inns of Chancery were variously attached. Less affluent or well-connected students and attorneys also resided there — as had Shakespeare's Justice Shallow, in the Second Part of *Henry IV*, in his youth. Although eight Inns of Chancery existed during our period, their importance was declining as more and more students enrolled directly with the Inns of Court. The name probably had its origins in the original function of the Inns of Chancery as residences for the medieval Chancery Clerks, who were legal officials in the king's courts.

Inns of Court. Residential colleges which, since the fourteenth century, had provided training in the COMMON LAW and which, unlike the UNIVERSITIES of our period, were situated in London, in a cluster to the west of the CITY. The Inner Temple and the Middle Temple derived their names from their proximity to the New Temple, originally occupied in the twelfth century by the Knights Templar (whose church they shared), while Gray's Inn and Lincoln's Inn occupied the one-time houses (or INNS, as defined in that article) of the Earl of Lincoln and Lord Gray de Wilton respectively. Only 'GENTLEMEN of blood' were admitted, and, as the name signifies, the Inns of Court were as much concerned with instilling the behaviour proper at COURT as with formal education, so that wealthier students often attended them as a kind of finishing-school, with no intention of proceeding to a career in the LAW. Dramatic entertainments, including ACADEMIC DRAMA and MASQUES, featured among the activities of the Inns, where *Troilus and Cressida* probably received its first performance, and the students were also strongly represented among theatre audiences, especially at the PRIVATE playhouses. The liking of Inns of Court students for SATIRE and EPIGRAM influenced the development of both these forms.

Inquisition. A special court of the Catholic church, established during the thirteenth century with responsibilities for putting down heresy. The use of torture for this purpose was quickly legitimized, and became widespread during the REFORMATION, when the Inquisition was reconstituted under the Holy Office in 1542. The activities of the Inquisition were especially virulent in SPAIN, where the ceremonial procession preceding the burning of condemned heretics at the stake became institutionalized as the AUTO DE FÉ.

Intentional Fallacy. Supposed critical heresy (so described by W.K. Wimsatt in an essay of 1946), whereby a work of literature is wrongly judged by its success or otherwise in fulfilling its author's intentions, rather than by its objectively-assessable qualities. The belief of the 'new critics' of the mid-twentieth century in the 'independence' that the created work of art thus assumed was a healthy corrective to the predominance in Shakespeare studies of the assumption (most influentially held and expressed by A.C. Bradley) that Shakespeare's mind could be entered through his plays. However, too resolute a denial of the relevance of 'intention' can also induce a lazy reluctance to understand any play — not least one of Shakespeare's — as in part (but essentially) a product of its historical moment, realized through the individual perception of its author's mind.

Interest. See USURY.

Interlude. Term used to describe several kinds of relatively short dramatic work. The word 'interlude' derives from the Latin *inter ludus*, literally meaning 'between play' — but with 'play' here signifying any form of recreational activity. 'Interludes' have thus variously been interpreted as originating in performances given *between* the courses of a banquet, as light relief *between* more serious episodes in a mystery PLAY, and even as any DIALOGUE *between* two or more speakers. In modern critical usage, the term is perhaps most helpfully reserved to distinguish the short, secular, and generally comic plays of such a writer as John Heywood (1497-*c*. 1580) from the more serious works of didactic intent (though of roughly similar length) known as MORALITY PLAYS. Some critics, however, regard certain of the 'moralities' as 'interludes', or use the term 'moral interlude' to describe any short play of the earlier Tudor period with a clear religious or polemical purpose. Companies of 'interlude-players' were kept at COURT as late as 1559, and, by our period, the term 'interlude' was used almost generically, though often derogatorily, to describe a play of any kind, as in PURITAN polemics against the stage.

Interval.   In the sense of a short break during a theatrical performance, this term is not found in our period, and it remains a matter of scholarly debate whether 'intervals' occurred in the Elizabethan PUBLIC THEATRES. Whether such breaks would necessarily have coincided with the ACT divisions imposed by modern editors on the plays of Shakespeare and many of his contemporaries is also doubtful. It is true that a STAGE DIRECTION in the FOLIO text of *A Midsummer Night's Dream* does require the players to 'sleep all the act', but scholars now consider the act divisions in this play to reflect changes made to the text after 1609, when the adult companies began to play indoors, and so probably to follow the practice of the PRIVATE THEATRES. Here, it was the custom to play MUSIC between the more regularly marked acts of the plays — which were also generally shorter to allow for this.

Intrinsic Value.   The inherent worth of a unit of currency, or of a commodity which supposedly had a constant relationship with the value of what could be purchased in exchange. Together with the concept of JUST PRICE, as formulated by Aquinas in the thirteenth century, the notion of 'intrinsic value' underlay much of the tension in our period between the medievally-derived belief in a stable economic state (subject though this was to occasional fluctuations caused by drought, pestilence, or other unavoidable divine intervention) and the emerging capitalistic need for USURY and the free play of market forces. The rampant inflation or PRICE REVOLUTION of the sixteenth century, during which prices rose by over five hundred per cent, destroyed any basis for confidence in the 'intrinsic value' of the currency, though a sort of folkloric belief survived, often expressed in COMPLAINT literature, and in SATIRES such as the CITIZEN COMEDIES of the JACOBEAN period.

Irony.   This ambiguous term, used to describe various kinds of intended, structured ambiguity, was defined during our period (perhaps as concisely as it has ever been) by Richard Puttenham, in his (or, ironically, possibly his brother George's) *The Art of English Poesy* (1589), as the 'dry mock'. The phrase nicely catches the combination of a slightly detached, laconic viewpoint with an underlying satiric or didactic intent that characterizes much irony, and also suggests appropriately that it is best understood as a 'tone of voice', easier to recognize than to analyze. It is to be distinguished from DRAMATIC IRONY, with which, however, it shares an element of deliberate or apparent concealment — in this case, of the author's or speaker's actual beliefs or attitude. In the Socratic DIALOGUES of PLATO, the *eiron* is thus the dissembling Socrates himself, pretending ingenuousness or doubt in order to encourage a discovery of the truth by means of the DIALECTIC thus induced. While concealing its point of view, much irony cultivates an urbane persona — in a dramatic context thus compounding the detachment of author from character by the introduction of a second level of 'simulated' communication. Although irony is more charac- teristically a mode of the later-seventeenth and eighteenth centuries than of the Elizabethan period, it is to be found as the 'tone of voice' of some SATIRE, in the qualities shared by such CHARACTER-types as the MALCONTENT, and in Shakespeare's works is most frequently to be found in the so-called PROBLEM PLAYS — the 'problem', so far as some critics are concerned, being their failure to recognize irony. It is also frequently to be found when characters are in DISGUISE, and is notably pervasive in *Macbeth*. Modern critics such as C. L. Barber argue that it is a much more fundamental Shakespearean mode — an 'exploitation of theatrical aggression', as, for example, in *Richard III*, where both Shakespeare's and his audience's attitude is an ironic compound of condemnation and applause.

Italy. As the birthplace of the RENAISSANCE, but at the same time the cradle and continuing home of the Roman Catholic church, Italy — considered as a concept rather than a country — evoked a curious mixture of admiration, loathing, and horrified fascination in the averagely loyal Englishman during our period. By the beginning of the fifteenth century, many of the older republics in this politically-segmented area had become mere satellites to its five major political powers — Venice, a city-state of enormous trading wealth; Florence, soon to come under the sway of the Medici; the Duchy of Milan; the Kingdom of Naples; and the so-called Papal States around and to the north of Rome. During the wars of the late-fifteenth and sixteenth centuries, these states came variously under the sway of French, Spanish, German, and Swiss invaders, and no less variously allied themselves with these foreigners against their fellow-countrymen. By the early seventeenth century (when Italy was at its most popular as the setting for JACOBEAN drama, especially TRAGEDY), the country itself was entering a period of exhausted decline, but continued to be represented by dramatists as a centre of internecine personal strife, often driven by the impulse for REVENGE, and of political duplicity irreligiously rooted in the supposed tenets of MACHIAVELLI. Plots based in either (or frequently both) kinds of conflict were further subject to the intervention of decorative cardinals, whose behaviour good PROTESTANTS might safely deplore while any kind of dramatic debate on matters affecting the theology of the Church of England remained taboo. Italian staging methods and theatre forms influenced Inigo Jones in his scenic embellishment of the Jacobean MASQUE: but (notwithstanding the elusive influence of the COMMEDIA DELL'ARTE), the strength of NEOCLASSICAL critical doctrines in Italy had stunted the growth there of any serious drama of note. It was therefore largely from such SOURCES as the HISTORY of Italy written by Guicciardini that the Jacobean dramatists derived their impressions and not a few of their plots. The many highly-cultured Italian immigrants to England — among them the jurist Alberico Gentili, the translator and lexicographer John FLORIO, and for a short time the philosopher Giordano Bruno — were presumably thought to have demonstrated by their sensible departures their superiority to their countrymen as perceived by most Englishmen. Perhaps even more despised were Englishmen who themselves cultivated an 'Italianate' style: as the HUMANIST scholar Roger Ascham put it, 'an Englishman Italianate is a devil incarnate'.

J

Jacobean. From the Latin form, Jacobus, of the name James, and so concerning the reign of James I (1603-25). This term is generally used rather more precisely by modern critics than is ELIZABETHAN — though it is not unknown to find plays by writers such as Ford and Massinger (actually products of the reign of Charles I, and so of the CAROLINE age) counted among 'Jacobean tragedies'. While no absolute distinctions are possible, the Jacobean period is generally considered to have been of a changed temper from the Elizabethan, partly owing to the different character of the monarch, partly to accelerating political and economic changes — while its ushering in by a severe outbreak of the PLAGUE, soon to be followed by the Gunpowder Plot, was scarcely propitious. It is, however, unhistorical to view the period as in some way 'in the shadow' of the coming civil war, which was in no respect anticipated at the time.

Jest Book. 'Jests' are etymologically related to 'gests', the English form of the Latin GESTA (as collected in the GESTA ROMANORUM), and for a long time was simply an alternative spelling. However, by the mid-sixteenth century the definition of a 'jest' had shifted to emphasize the comic element, and the term 'jest book' is now used to describe collections of comic, sometimes bawdy anecdotes, generally of middle-class life, which are often more reminiscent of encapsulated FABLIAUX. The earliest English collection is *A Hundred Merry Tales* (c. 1526), while later in the sixteenth century CLOWNS gave their names to such works as *The Gests of Skoggan* (c. 1565) and *Tarlton's Jests* (c. 1592). Peele, one of the UNIVERSITY WITS, was the reputed author of a collection of *Merry Conceited Jests* in 1607.

Jester. See CLOWN and FOOL.

Jews. While Jewish communities had been widespread throughout Europe in the early Middle Ages, they were 'tolerated' largely because of the Christian prohibition on USURY, on which many of the communities were thus forced to become dependent. Increasingly, this ban was circumvented by Christian bankers, and by the end of the fifteenth century few practising Jews remained in Europe, having been expelled from England in 1290, from FRANCE in 1394, from SPAIN in 1492, and from Portugal in 1496. Most of the states of GERMANY had also banished their Jewish communities by this time, and it was only in ITALY, especially in Venice and Mantua, that they were still able, within severe constraints, to live and even sometimes to prosper. A Jewish community was re-established during the later sixteenth century in Amsterdam, but the Jews returned to England only under Cromwell in 1655. Most Englishmen of the Elizabethan period would thus have had no personal acquaintance with Jews, though a certain number of (often nominal) converts, many exiled from Portugal, were to be found in London — among them, unfortunately, Roderigo Lopez, whose trial and execution for supposed complicity in a plot to poison the Queen in 1594 boosted residual prejudice. Otherwise, the TYPOLOGY of the Jew was derived from folk myths concerning Jewish responsibility for the Black Death and for various forms of ritual murder. How far Marlowe was ridiculing such myths, and examining Christian as much as Jewish greed in *The Jew of Malta* (*c.* 1589), remains debatable, as does the question of how far Shakespeare 'ennobled' the largely stereotyped Shylock in *The Merchant of Venice*. Lesser works such as the lost play *The Jew* (1579) evidently represented what one PURITAN source called 'the greediness of worldly choosers and bloody minds of usurers' with no such redeeming ambiguity.

Jig. In the Elizabethan PUBLIC THEATRES, a brief, usually farcical afterpiece, accompanied by dancing, and performed following the main play. Generally sung in a simple BALLAD meter, the jig derived from a variety of SONG and DANCE forms, popular in village pastimes and itinerant stage performances: often these were also referred to as jigs, and in turn influenced the *Singspiele* of continental Europe. The solo dance remained one of the many forms of the jig, as evidenced by the CLOWN William Kempe's legendary dance from London to Norwich in 1600 (though this was described on the title-page of the book attributed to Kempe as a 'morrice'). Thomas Platter, a German visitor to London in 1599, records seeing a jig performed after Shakespeare's *Julius Caesar* at the Globe, and, according to Dekker in 1613, jigs were 'often seen after the finishing of some worthy tragedy'. The prevalence of this custom remains one of the most widely-ignored aspects of Elizabethan theatre practice, although it provides a potentially tantalizing analogy with the practice in the Ancient GREEK theatre, where a comic SATYR PLAY was performed following each TRILOGY of TRAGEDIES.

Journeyman. The intermediate status occupied by the APPRENTICE who had worked out his INDENTURES, but not yet become a MASTER CRAFTSMAN of his GUILD. Although this progress, given goodwill and endeavour, was supposedly as of right, increasingly during our period the journeyman unsupported by family connections or wealth remained a mere day-labourer, thus hastening the creation of an urban working class.

Just Price. A religious-cum-economic concept, most clearly formulated by the thirteenth-century theologian St. Thomas Aquinas, and intended to govern the price over and above the cost of his materials that it was lawful for a seller to charge for goods of his own manufacture, in order to maintain his state of life. Early Christian thinking had held that not only USURY, but even trade in goods, if for the express purpose of making a profit, was sinful — and so too, it followed, was an excessive charge for the products of one's own labour. The concept of 'just price', together with that of INTRINSIC VALUE, survived into our period long after they had been whittled away by emerging capitalist practice, and continued to underlie attacks in SATIRE, CITIZEN COMEDY, and elsewhere against the supposed greed of the profiteering MERCHANT.

Justice of the Peace. Lay (untrained) magistrate appointed by the sovereign to keep the peace and administer the LAW in each county. Originally this was a function of the KNIGHTS of the county, but by the early part of our period the justices were more widely drawn from the ranks of the minor GENTRY, the only qualification being an annual income of at least twenty pounds from FREEHOLD land. There were usually from twenty to sixty justices for each county, who met formally four times a year at the Quarter Sessions, but dispensed summary local justice as required — though for certain major functions a justice of the QUORUM had to be present. In practice, the administrative duties of the justices (which ranged from collecting taxes and determining wages to the levying of troops in times of war) were probably more important than their judicial functions when, during the reign of Elizabeth, they became important instruments of GOVERNMENT policy — which, however, they helped to shape as well as to oversee, often combining their duties with membership of the House of Commons. The disturbance of this delicate balance by the Stuarts is considered by some historians to have been a major cause of the unrest which led to the civil wars.

Justification by Faith. One of the fundamental tenets of PROTESTANT theology, by which it was held that man obtains his divine salvation through 'faith alone' (*sola fides*), rather than through the 'good works' emphasized by the Catholic church. While the doctrine of 'justification by faith' was originally formulated by LUTHER, the concomitant principle of each individual's PREDESTINATION (to salvation through God's grace, or to damnation) was largely elaborated by CALVIN.

K

Kempe's Jig. See JIG.

Kind. Term used synonymously with GENRE, and the more usual description for a distinct literary FORM in NEOCLASSICAL critical usage, which was especially concerned with determining whether a work was true to the rules of its 'kind'. During the early part of our period, Sir Philip Sidney in the APOLOGY FOR POETRY unsuccessfully (so far as English playwrights were concerned) warned against the mixing of the dramatic kinds.

King's Evil. The name popularly given during our period to scrofula, because of the belief that it could be cured by the royal touch. The practice of 'touching', which went back to the reign of Edward the Confessor (d. 1066), was especially cultivated by the Stuart monarchs as a mark of the DIVINE RIGHT OF KINGS, but lapsed after the reign of Queen Anne.

Knight. By our period, a lower, non-hereditary rank of the NOBILITY, whose function and, indeed, self-perception had changed drastically over the centuries. Deriving from the Old English *cnicht*, meaning simply a military servant of the king or a great lord, a 'knight' after the Norman Conquest was a nobleman bound by his 'knight's fee' to provide an armed horse-soldier for the king's army from his estates. With the advent of the Crusades, knighthood became a formalized rank of CHIVALRY, denoting the status finally acquired by a page — who, having then become an ESQUIRE, was finally given his ACCOLADE and ARMS as a full knight. Many of the different 'orders' of knighthood derive from this time. Edward I was given to mass creations of knights, on one occasion in 1306 elevating 267 esquires to that rank, along with the Prince of Wales. With the decline of feudalism, and the putting-down of private retainers by Henry VII under the Statutes of LIVERIES, knighthood became relatively less important. Then, Elizabeth's legendary parsimony over the award of honours, combined with the Earl of Essex's profligacy in exercising his commander's right to distribute knighthoods in battle (a major cause, however, of his fall from royal favour), led to ill-feeling among those worthies in civil life who felt such a distinction their due. To the total of some 550 knights at the end of Elizabeth's reign, James I added over 900 (largely in exchange for ready money) in the first four months of his own, and so only succeeded in bringing the rank into disrepute — for which he was duly lampooned in the CITIZEN COMEDY *Eastward Ho!*. But James continued to distribute honours for cash throughout his reign, and although Charles I discontinued the practice of selling honours in 1629, the rank of knighthood was by then thoroughly debased, and the new, hereditary knighthoods known as baronetcies (first created in 1611) not much less so.

Knox, John (1505-72).   Scottish PROTESTANT, and leading figure in the REFORMATION, both in England, where he was a supporter of Cranmer, and in his native country. In exile during the reign of the Catholic Queen Mary, he came under the influence of CALVIN in Geneva, and in 1588 published his notorious *First Blast of the Trumpet Against the Monstrous Regiment of Women* — 'regiment' here meaning the function of ruling, and so referring to the Catholic queens then governing his own Scotland and France, as well as England. The work was controversial not for the anti-feminism which may first strike a modern reader, but for the theological support it gave to resisting by force an unlawful PRINCE, in subversion of the supposed DIVINE RIGHT OF KINGS. After 1559, Knox began his reorganization of the church in SCOTLAND on presbyterian, Calvinistic lines.

L

Label Name. Another (and simpler) term than APTRONYM or CHARACTO-NYM for the frequent ONOMANTIC device of naming a character in a play after his distinguishing trade, physical appearance, or dominant HUMOUR.

Land. Still regarded during our period as the measure of the power and prosperity of the NOBILITY. However, the inflationary pressures of the PRICE REVOLUTION of the sixteenth century, especially on the cost of food, led to radical changes in the management of the great estates. Landlords (many of them now absent for at least part of the year in LONDON) became less concerned with the welfare of their tenants than with the need to make greater profits through speculative enterprises, not only through ENCLO-SURES but by imposing increases in rents and harsher tenancy agreements, particularly under the manipulable COPYHOLD system. Meanwhile, the dissolution of the monasteries under the REFORMATION had added between a quarter and a third to the total landed area of England in private hands. Historians continue to disagree about the extent and effects of the consequent changes in the income and power of the nobility. Some landlords enjoyed personal prestige at the expense of economic decline by continuing to run their estates on traditional, paternalistic lines, while others recognized, if only by their changed style of management, the increasing importance of money over land as the chief indicator of real wealth. As against the increase in the wealth of many YEOMEN who held their land by FREEHOLD must be set the dispossession of poorer tenants, and the consequent increase in those dependent solely on wage-labour for their income, reducing wages at the beginning of the seventeenth century to their lowest levels for three hundred years.

Latin. The language spoken in Ancient Rome, which continued in ecclesiastical, scholarly, and literary usage throughout the Middle Ages and into the Tudor period. In the process it had been modified by its contact with the VERNACULAR, and PETRARCH with other scholars of the RENAISSANCE accordingly wished to restore the CLASSICAL purity of the language, towards which end new editions of the great classical writers and scholarly Latin grammars were prepared. Colet asked the HUMANIST scholar John Linacre to compile a new grammar when he founded St. Paul's School in London in 1510, but it was William Lily's which after 1540 came into almost universal use at St. Paul's and most of the other English GRAMMAR SCHOOLS. The great Latin authors remained, even more than the GREEK, models for study and IMITATION, and Latin remained the language not only of schools and UNIVERSITIES, but of the LAW and theology as well. However, the REFORMATION, and the accessibility in PROTESTANT countries of translations of the BIBLE into the vernacular, ended its everyday use in the Church of England. In the drama, it is still occasionally to be found employed for SENTENTIAE and other TAGS.

Law.   Of the three branches of the law which had become established in the medieval period, ecclesiastical (or canon) law had been made redundant following the REFORMATION. The study of Roman or CIVIL LAW had thus become by our period the sole concern of one of the three higher faculties in the UNIVERSITIES of Oxford and Cambridge (where it was second in popularity only to theology), since instruction in the remaining branch, the COMMON LAW, was confined to the INNS OF CHANCERY and the INNS OF COURT. So far as the actual dispensing of justice was concerned, the superior courts, which all met in WESTMINSTER Hall, were the Court of Queen's Bench, which dealt with criminal matters; the Court of Common Pleas, which dealt with civil disputes; the Court of Chancery, which was concerned with matters outside the redress of the COMMON LAW; and the Court of Exchequer, which dealt with matters arising from the collection of revenues. Circuit courts, held in county towns, dealt with all kinds of cases at a local level, two judges presiding at each such court in the Lenten and midsummer vacations, between the LONDON law terms. The Court of STAR CHAMBER (named after the chamber at the Palace of WESTMINSTER where it sat), which included members of the PRIVY COUNCIL along with the chief judicial officers, was chief among the so-called PREROGATIVE courts — which sat without a jury, and so, for that reason (since they could deal with powerful offenders whom juries might be reluctant to convict), were often more popular with ordinary people. Other prerogative courts included the Court of Requests, for the impoverished, and the controversial Court of WARDS. Locally, JUSTICES OF THE PEACE dealt summarily with minor offences, and at Quarter Sessions with matters for trial by jury.

Lazzi.   Stock pieces of comic theatrical business, the speciality of the comic servants of the COMMEDIA DELL'ARTE. The term is sometimes found in critical usage to denote any combination of word, action, expression, gesture, or by-play for comic effect which is characteristic of a particular player, and where the verbal ingredient, if present, is of much less importance than in such narrative 'jokes' as are recorded in the JEST BOOKS. The CLOWNS in our period would certainly have had their distinguishing *lazzi*, but these are very difficult even to attempt to reconstruct from the written texts of the plays in which they performed.

Length of Performance.   In our period, probably between two and three hours, as seems affirmed by a promise of 1594 by the LORD CHAMBERLAIN to the CITY that plays 'will now begin at two, and have done between four and five'. The shorter time was the more usual if 'the two hours' traffic of our stage' mentioned in the PROLOGUE to *Romeo and Juliet* and the 'two short hours' of *Henry VIII* are allowed to carry any weight. Although some scholars believe these to be severe underestimates, even Jonson's *Bartholomew Fair*, textually one of the longest plays of its time, is declared by its author to have occupied only 'the space of two hours and a half and somewhat more', according to the mock-contract made with its audience in the INDUCTION — and this, from the context, could scarcely have been omitted to shorten the performance, though cuts of some sort to the longer plays were almost certainly made, and may account for the form taken by some of the BAD QUARTOS of Shakespeare. Plays for the PRIVATE THEATRES were generally shorter, to allow time for the MUSIC in the INTERVALS — but audiences seem to have expected a certain minimum length, as is suggested by the 'additions' Webster contributed to Marston's *The Malcontent*, in order to compensate for the absence of music when the play was taken over by a PUBLIC THEATRE.

Lent. After the CARNIVAL period of Shrovetide which preceded it, this was (and of course still is) the period of forty days (excluding Sundays) leading up to Easter, on whose moveable place in the Church calendar its exact dates thus annually depend. During our period, the MASTER OF THE REVELS was responsible for enforcing the prohibition against theatre companies playing during Lent — or, as seems to have become the accepted custom later, for collecting the cash in return for which dispensations could be granted, except for the 'sermon days' of Wednesday and Friday, and during Holy Week itself. Even before this, and in spite of frequent PRIVY COUNCIL orders, the ban was less than fully observed, and in 1607 a COURT performance was actually given by the King's Men before James I. On occasion it seems that other entertainments than plays were given, perhaps as less liable to incur the wrath of the PURITANS.

Liberal Arts. See SEVEN LIBERAL ARTS.

Liberty. Not, in our period, freedom from restraint, but a clearly-defined and so limited right. Also, by extension, a particular kind of local government area: thus, those districts outside the CITY of LONDON known as 'liberties' were not beyond the jurisdiction of the City authorities, as is sometimes claimed, but rather subject to certain legal exemptions from constraint, usually of ecclesiastical origin. However, one 'liberty' — Blackfriars — was, paradoxically, both within the walls yet at first outside the City's control, since following the ending of its monastic function it had become a 'liberty' subject to the personal PREROGATIVE of the king. It was finally transferred to the City in 1608 — ironically, just before the King's Men began performing there, finally breaching the City's previous prohibition on playing within its jurisdiction. The 'Liberties of the Fleet' were those areas around the Fleet Prison in which the prisoners were permitted to move and reside. However, the 'Liberty of the Clink', where the PUBLIC THEATRES on Bankside (not to mention its brothels) were built, and which also derived its name from its prison, was a 'liberty' in the judicial sense, within the jurisdiction of the Bishop of Winchester.

Licensing. During our period, the MASTER OF THE REVELS was responsible for authorizing the stage performances of all plays. By *c.* 1606 he seems also to have been given responsibility for permitting their publication, though this was legally within the jurisdiction of the Archbishop of Canterbury and the Bishop of London, who delegated the task to lesser clergymen. An entry in the STATIONERS' REGISTER supposedly secured the copyright of a work in print, though performing rights, which were owned by the theatre companies rather than dramatists, were in fact more difficult to maintain once a play was published, and its text thus no longer in the BOOK-KEEPER'S sole keeping.

Light Ending. A line in BLANK VERSE concluding with a single-syllable word, such as a pronoun or auxiliary part of a verb (can, should, etc.), *lightly* stressed, and running-on to the next line to form an ENJAMBMENT — as distinct from a WEAK ENDING, where the final syllable, usually in this case a conjunction or preposition, is unstressed, or a FEMININE ENDING, where the syllable is metrically irregular. 'Light endings' began to proliferate in Shakespeare's plays from *Antony and Cleopatra* (*c.* 1607) onwards.

Light Stress. In BLANK VERSE, a STRESS (often marked in modern printed texts by an ICTUS) on a syllable which would not usually be emphasized.

Lighting. Plays at the PUBLIC THEATRES began at two o'clock in winter, and contemporary references to LENGTH OF PERFORMANCE suggest that they would normally have been over by five: thus, despite later starts on occasion in the summer, the performances would only have needed natural lighting. Although also given in the afternoons, plays in the PRIVATE THEATRES, as also at COURT (where performances were usually given quite late in the evenings, as part of a programme of entertainments), were functionally lit by candelabra and lanterns.

Lines. Not, in our period, that portion of a playtext which makes up an actor's PART, but rather — in the way that today one might talk of some-

body's 'line of business' — the distinguishing *kind* of roles or 'parts' which made up each player's contribution to the crowded repertoire of the Elizabethan theatre. Shakespeare's own 'line', according to tradition, comprised small but significant roles, such as that of the Ghost in *Hamlet*, while the lines of most CLOWNS or FOOLS are fairly readily distinguishable. The modern scholar Andrew Gurr suggests that, on the basis of the few cast-lists of the King's Men that survive, for the period 1623 to 1632, the leading actors' lines could be categorized as 'hero', 'blunt foil for the hero', 'tyrant or soldier', 'smooth villain', 'dignitary or old king', 'young man or lover', and 'comic figure'.

Lists. The area enclosed by the BARRIERS at a TOURNAMENT.

Literae Humaniores. Literally, from the Latin, 'humane letters' — that is, studies in the CLASSICAL languages and literatures, philology, logic, ethics, and metaphysics. See also SEVEN LIBERAL ARTS.

Litotes. Term in RHETORIC, derived from the Greek *litós* ('simple, moderate'), and so, by contrast with HYPERBOLE, denoting the achievement of a desired effect by means of understatement, or by a denial of the contrary, as in the remark, 'it wasn't a bad play'.

Livery. The distinctive COSTUME worn by the attendants upon a KNIGHT or other member of the NOBILITY. Laws of Henry VII's reign designed to curb the power of the barons by restricting the number of their retainers were called the 'Statutes of Livery and Maintenance', and the Court of STAR CHAMBER was originally established to examine abuses of these acts. The most powerful of the GUILDS were known as the twelve 'livery companies' of the CITY of LONDON.

Livy (59 BC-AD 17). Roman writer, whose *Ab Urbe Condita Libri* traced the HISTORY of Rome from its mythological beginnings down to AD 9. Although only 36 of the original 142 books were preserved in their entirety, they formed a frequent model for IMITATION by writers of the RENAISSANCE.

Logic. One of the SEVEN LIBERAL ARTS of the Middle Ages. Although part of the TRIVIUM, comprising subjects considered less advanced than those of the QUADRIVIUM, logic was by our period increasingly being taught in the UNIVERSITIES rather than the GRAMMAR SCHOOLS.

London. In popular usage, the whole of that built-up metropolitan area along the Thames which in our period stretched roughly from Wapping and Shadwell in the east to Tothill Fields in the west. The Borough of

Southwark was the only major centre of population south of the river, thanks to its proximity to the single point of crossing at London Bridge, but to the north rapid development was taking place towards Finsbury and Shoreditch, the earliest London theatres being built in these neighbourhoods, outside the jurisdiction of the CITY. Much of this growth had been relatively recent, despite various proclamations against new building after 1580, intended to curb the risks of fire and disease caused by overcrowding. Historians agree that the population of the metropolitan area *c.* 1600 was probably around 200,000 — a total which was to triple over the next century. In administrative terms, the City of London remained powerful and virtually self-governing 'within the walls', but other local government, apart from the special cases of the LIBERTIES, was largely on a PARISH basis, so far as such matters as the administration of the POOR LAWS and compilation of the BILLS OF MORTALITY were concerned, and even WESTMINSTER had no charter of its own, despite its abbey and its special position as the seat of GOVERNMENT and COURT. Socially, the distinctions between the MERCHANT classes, who tended to dwell in the City and the northern and eastern suburbs, and the NOBILITY and GENTRY whose homes were even now beginning to spread westwards from the Strand, were already clear, though not yet so theatrically important as they were to become during the Restoration.

Long Line. In BLANK VERSE, an interpolated ALEXANDRINE (line of six iambic feet), or simply a line containing more than one unstressed syllable at its close (as distinct from the simple FEMININE ENDING).

Lord Chamberlain. One of the three great officers of the royal household, whose functions included all matters relating to royal entertainments. He had to deal not only with the maintenance of the CHAPEL ROYAL and the arrangement of theatrical performances at COURT, but with matters relating to the royal PATRONAGE of theatrical companies — members of the King's Men thus being officially sworn-in as 'grooms of the chamber in ordinary without fee'. Many of his powers during our period were in practice delegated within his department to the Master of the REVELS, including those of the LICENSING or censorship of plays — with which 'duty' future Lords Chamberlain were to be so much more closely associated for more than two centuries after the passing of the Licensing Act of 1737.

Lord Mayor's Show. An important civic occasion and annual celebration in London, marking the election of the Lord Mayor (then at the end of October), and his journey from the CITY of LONDON to 'swear fealty' to the sovereign at WESTMINSTER. PAGEANTS became a regular part of the occasion probably during the fifteenth century, and in 1422 the route was for the first time by water. The show reminds us of the many forms of 'theatricality' celebrated by the Elizabethan Londoner: but it was also of importance in providing an alternative source of income for professional dramatists (including Dekker, Middleton, and Anthony Munday), and provided some opportunity for the exercise of scenic art at a time when it remained largely neglected in more conventional theatre forms, other than that of the MASQUE.

Lord's Room.   Probably a 'box', or separated-off section of the first tier of the gallery in the earlier Elizabethan PUBLIC THEATRES. Some scholars hold that it was situated directly facing the front of the stage, while the majority believe it to have been immediately above the stage itself, thus also functioning when needed as the UPPER STAGE. The singular form, Lord's Room, would appear to suggest a special sanctum reserved for the theatre's noble PATRON and his friends, but plural references rather suggest that there were several 'Lords' Rooms' available, at the highest admission price (for the outdoor playhouses) of sixpence. 'Gentlemen's Rooms' were apparently later situated in the side galleries closest to the stage, though the habit in the PRIVATE THEATRES of the most fashionable spectators sitting on the sides of the stage itself does not seem to have been followed in the public playhouses.

Lute.   Stringed musical instrument, probably the most widely utilized for serious solo MUSIC in the Elizabethan period. Like a mandolin or half-pear in section, its strings are plucked rather than played with a plectrum.

Luther, Martin (1483-1546).   German theologian and reformer, who, as Professor of Theology in the University of Wittenberg, developed, through biblical study, the precepts which came to characterize PROTESTANT belief, most notably JUSTIFICATION BY FAITH. He was also strongly opposed to the sale of indulgences and to any claim by the church to be able to remit sins, which he held to be a matter for divine forgiveness. Luther's famous '95 theses' were pinned to the doors of the Castle Church in Wittenberg in 1517, and he further challenged church authority in a DISPUTATION in 1519, when he denied the infallibility of the pope. During the 1520s the breach with Rome became formalized in the struggle for REFORMATION in GERMANY, and its subsequent spread throughout much of Europe. Luther's translation of the BIBLE into the VERNACULAR, published in 1534, was also widely influential. He was strongly opposed to movements for popular political reform (notably through his support for the authorities during the Peasants' War of 1524-25), and he has been accused of inciting prejudice against the JEWS: however, he was notably more moderate in putting his theology into practice than his near-contemporary CALVIN.

M

Machiavelli, Niccolò (1469-1527). Italian statesman, playwright, and philosopher, acquaintance of Leonardo and Michelangelo, who served as an envoy for the Florentine republic under Cesare Borgia, but devoted himself to writing after the Medici returned to power in 1512. In *The Discourses* and, primarily, *The Prince* (1513, but unpublished until 1532) he was the first writer to attempt a systematic and undogmatic analysis of the politics of power — to exercise which effectively, the ideally strong PRINCE needed the distinctive quality of VIRTU. Machiavelli believed that the inherent evil in mankind could only be subverted by God-given grace, or through the constraints of the law, and he opposed those Christian doctrines which advocated humility, preferring expedient strength of action, which could be ruthless if that was needful to attain a desirable end. Queen Elizabeth herself often acted in accordance with the tenets of *The Prince* — and certainly knew the book, probably in its French translation, since it was not published in English until 1640. But Machiavelli's principles were widely misrepresented (or, more charitably, misunderstood) by English writers, and the dramatists of our period were not alone in treating him as the embodiment of evil opportunism — though quite probably deriving their views from Gentillet's attack in *Contre-Machiavel* (1576) rather than from the original. The 'Machevil' who serves as PROLOGUE to Marlowe's *The Jew of Malta* is the first known representation on the English stage, but the unscrupulous villains of later REVENGE plays, which were often set in ITALY, provide several later examples of what came to be regarded as the Machiavel type. In fact, Machiavelli's disciple ARETINO may with a greater degree of justice be accused of the amoral and atheistical opportunism usually attributed to Machiavelli himself.

Macrocosm. Literally, the 'great world', a term sometimes used simply as synonymous with the 'universe', but more often, within the context of assumptions of the CHAIN OF BEING and the theory of CORRESPONDENCES, as signifying a larger pattern which may be deduced by ANALOGY from a pattern in the 'little world' or 'microcosm'. In the concept of the BODY POLITIC, the 'macrocosm' is thus the STATE, whose characteristics may be derived from the 'microcosm' of the human body.

Madrigal. Elizabethan SONG for up to six voices, without instrumental accompaniment, usually sung one voice to a 'part', or melodic strand. A 'four-part madrigal' was thus a part-song composed for that number of voices, each with its own melodic line, but combining to create a musical whole. Madrigals were among the most popular forms of secular Elizabethan MUSIC, the words usually being less literary in style than in earlier, Italian examples. The AYRE was a simpler form.

Magic.   No such absolute distinction was felt in the Elizabethan age as in our own between the supernatural and the everyday. But whereas the medieval church had insisted that God was the source of the magic realized through exorcism, transubstantiation, or the powers of a saintly relic, the REFORMATION in England had made the element of the supernatural in the Christian religion far less immediate and tangible: as the modern critic Gamini Salgado expressed it, 'the Church of England took the magic out of Christianity'. This may well account for the rise in other supposed means of access to the supernatural during the later sixteenth century, and for a fascination with the subject which resulted in even James I compiling a treatise on DEMONOLOGY (1597). The methods of WITCHCRAFT were not always much different from pursuits still regarded as scientific, notably ALCHEMY and ASTROLOGY, while magical powers were even ascribed by the credulous to itinerant jugglers and other harmless practitioners of what we should today call conjuring (a term which then denoted the calling-up of evil spirits). Interest in astrology seems greatly to have increased in the sixteenth century, and astrological handbooks and almanacks appeared in considerable numbers, with such practitioners as Simon Forman and Nicholas Culpepper amassing a good deal of wealth from their 'consultations' and casting of nativities. Forman, who gave his 'services' free to the poor, and remained in London to tend those suffering from the PLAGUE (not to mention prophesying the exact date of his own death) is only the most prominent of those it is difficult to castigate merely as charlatans. Folk-lore also played an important part in magical beliefs, and it is notable that in *A Midsummer Night's Dream* the fairies are named after the common insects and flowers of the countryside — while Puck's other name of Robin Goodfellow links him clearly with hobgoblins and the devil, just as Ariel in *The Tempest* has affinities with the demons thought to 'live in the air about us'. However benign the intent of Prospero's magic in that play, it is no less derived from the BLACK tradition than that of Mephistopheles in Marlowe's *Doctor Faustus*.

Magistrate.   Not, in our period, simply synonymous with a JUSTICE OF THE PEACE, but (from the Latin *magistratus*, 'master' or 'ruler') any person in a position of 'magisterial' authority. The sovereign was thus the 'chief magistrate' of the nation, and it is in this sense that the word is used in the title of A MIRROR FOR MAGISTRATES.

Malcontent.   A 'type' or CHARACTER in the JACOBEAN sense, but also a real-life dissident (the Earl of Essex being so described before his execution in 1601), or, more pervasively, a sufferer from the prevalent complaint of MELANCHOLY. The EPONYMOUS hero of Marston's play *The Malcontent* (1603) was not the earliest malcontent of the dramatic kind, nor the first to assume his railing HUMOUR as a DISGUISE. And Marston's Malevole has been given a 'privileged' position at court not unlike that of Jaques in *As You Like It*, though both plays have their own FOOLS besides. There are other malcontents in COMEDY, such as Macilente in Jonson's *Every Man out of His Humour* and Malvolio in *Twelfth Night*, but they are to be found also in the character of Thersites in the so-called PROBLEM PLAY of *Troilus and Cressida*, while in TRAGEDIES malcontents range from the 'melancholy Dane' himself in *Hamlet* to the disaffected protagonists of Webster, or Middleton's De Flores in *The Changeling*. Perhaps Tourneur's Vindice in *The Revenger's Tragedy* comes closest to diagnosing the relationship between the stage type and the 'real-life' malcontent when he describes his own father's death from 'discontent, the nobleman's consumption' — in short, a condition caused by an imbalance between social position or expectations and fortune.

Manet, Manent. A STAGE DIRECTION indicating, from its Latin meaning, that a character or characters (respectively) should remain behind at the end of a SCENE, or after some other mass-departure from the stage — when alone, usually in order to deliver a SOLILOQUY.

March. As a form of MUSIC in the theatre, this would usually have been played by fife and drum. The STAGE DIRECTION for a 'dead march', or solemn music for a funeral procession, is frequently found at the end of a TRAGEDY.

Marprelate, Martin. Pseudonym adopted by the authors of some half-dozen pamphlets in the extreme PURITAN cause published between 1588 and 1592 in defiance of the LICENSING procedures for books. It is possible that a lost play by Lyly concerning the resulting controversy, staged by the CHILDREN'S COMPANY of Paul's Boys, was the reason for that company's suppression in 1590.

Marriage. Contrary to the evidence of most theatrical COMEDY of our period, marriage was generally (so far as the upper and middle classes were concerned) an arrangement between families for mutual economic and dynastic advantage, rather than a matter of ROMANTIC love. Paternal insistence was becoming less rigorous than in earlier times, however, and most children appear to have been permitted the right of veto if not of free choice: but it remains a matter of scholarly debate how closely what Lawrence Stone has called 'affective relationships' were approaching the norm, while the PURITANS' advocacy of greater equality in marriage and condemnation of the 'double standard' did not, of course, advance such causes among their opponents. However, many arranged marriages seem to have turned out surprisingly well — fortunately so, in view of the near-impossibility in normal circumstances of obtaining a divorce. Writers tended to follow established TYPOLOGY in showing married WOMEN as shrewish, despite marriage being the guiding impulse behind so much theatrical comedy.

Martyrs, Book of.   Popular title for the work of PROTESTANT theological history first published by John FOXE in 1563.

Masque.   Form of dramatic spectacle in which spoken DIALOGUE, MUSIC, SONG, and DANCE, were combined into an entertainment embellished with lavish COSTUMES and impressive sets. For these decorative elements, Inigo Jones became largely responsible at the height of the popularity of masques at COURT during the JACOBEAN period, when the parts were taken by members of the royal family and household. Ben Jonson was the most notable writer of masques, into which he also introduced the more realistic and ribald ANTI-MASQUE, for which professional actors were employed. Masques usually took the form of an ALLEGORY, often derived from mythological sources, and designed to frame an elaborate compliment to the qualities of the King and Queen. The masque had its origins in earlier, simpler PASTORAL and neighbourhood entertainments, deriving its name from the masks generally worn in the processions which preceded these so-called 'disguisings'. The 'Masque of the Nine Worthies' at the close of *Love's Labour's Lost* (*c.* 1594) makes dramatic use of this earlier type, while the masque of Juno and Ceres in *The Tempest* (*c.* 1612) exemplifies the subsequent changes in style and emphasis, as these were now coming to be incorporated into 'regular' plays for the commercial theatre. Sadly, while the texts of many masques have survived, the dance notation has not, and only a little of the music.

Master.   Prefixed to a name, this was simply the mark of any GENTLE-MAN of rank, distinction, or learning (as in Master of Arts) during our period, and did not denote the youth of the person addressed, as today. Its gradual extension to any addressee coincided with the term commonly being abbreviated to 'Mr.' in written form, and eventually to its being so-pronounced. Among its various other usages, it was also a short form for MASTER CRAFTSMAN.

Master Craftsman.   After taking back his INDENTURES, the APPRENTICE in a craft would then work as a day-labourer or JOURNEYMAN, during which time he would in due course hope to complete his MASTERPIECE. Its acceptance as such by others of his GUILD marked his rise to the rank and independence of a 'master craftsman'. Regulation was achieved at the lower end of this scale by the limits placed on apprentices entering a craft, so that progress to mastership was supposedly subject only to hard work and time: by our period, the decline of the guild system, together with other economic changes caused by the PRICE REVOLUTION, meant that this (if it had ever fully been so) was no longer the case.

Master of the Revels.   See REVELS.

Masterpiece.   The craft object, or demonstration of specialist skill, through which the JOURNEYMAN hoped to persuade the MASTER CRAFTSMEN who were the freemen of his GUILD that he was qualified to join their number. Although such 'masterpieces' might on occasion resemble the kind of 'high art' product to which the term is now applied — the work, say, of the journeyman mason or carpenter — they could equally well include a butcher's skilled dismembering of a carcass, or the completion of a pair of shoes or a hat. This test of the 'mastery' of one's craft seems to have been rigorously applied in the later Middle Ages, but during the sixteenth century favouritism on grounds of family or status became more common, while the less fortunate were tested more and more exactingly. As skills became more specialized, the sheer range of experience needed to complete a 'masterpiece' entirely from one's own resources (a crucial criterion) became rarer, and, indeed, less relevant to the needs of the emerging capitalist system.

Measure.   A literal translation of the Greek word, *meter*, with whose English sense in PROSODY it is synonymous, 'measure' is the general term for the regular patterns of STRESS in a line of verse, each unit of which constitutes a verse FOOT. In English, the commonest measures are the ANAPEST, DACTYL, IAMB, SPONDEE, and TROCHEE. The quantity of any of these patterns of stress, or feet, in any one line may be described through more straightforward combinations of numerals, with '-meter' as suffix — most commonly, tetrameter for a line of four feet, PENTAMETER for five, and HEXAMETER for six. The distinctive verse form of the plays of our period was thus the iambic pentameter of BLANK VERSE.

Melancholy.   Almost endemic in the JACOBEAN period, according to some historians, who have even suggested that dietary deficiencies may have been among its possible causes. Yet a certain luxuriance in unhappiness was also a characteristic of the later Middle Ages, as much in the formalized unfulfilment of COURTLY LOVE as in such cautionary reminders of MUTABILITY as the DANCE OF DEATH and the MEMENTO MORI. In this wider context, the RENAISSANCE represents a relatively brief interlude of optimism and aspiration, only lingeringly declining, as did the Elizabethan age itself. Of course these are huge generalizations: yet the impulse felt by Robert Burton to write an *Anatomy of Melancholy* in 1621, and, in theatrical terms, the presence of such CHARACTER-types as the MALCONTENT in plays of all kinds, provide some of the period's own testimony to its melancholic disposition or HUMOUR.

Memento Mori.   Literally, from the Latin, a 'reminder of death', which might take historical, aesthetic, or EMBLEMATIC form — as, respectively, in reflections upon past heroes now turned to dust, in a dwelling upon the inevitable decay (or MUTABILITY) of physical beauty, and in the motif of the DANCE OF DEATH, in which all sorts and conditions of men were inescapably destined to join. A stress on mortality had been popularized since the thirteenth century by the preaching of the mendicant orders, and since the fifteenth by the use of the WOODCUT, with its crude but widespread ICONOGRAPHIC appeal. A product of the MELANCHOLY cast of the late-medieval imagination, the *memento mori* remained widely utilized as a motif in visual and literary art forms, whether through the presence of skeletons and naked corpses on tombs or in the frequent reflections on mortality in many plays, notably of the JACOBEAN period, where its corrective, religious purpose is lost in a more EXISTENTIAL, secular awareness of the 'long silence' of death. The skull of his beloved carried by Vindice in Tourneur's *The Revenger's Tragedy* is an emblematic *memento mori* typical of the REVENGE tradition.

Memorial Reconstruction.   See REPORTED TEXT.

Merchant.   In the medieval period, a buyer and seller of goods not of his own manufacture, who therefore could not claim the moral sanction of JUST PRICE in making the 'unproductive' profit essential to his living, and so be exempted from the Church's condemnation of such forms of gain as USURY. However, the activities of those who shared the risks of trading by sea to foreign lands (and so stood to lose all as well as to gain) won the influential approval of St. Thomas Aquinas — and so, by our period, 'merchant' tended increasingly to denote those whose trade was with overseas markets, as was that of Shakespeare's EPONYMOUS *Merchant of Venice*. Many foreign merchants of this kind achieved immense political power, as did the Medici and, less ostentatiously, the members of the HANSA, or 'Hanseatic League', whose strong foothold in London was opposed by the emerging native GUILD of 'Merchant Adventurers', and eventually relinquished in 1597. By this time, English sea power had enormously boosted the potential for trade, and 'joint stock companies' were emerging to spread the risks (and the gains) of entirely individual enterprise. The wealth of middle-class merchants, as of other rich CITIZENS of the CITY of LONDON, was a frequent target for theatrical SATIRE, particularly in CITIZEN COMEDIES. Compare GUILD MERCHANT.

Metatheatre.   Term coined by Lionel Abel in his book of that title (1963), by analogy with such words as 'metaphysics' and 'metapolitics', to describe plays which investigate the nature of theatricality itself. Shakespeare, notoriously, tends to intensify the sense of his play's reality when he employs theatrical references or IMAGERY, whereas other writers of our period, such as Jonson and Marston, deliberately seek to 'distance' an audience when stressing the theatrical nature of their own works. Despite the use of a play-within-a-play in HAMLET, to this extent Tom Stoppard's *Rosencrantz and Guildenstern Are Dead* (1963) is the more 'metatheatrical' of the two plays.

Meter.   See MEASURE.

Microcosm.   See MACROCOSM.

Mighty Line.   Term first used by Jonson (in comparing Shakespeare's work with that of his contemporaries in the commendatory poem he wrote for the First FOLIO), to describe the BLANK VERSE of Christopher Marlowe. It usefully, if somewhat vaguely, conveys the impression particularly of Marlowe's earlier style, in which, though in chiefly regular END-STOPPED lines of momentous rather than colloquial RHYTHM, the 'might' is in the sheer cumulative force of the RHETORIC. In William Empson's evocative summary: 'after one subordinate clause has opened out of another with inalterable energy, it can still roar at the close with the same directness as in the opening line'.

Miles Gloriosus.   The 'braggart soldier', so called by the Roman drama-tist PLAUTUS, a CHARACTER-type perpetuated in the *Capitano* of the COMMEDIA DELL'ARTE, and recognizable in certain characters of the English drama of our period, such as Bobadill in Jonson's *Every Man in His Humour* and (as part of his complex ancestry and ultimate uniqueness) Falstaff in Shakespeare's *Henry IV*.

Minion.   From the French *mignon*, the favourite or beloved of a PRINCE or king, but a term also used affectionately of each other by lovers or by intimate friends of the same sex. The usage had tended to become more derogatory by our period, implying a homosexual element in the relationship, as between Gaveston and the king in Marlowe's *Edward II*.

Miracle Play.   A term sometimes found in critical usage as synonymous with MYSTERY PLAY, but most helpfully reserved to distinguish this latter form (as also the allegorical MORALITY PLAY) from short dramatizations of saints' lives and other sacred themes, usually drawn (unlike those of the mystery plays) from SOURCES other than the BIBLE. Miracle plays were particularly popular in France during the later medieval period, when 'cycles' of miracle plays also occur (each ending with the appearance of the Virgin Mary), but extant English examples are rare.

Mirror for Magistrates. A collection of dramatic 'self-portraits', in the form of verse monologues, of subjects drawn mostly from English HISTORY. The text was expanded in successive parts from an original 19 subjects in the 1559 edition by William Baldwin to a total of 33 by various writers in later editions dating from 1563 to 1610. The work was indebted to contemporary CHRONICLES, and also to John Lydgate's version of the *Falls of Princes* (after BOCCACCIO, *c*. 1430). An INDUCTION was contributed by Thomas Sackville, author with Thomas Norton of the first TRAGEDY in BLANK VERSE, *Gorboduc* (1561), whose 'cautionary' purpose it somewhat anticipated. MAGISTRATE is here used in its sense of 'ruler', and the 'mirror' is one in which contemporary rulers may thus see present events reflected, in order to avoid repeating past mistakes. Sackville's *Complaint of Buckingham* was probably known to Shakespeare when he wrote *Richard III*, while the rise and fall of the final subject, Sir Thomas Wolsey (seen as a very recent example of the operation of the WHEEL OF FORTUNE), was also utilized by Shakespeare, for *Henry VIII*.

Monarchy. See GOVERNMENT.

Monopoly. An exclusive right granted originally to a GUILD for the manufacture of a certain kind of goods. The system in its medieval origins was intended to protect standards by self-regulation; but during the earlier Elizabethan period, when monopolies or PATENTS were also given to individual MERCHANTS — ostensibly as a stimulus intended to encourage new materials and techniques — it was also used as a form of PATRONAGE for COURT favourites. The extension of the system under James I, despite attempts at statutory limitations, was one of the aggravating causes of the unrest which led eventually to the civil wars, and a bill to abolish the 'mountains of monopolies' was among the earliest concerns of the Long Parliament which met in 1640.

Montaigne, Michel de (1533-92). French writer, whose three books of *Essais* (published in 1580 and 1588, but not translated into English, by John FLORIO, until 1603) brought the prose ESSAY to a perfected and self-acknowledging form. Variously concerned with personal experiences, reflections on the natural world, and discussions of the qualities and habits of humankind, they were widely influential in England, notably on the dramatist John Webster — but not least, also, on Shakespeare, who was doubtless attracted by their combination of formal balance with humane tolerance and rational judgement. (A copy of Florio's translation in the British Library bears Shakespeare's possible signature.) While the essays displayed the best HUMANIST qualities, they were written in an era of extreme intolerance in FRANCE, during which Montaigne even landed himself briefly in jail.

Moor.   See AFRICA and BLACK.

Moral Interlude.   See INTERLUDE and MORALITY PLAY.

Morality Play.   A form of short, didactic play which emerged during the fifteenth century, and reached a peak of popularity roughly coincident with the REFORMATION. In length similar to that of the INTERLUDE, of which some critics feel the morality plays were simply one manifestation, they were distinguished by the use of ALLEGORY, and by their PERSONIFICATION of human qualities of good and evil, usually competing for the soul of a fallible central character such as the EPONYMOUS *Everyman* (*c.* 1500). In *Mankind* (*c.* 1475) the blending of comic and deeply serious elements within a subtle dramaturgical framework displays the flexible potential of the form, as turned to political purposes by Skelton in *Magnificence* (1516) and, notably, by Sir David Lindsay in his *Satire of the Three Estates* (1540). The VICE became an especially popular figure in these plays, and his descendants are to be found in plays of our period from Marlowe's *Doctor Faustus* (*c.* 1588) to Jonson's *The Devil Is an Ass* (1616).

Motion.   In our period, a puppet or puppet-show. Motions were popular entertainments, especially at FAIRS, and Jonson even includes a puppet-show — a BURLESQUE dramatization of Marlowe's *Hero and Leander* in doggerel couplets — in *Bartholomew Fair*.

Motley.   The distinguishing COSTUME of the theatrical FOOL. During our period, this is not now thought to have been the bright, regularly-chequered affair of later tradition, but a coat of variegated cloth — as Dekker puts it, 'full of stolen patches, and yet never a patch like one another'. However, the nature of 'motley', and even whether it properly signified colour or cloth, continues to be debated by scholars, though Leslie Hotson's theory that it was a particular kind of tweed, made up into a long, petticoat-like garment, is now no longer generally accepted.

Music.   Although English music of the Elizabethan period has not received the same attention in our own times as its literature and drama,

Mutability

the work of such composers as Thomas Tallis, William Byrd, Orlando Gibbons, and John Dowland contributed to the sense of creative ferment of the late-RENAISSANCE in England. The MADRIGAL and other part-songs became the most characteristic kind of secular vocal music, though the simpler AYRES and CANZONETS were also popular. Forms of social dance included the CORANTO, GALLIARD, and PAVAN, for which most great households would have possessed the requisite instruments, such as VIOLS, recorders, LUTES, VIRGINALS, brasses and woodwind, and even, on occasion, a 'great organ'. These, and other instruments such as fifes, HAUTBOYS, TABORS, trumpets, drums, and SACKBUTS, were also among the likely possessions of the playhouses of our period, though the PUBLIC THEATRES lacked an adequate acoustic for the stringed and woodwind instruments. Indeed, the INDUCTION to Marston's *The Malcontent* in its Globe version refers to the 'not-received custom' of music in the outdoor houses: the reference here, however, is to the lack of music before the performance or in the INTERVALS between the ACTS, a tradition at the PRIVATE houses which derived from the ostensible status of the actors in the CHILDREN'S COMPANIES as choirboys. But music integral to the play is frequently called for in texts for the public theatres, and this has given rise to speculation over the existence and nature of a music room. Most public-theatre music in the earlier part of our period, however, seems to have been played WITHIN, and was largely functional — as in the case of the successive 'alarums', 'parleys', and 'retreats' sounded by trumpet and drum during battle scenes. Later, the move of the King's Men indoors for the winter season, together with the vogue for TRAGI-COMEDY, saw an increase in musical elements in the plays of the adult companies. SONGS were also popular, mainly to signify mood rather than as incidental music. But it should not be forgotten that the neglected form of the JIG was a popular part of a visit to the public theatre for the ordinary person, just as, at the other extreme, was the MASQUE of the entertainment expected at COURT.

Mutability. The condition of gradual decay seen in our period as governing the world through the passage of time (curiously comparable to the modern scientific concept of entropy). As in Spenser's *Faerie Queen*, this is seen at once as poignantly regrettable, yet also properly productive of a sense of CONTEMPTUS MUNDI. Only the heavenly SPHERES beneath the moon were regarded as mutable, because of an ill-mixture of the four ELEMENTS, whereas their perfect combination in the spheres beyond made these eternal. The concept meshed also with the NEOPLATONIC belief in ideal forms, as contrasted with the 'unreal' corruptibility of the material world.

Mystery Plays. Cycles of short, EPISODIC plays (up to 48 in number, to judge from the four English cycles which have come down to us intact) which, during the later medieval period, constituted the entertainments presented by amateur players from the GUILDS at the great festivals of the Church, notably Christmas, Easter, and, in particular, CORPUS CHRISTI. The plays of the mystery cycles were drawn almost exclusively from the BIBLE, but are now thought to have derived their generic name from the Latin *misterium*, indicating their association with the 'mysteries' of the crafts responsible for their presentation, rather than from *ministerium*, or 'church office', once thought to suggest their development from the liturgical drama of the earlier medieval period. In fact, this 'evolutionary' view of the plays — perceived as part of a movement 'from the church to the churchyard to the marketplace' — is almost certainly oversimplified. So too is the frequently-repeated assertion that the cycles were exclusively presented on 'PAGEANT-wagons', drawn from place to place before a stationary audience, since the so-called *Ludus Coventriae* is clearly intended for static presentation. The collaborative, amateur, and generally itinerant nature of these plays associates them properly with their civic origins, and with such other spectacles as the LORD MAYOR'S SHOW, more than with the emergence of the permanent professional theatre companies in London.

N

Nation State. The nation understood as an independent and unified political entity, comprising citizens of common breeding and culture. The term is often used in a historical or critical context to distinguish the STATE, as it was in process of becoming during the RENAISSANCE and the REFORMATION from the looser agglomeration of feudal powers and principalities of the medieval period — which were at least in theory bound together by their shared acknowledgement of the supremacy of the Catholic church. England was among the earliest of the European powers to undergo the process of becoming a 'nation state': it was not to be until the nineteenth century that ITALY and GERMANY became so.

Natural. In addition to the adjectival usages derived from the multiplicity of senses in which NATURE was used during our period, a 'natural' was also an idiot, or rustic CLOWN.

Naturalism. A term used frequently and all too often imprecisely in modern criticism. Generally speaking, it is inappropriate in discussion of the plays of our period: however, 'naturalism' did have an emerging sense at that time, as the study of the works of man and NATURE, explained and justified without reference to a divine cause, and so generally denounced as atheistic — although a 'naturalist' by this definition was really only a scientist, in the modern sense. The term came into more general currency during the nineteenth century to describe the belief that it was possible to apply scientific method to the literary presentation of man and his society, and to show human behaviour as itself subject to scientific laws — in other words, to 'natural causes'. There is, in consequence, a stronger element of DETERMINISM (man's behaviour being perceived as conditioned by the circumstances of his upbringing and environment) in naturalism than in REALISM, though their shared scrutiny of the perceived surface of life, and of the details of human relationships, brought the movements close together, and in general usage the two terms are often used as if interchangeable. What is important to stress here is that 'naturalism' was a product of its historical moment, and is not to be regarded as an ultimate test of artistic endeavour in general, or of theatrical technique in particular. Thus, although Elizabethan drama is at times 'realistic' it is very seldom 'naturalistic'. Aesthetically, this is because the function of ART was not regarded at the time as the representation of the surface of life. Theologically, it is because human society was believed to be subject to divine laws, and to the aims and ambitions of 'fallen' man, but not to forces or laws which operated independently of either god or man. Plays of our period which may arguably be perceived as portraying a godless universe are thus usually better understood in terms of EXISTENTIALISM than of naturalism or other deterministic philosophies.

Nature.   Described by the modern critic Raymond Williams as 'perhaps the most complex word in the language', 'nature' is especially difficult to use meaningfully in a critical context. What, generally speaking, during our period it is *not* is an object of poetic contemplation and celebration, so close to the later, ROMANTIC sensibility. Medieval art and writing seldom dealt with nature in this sense, other than as a conventionalized setting for human activity, and medieval man was more concerned with subduing 'nature' in the raw than with admiring it — just as he feared the forces of the 'natural' MAGIC still being practised by the witches in *Macbeth*. By the Elizabethan era, 'civilized' nature had become a proper subject for appreciative art, as in PASTORAL, but 'nature' as an elemental force was still perceived as fraught with dangers, omens, and capriciously-exercised powers. There were many related and distinct senses in which the word was also used during our period, and perhaps it may best be understood by distinguishing it from its possible opposites or contraries. Thus, 'nature' was perceived to be distinct from 'art' (as in 'natural' *versus* 'artificial'); from 'nurture' (that is, characteristics inherent in one's birth or 'quality', rather than instilled through education or upbringing); from CIVILITY or proper breeding, which thus required that uncontrolled 'natural' (often implying sexual) instincts should be subject to ethical constraints; and, conversely, from man's fallen state, his 'natural' condition being one of primal innocence. 'Nature' could represent a divine but sensually-driven force, as in Edmund's 'Thou Nature art my goddess', in *King Lear* — but might also simply suggest 'the common denominator of primitive humanity', as in Lear's own 'Allow not nature more than nature needs'. All these uses are further complicated by the different senses in which the concept tends to be used in critical rather than creative writing, where a work of art might be understood, after ARISTOTLE, as the imitation of an ordered nature, with the POET as intermediary — at the same time as being recognized, after PLATO, as a separate construct, or, after the NEOCLASSICAL critic Scaliger, as creating 'quite another sort of nature', subject to its own rules of IMITATION, deduced from the practice of the ANCIENTS.

Nemesis.   The Greek word for 'retribution', and so signifying the gods' punishment for the HUBRIS of the PROTAGONIST in Ancient GREEK and some other TRAGEDY.

Neoclassical.   As distinct from CLASSICAL, 'neoclassical' signifies the reinterpretation and often the extension, during and after the RENAISSANCE, of the critical precepts of the ANCIENTS. The tendency for art to find itself subject to the pressures of 'neoclassical' doctrines in fact followed a westward movement in time from its origins in ITALY during the sixteenth century (in the work of such writers as Scaliger and Castelvetro), through its peak of influence in FRANCE around the mid-seventeenth century (as exemplified in the TRAGEDY of Racine and Corneille), and so to its absorption into the English consciousness during the later-seventeenth and earlier-eighteenth centuries, conventionally 'from Dryden to Johnson'. However, such earlier English writers as Sir Philip Sidney (in the APOLOGY FOR POETRY) and Ben Jonson ensured that many of the principles of neoclassical thought were current during the Elizabethan and Jacobean period, ignored though they generally were, particularly by the POPULAR SCHOOL of dramatists which included Shakespeare. Often blending the descriptive comments of ARISTOTLE with the more formulaic approach of HORACE, the neoclassical critics stressed the aim of pleasurable instruction in art and the governing principle of DECORUM, while attempting to impose rigid 'rules', which, for the drama, included those of the three UNITIES and of VERISIMILITUDE.

Neologism.   The coining of a new word — a process far less self-conscious during the Elizabethan period, when the language was in a flexible state only gradually becoming more 'fixed' by such factors as the growth of the printing industry. Some dramatists are more given to neologisms than others, in no necessary relationship to their importance: thus, Shakespeare's vocabulary actually included a relatively smaller proportion of neologisms than that of John Marston (whose often congested but innovative style was derided by Ben Jonson in *The Poetaster* during the WAR OF THE THEATRES).

Neoplatonism.   The renewed study of the philosophy of PLATO, which is usually dated from the forming of the Platonic Academy in Florence by Cosimo de Medici in 1459. Neoplatonism spread throughout RENAISSANCE Europe in the following century through the work of such HUMANISTS as Erasmus, Thomas More, and Giordano Bruno, who argued that Plato's conception of a 'demiurge' who created the universe was close to the Christian belief in a divinely-created but 'fallen' world. Neoplatonism also emphasized the importance of the ideal over the material world, which it considered 'unreal' because of its corrupt MUTABILITY. Hence the 'neo-platonic' vogue for idealized forms of love, as described in Plato's *Symposium*, at the COURT of Charles I and Queen Henrietta Maria, as reflected in (or arguably satirized by) Jonson's late comedy *The New Inn* (1629).

Nine Worthies.   A group of heroes comprising (with a characteristic

119

medieval love of symmetry and CORRESPONDENCES) three from the CLASSI-CAL or pagan world (Hector, Caesar, Alexander), three Jews (Joshua, David, Judas Macabeus) and three Christians (Arthur, Charlemagne, Godfrey of Bouillon). Nine female heroes were added when the cult was at its height, in fifteenth-century France. By our period the concept had drifted from its origins in CHIVALRY into popular folklore, as evidenced by the 'Masque of the Nine Worthies' performed towards the end of *Love's Labour's Lost*.

Nobility. The general term for those of the higher secular ESTATE, in England by hereditary descent through first-born males, or PRIMOGENI-TURE, rather than (as in FRANCE and ITALY) primarily through ownership of LAND, though this of course remained the measure of wealth. To the five ranks of the English nobility — duke, marquis, earl, viscount, and baron or KNIGHT — James I added the hereditary title of baronet in 1611, having himself devalued non-hereditary knighthoods by his widespread sale of titles (about whose distribution Elizabeth had been notoriously parsimonious). In general, the English nobility was far less exclusive (and far less rigorously demarcated) than the continental: thus, in our period the minor GENTRY were usually also considered of noble birth, and aspired towards the essential attribute of GENTILITY. Entry into the ranks of the nobility might be through PATRONAGE or simply economic status — resulting in a social mobility far greater than in the French aristocracy, whose atrophied condition was later to be a contributory cause of the French Revolution. However, the English nobility — thanks in no small part to the deliberate policy of the Tudor monarchs, as sustained by Elizabeth — lacked the political authority enjoyed by the nobility of France and (most notably) the many princelings of the fragmented territories of GERMANY. In England, such local jurisdiction was still exercised only (and residually) in the so-called 'counties palatine'. Shakespeare's works are suffused with references to nobility: in them, as the modern scholar Gary Taylor helpfully enumerates, he employs 'variations of the word "lord" 3296 times, of "king" 1830 times, of "noble" 843 times, of "prince" 672 times, of "queen" 495 times, of "royal" 263 times, of "knight" 219 times'.

Nocturnals. A shorthand term to describe the 'mistakes of a night', a popular CONVENTION in Elizabethan COMEDY since *Gammer Gurton's Needle* (*c.* 1555). Favourite later examples were *The Two Angry Women of Abingdon* and *The Merry Devil of Edmonton*, though the best remembered today is, of course, Shakespeare's *A Midsummer Night's Dream*.

Novella (plural, *novelle*). Italian term for a short, often anecdotal prose narrative, at first distinguished (as the name suggests) by originality or newness of plot, at a time when IMITATION in the other GENRES often extended to thematic SOURCES as well as to matters of style. The earliest, medieval *novelle* were anonymous, but collections by individual writers soon appeared, notably by Sacchetti (*c.* 1330-1400), in the linked sequence of the *Decameron* by BOCCACCIO, and in the collection of 214 such stories by Bandello (1480-1561). *Novelle* provided useful raw-material for plots (or sub-plots) of plays during our period, often *via* the popular collection assembled by William Painter as THE PALACE OF PLEASURE (1565-67); but the form did not develop as such in England, although the prose narratives of Deloney, Greene, and Nashe are sometimes so-described.

Number.   Observance of beat or MEASURE. By extension, the term is thus often used in its plural form to describe verse or poetry in general — as when Hamlet declares to Ophelia that he is 'ill at these numbers'.

O

Oaths. See ABUSES OF PLAYERS.

Objective Correlative. Term coined by T.S. Eliot, which has since entered into general critical currency to describe the balance that Eliot felt to be necessary between an emotion portrayed in a work of art and the circumstances evoking that emotion. Eliot thus objected to *Hamlet* because the central character was 'dominated by a state of mind which is inexpressible because it is in *excess* of the facts as they appear'. Surprisingly, it does not appear to have occurred to Eliot that many (probably most) 'states of mind' in real life lack so scrupulously correspondent an 'objective correlative'. Compare DISSOCIATION OF SENSIBILITY.

Onomantic. Literally, from the Greek, 'divined from names' — as are attributes of personality or occupation when a playwright chooses to give a CHARACTER an APTRONYM, CHARACTER NAME, or LABEL NAME, all of which are thus 'onomantic'.

Onomatopoeia. This term, derived from the Greek and literally meaning 'the making of words', is used to describe words whose sounds resemble those they are supposed to describe. When the sense-impression conjured by a passage in a play evokes (say) haste or ponderousness or luxuriance, it is similarly said to be 'onomatopoeic'.

Op. Cit. Abbreviation for *opera citato*, a Latin term meaning 'in the work cited'. The abbreviated form is frequently to be found in the footnotes of books or articles, indicating that the full bibliographical details of the work in question will be found in an earlier reference — but IBID is generally preferred if the detailed reference is the one immediately preceding.

Oratory. See RHETORIC.

Ordinary. In addition to its present sense, of an everyday or commonplace occurrence, the term during our period had a profusion of other meanings, from its emerging colloquial sense of a set meal taken at a regular time at a TAVERN (and hence, by extension, the tavern itself) to its precise legal usage signifying a defined legal right as distinct from one of the 'absolute', PREROGATIVE rights of the sovereign.

Ordinary Poet.   Term used in our period to describe what today might be called the 'house dramatist' — that is, the POET regularly attached to a theatrical company. Some, like Shakespeare, were also SHARERS in their companies, while others were under a renewable legal contract — of which only one example, Richard Brome's contract with the Salisbury Court Theatre for 1635, has survived, stipulating conditions under which he was supposed to provide three plays annually, and remain in the exclusive service of the company.

Original Sin.   The Christian doctrine that all human beings, as hereditary descendants of Adam, are born endowed with his, the 'original' sin. Whereas the Catholic church held that baptism cleansed the infant of this 'original sin', PROTESTANT theology as defined by LUTHER and CALVIN gave the doctrine a more DETERMINIST interpretation, from which in part derived their insistence upon JUSTIFICATION BY FAITH rather than by works, and the particular stress placed by Calvin upon PREDESTINATION.

Ovid (43 BC-AD 18).   Roman poet, influential on later thought and behaviour and a model for IMITATION even before the RENAISSANCE. His work of amorous 'instruction', *The Art of Love*, became a major source for the conventions of COURTLY LOVE. The fifteen books of the *Metamorphoses*, dealing in a semi-chronological manner with the 'transformations' undergone by characters from myth, legend, and HISTORY, were translated into English by William Golding in 1567, and served as a popular SOURCE for the MASQUES, PAGEANTS, and other entertainments of our period.

Oxymoron.   A term in RHETORIC for a figure of speech or statement in which two apparently contradictory elements give a paradoxical slant to the sense, as in Hamlet's now-proverbial 'I must be cruel only to be kind'.

P

Pageant. This term is variously used to describe the cart on which an episode in a cycle of medieval MYSTERY PLAYS was performed, one of its regular stopping-places, and also the play itself. By our period, a 'pageant', comprising tableaux or other celebratory entertainments, was a popular part of any royal PROGRESS, a regular feature of the annual LORD MAYOR'S SHOW, and a frequent element of other festive occasions such as royal weddings and investitures. Peele, Jonson, Dekker, Middleton, and Anthony Munday were among the playwrights who devised such festivities. The term 'pageant' also continued in use to describe the structures, usually built of wood and canvas, which housed these entertainments.

Paired Words. Term used to describe the stylistic device of linking two nouns both modified by the same adjectival phrase, or simply joined for rhetorical effect. As a stylistic mannerism, this was characteristic of Shakespeare's middle period — in the words of the modern scholar F.E. Halliday, 'one of the nouns being typically Latin, abstract, polysyllabic, and general, the other Saxon, concrete, monosyllabic, and particular, as in "accident of flood and fortune", "catastrophe and heel of pastime".'

Palace of Pleasure, The. Collection of 101 tales translated by William Painter (c. 1540-94), and published in 1565-67. These were widely plundered as SOURCES for plot material by the dramatists of our period. Among Painter's own sources were PLUTARCH, the *Decameron* of BOCCACCIO, and NOVELLE by Bandello and Cinthio.

Panacea. See ALCHEMY.

Parish. The oldest surviving district of English local administration, dating back to the seventh century. However, it was not until the fourteenth century that the whole of the country had been divided into 'parishes', small ecclesiastical units each with its own priest and church. Under the Tudors parishes were also used for purposes of local GOVERNMENT — notably the upkeep of highways, and the administration of the POOR LAWS — both in rural areas and in parts of LONDON outside the CITY.

Parliament. See GOVERNMENT.

Parnassus Plays.   Collective term for three anonymous plays performed at St. John's College, Cambridge, between 1598 and 1602. These contained numerous topical references to UNIVERSITY and cultural life, including the theatre. The third in the sequence, *The Return from Parnassus*, was published in 1606, and contains an 'audition' of two students by players from the King's Men, Will Kempe and Richard Burbage, and references to Shakespeare, as also to the WAR OF THE THEATRES.

Part, Actor's.   This term did not simply denote an actor's role in a play, though its present usage in this sense derives from its more specific Elizabethan meaning, of one of the long scrolls prepared by the BOOK-KEEPER for each player, containing only his own cues and lines in the play, together with relevant STAGE DIRECTIONS. The one extant example of such a 'part', for a role in Greene's *Orlando Furioso* (probably created by Alleyn in 1592) is some seventeen feet long. Apart from reasons of economy, it was in a company's interests to preserve only a single, complete BOOK of the play, to protect its ownership of the piece from PIRACY.

Passing Over.   A STAGE DIRECTION found in the drama of our period, presumably indicating a passage from one side of the stage to the other. Conjecturally, the actors involved, often in procession, would enter from one side of the theatre's yard, by means of the 'corner-steps' postulated by the modern scholar Richard Southern, and return down the steps opposite.

Pastoral.   Literally, from the Latin, 'concerning shepherds', and thus a term denoting the recurrent artistic concern to construct an idyllic version of rural life. The precedent was rather that of the CLASSICAL *Idylls* of Theocritus than of Christian TYPOLOGY, in which (as in the shepherds' plays of the MYSTERY cycles) NATURE and the countryside are presented altogether more earthily. RENAISSANCE versions of pastoral in English range from the poetic 'chronology' of Spenser's *Shepherd's Calendar* (1579) to Sidney's ROMANCE, the *Arcadia* (1590) and Marlowe's slightly plodding lyric, *The Passionate Shepherd* — to which Raleigh's ironic response was an example of the 'mock-pastoral' which was to become so popular a mode in the eighteenth century. The 'pastoral' in Renaissance painting is exemplified by such idealizations of the countryside as Giorgione's *Fête Champêtre*, while pastoral drama first emerged in ITALY in Tasso's *Aminta* (1581) and Guarini's *Il pastor fido* (1585) — the latter in particular exerting a strong influence on English pastorals, and their often close relation, the TRAGI-COMEDY. John Fletcher, a master of both types, wrote his own *The Faithful Shepherdess* (*c.* 1608), and even Ben Jonson attempted the form, in his unfinished *The Sad Shepherd* (1641), while there are obvious (though not uncritical) elements of pastoral in such of Shakespeare's plays as *As You Like It* and *The Winter's Tale*. But the mode was primarily an aristocratic one, and so found itself well-expressed in the MASQUE. Nobody who had actually had much acquaintance with sheep could take pastoral too seriously.

Patent. From the Latin for 'open', the full form is 'letters patent', a royal warrant of privilege, office, or MONOPOLY. The Act of 1572 legitimizing theatrical companies stipulated only the formal PATRONAGE of a member of the NOBILITY, but James I, upon his accession in 1603, authorized playing only under a 'patent' from the crown. The Master of the REVELS was also appointed by 'letters patent'.

Patronage. Literally, from the Latin *patronus*, a 'protector' of favoured clients. Patronage, either direct or indirect, was the main form of support for a POET or theatrical company. Direct patronage was often acknowledged or solicited in the form of dedications to printed works — Shakespeare's *Venus and Adonis* and *Lucrece* being dedicated to his patron, the Earl of Southampton. Indirect patronage was required under the Act of 1572, whereby, in effect, a member of the NOBILITY lent his name (and usually little more) as legal protection for a theatrical company. So far as the arts were concerned, England never enjoyed patronage to the extent that it flourished in ITALY during the RENAISSANCE, but it continued to be an important source of protection or income into the eighteenth century — sometimes, for those in political favour, in the form of sinecures at COURT or in GOVERNMENT office.

Pavan. A slow and stately, four-in-a-measure processional DANCE, popular during our period on ceremonial and celebratory occasions. It was often associated with the GALLIARD in the work of Elizabethan composers, who, in adapting these dance forms for instrumental composition, were thus responsible for the emergence of the suite.

Pentameter. Literally, from the Greek, 'five to a meter', and so, in PROSODY, denoting the five-foot verse line. In its IAMBIC form, the basic MEASURE of dramatic BLANK VERSE.

Peripeteia. Literally, from the Greek, the 'sudden change' in TRAGEDY which occurs, according to ARISTOTLE, when the fortunes of the PROTAGONIST undergo a reversal — usually, though not necessarily, for the worse. The related 'change from ignorance to knowledge' is the *anagnorisis*, or DISCOVERY.

Personation. One of several terms employed during our period to describe what today would simply be called ACTING, this latter word at first being more closely associated with the gestic component in RHETORIC.

Personification

'Personation' was a NEOLOGISM, recorded in 1598 by John FLORIO and employed by John Marston (in the INDUCTION to his *Antonio and Mellida*, 1599), seemingly to distinguish the more psychologically subtle PLAYING of such an actor as Burbage from the more 'presentational' style associated with Alleyn. Slowly, 'acting' became the generic term, while the previously neutral 'playing' began to acquire a derogatory sense.

Personification. In RHETORIC, the giving of human attributes to an inanimate object or moral quality — the MORALITY PLAY depending on the latter usage as its governing CONVENTION. Caroline Spurgeon enumerated some 70 examples of personification in *King John*, a far higher number than in any other of Shakespeare's plays.

Petrarch (Francesco Petrarca, 1304-74). Italian poet and HUMANIST, often regarded as father of the RENAISSANCE, notably in his abiding interest in classical LATIN language and literature — and even in his valiant failure to acquire facility in GREEK. A more distinctively personal achievement was his development of the SONNET, inspired by his love, in life and death, for the Laura immortalized by his poems in this form. 'Petrarchism' is a term occasionally found to describe the style developed by Petrarch — somewhat artificial in diction, and marked by CONCEITS and often forced antitheses — which is to be found in some of the more mannered of Shakespeare's sonnets.

Petty School. General term for any school offering elementary education during our period. The petty school would usually be entered at the age of four or five by both boys and girls, when the alphabet and rudiments of reading would be taught from the HORNBOOK. Often, only two other books were subsequently used — an *ABC with the Catechism*, and a *Primer* of devotional readings — and it is evident that considerably more attention was paid to the acquisition of reading skills than to writing. Some elementary LATIN might also be taught from the third year. Petty schools continued under ecclesiastical supervision after the REFORMATION, but by our period were sometimes attached to a GRAMMAR SCHOOL, to which boys of wealthier parents would proceed at seven or eight, while girls received any further education at home, and poorer children probably began work with their parents or entered the APPRENTICE system. Some petty schools were 'song schools', in which promising choristers would receive their elementary education.

Philosophy. During our period, this term denoted knowledge of all kinds, and its systematic pursuit. For the higher degree of 'Doctor of Philosophy' in the UNIVERSITIES, the three branches of moral, natural, and metaphysical philosophy were studied at an advanced level. Curiously, there were few major exponents of 'philosophy' in its usual present-day sense of the speculative study of ultimate causes and realities (then the preserve of the 'metaphysical' branch of the subject), between Aquinas in the thirteenth century and Descartes, Spinoza, and Leibnitz in the seventeenth, apart from the exponents of the ideas of PLATO and ARISTOTLE during the RENAISSANCE — presumably because the period was one of primarily HUMANIST concern with the study and advancement of mankind itself. Edward Herbert's *De Veritate* (1625) was the first work of pure metaphysics by an Englishman.

Picaresque. This term is derived from the Spanish *picaro*, a 'rogue', and, in English usage since the nineteenth century, has been applied to a literary work, usually of prose fiction, concerned with the travels, adventures, and employments of a central character from low life (or 'picaroon'). Full of earthy REALISM, and usually EPISODIC, picaresque novels were in marked and often refreshing contrast to ROMANCES, as also to the literature of COURTLY LOVE. Thomas Nashe introduced the form into England with his *The Unfortunate Traveller* in 1594.

Pietà. An Italian term meaning 'pity' (and so to be distinguished from the Latin PIETAS, below), used to denote the representation, frequent in the art of the RENAISSANCE, of the dead Christ in the arms of the Virgin Mary.

Pietas. Literally, from the Latin, 'piety', denoting in particular the Roman concept of duty — towards the gods, the family, and the state. To be distinguished from PIETÀ, above.

Piracy. The publication of a play in a text thought to have been derived by unauthorized means, rather than by permission of the theatrical company which (rather than the dramatist) normally owned its copyright. Thus, there are up to six pirated BAD QUARTOS among the earlier editions of Shakespeare's plays, which were probably put together by means of REPORTED TEXTS.

Pit. This term was used to describe the ground-floor area fronting the stage in the PRIVATE THEATRES. Its use in this sense probably derived from the area's similarity in form to an actual cockpit, one of which was converted into the Phoenix Theatre, Drury Lane, *c.* 1616. Unlike the YARD of the PUBLIC THEATRES, the pit in the private houses was furnished with seats, and was the most expensive and fashionable part of the house.

Plague. This was an endemic affliction both economically and physically during our period — economically, so far as the theatre was concerned, in that severe outbreaks of the plague, as measured by the BILLS OF

MORTALITY, necessitated the closure of the theatres. Although never entirely dormant, plague caused no lengthy closures between the severe outbreaks of 1563 and 1592, but no playing was permitted from June 1592 to May 1594, when a vigorous epidemic caused some 10,000 deaths in 1593 alone. The next bad outbreak, coinciding with the accession of James I, came in 1603, when the theatres were closed for over a year from March, but apart from one less contagious outbreak in 1609, there were only brief closures due to plague until 1625 — when, unpropitiously, one of the worst recorded outbreaks, killing 35,000 people, coincided with another change of monarch, and caused the postponement of the coronation of Charles I. There was a further interruption of playing lasting nine months during the plague of 1636. While, during lengthy outbreaks, some companies might (if the spread of the disease permitted) tour in the provinces, the playwrights often had to fall back on other work — perhaps, like Shakespeare in 1592-94, turning to verse, or, like James Shirley in 1636, attaching themselves to a company in the less affected area of Dublin. Some closures — notably during the outbreaks of 1592-94 and 1636 — also precipitated major shake-ups in the management and character of the theatrical companies.

Plat. See PLOT.

Plato (*c*. 427-*c*. 348 BC). Ancient GREEK philosopher, who during his extensive travels after the execution of his teacher Socrates began to write in the DIALOGUE format through which most of his works achieve their philosophical DIALECTIC. On returning to Athens, Plato founded the Academy, where ARISTOTLE studied under him for twenty years. At the heart of his philosophy is the doctrine of ideas (or forms), denoting the unchanging state of reality which Plato believed to transcend the physical, earthly manifestations of material objects and, indeed, spiritual qualities. Thus, a Platonic 'idea' is not something which emerges from human thought, but is resident in an ultimate realm of truth, to which the human soul provides the only means of access. Plato's objections to POETS, most of whom he would have excluded from his *Republic*, are thus that their work can attempt IMITATIONS only of mundane, everyday reality, and so offer merely 'imitations of an imitation'. The attempt in the RENAISSANCE to reconcile Platonic and Christian thought is usually distinguished as NEOPLATONISM.

Platonic Love. A concept which, through a misinterpretation of Plato's references in the *Symposium* to his purely spiritual care for the young male pupils in his charge, came to be understood as signifying a purified, non-sexual form of love between man and woman, in which each contemplates the spiritual beauty of the other's soul. An aspect of NEOPLATONISM rather than of Plato's own teaching, it inspired certain aspects of COURTLY LOVE — and, as manipulated by Queen Henrietta Maria, became almost a political weapon at the COURT of Charles I.

Plautus, Titus Maccius (*c.* 254-184 BC). Roman dramatist, responsible for creating (or adapting, through the GREEK New Comedy of Menander) many of the character-types which have endured in COMEDY down to the present day. Rediscovered during the RENAISSANCE, his plays were much utilized in SCHOOL and ACADEMIC DRAMA in the sixteenth century, while for the dramatists of our period his plots were valuable SOURCES of comic raw material. Perhaps most famously, Shakespeare based his own *The Comedy of Errors* on the *Menaechmi* of Plautus, whose MILES GLORIOSUS had provided a source not only for Nicholas Udall's *Ralph Roister Doister* as early as *c.* 1550, but a CHARACTER-type found in many plays of our period — as are numerous Elizabethan equivalents of such 'cunning servants' as Pseudolus and Tranio.

Playing. A term originally synonymous with ACTING, and generally preferred to it during the earlier part of our period. Later, however, as the modern scholar Martin Butler has noted, 'acting' became a 'professional qualification', whereas 'playing' began to carry the suggestion of a 'holiday skill' — hence Jonson's protest against the performances of his *The New Inn* (1629) which, he claimed on its title-page, was 'never *acted*, but most negligently *played*'. Compare PERSONATION.

Plot, Plat. Although used, notably in translations of ARISTOTLE, in its present sense of the developing ACTION of a play, during our period it described the synopsis of a play, sometimes denoting the author's preliminary scenario, but more usually the outline hung backstage during a performance. This 'plot' or 'plat', which was primarily concerned with the changing composition of the characters present on stage, was compiled by the BOOK-KEEPER from his PROMPT-BOOK, and enabled the players to fit their own segmented PARTS into the context of the action. Seven 'plots' of this kind have survived.

Pluralism. The holding of several benefices in the church by the same person.

Plutarch (*c.* 46-*c.* 120). Roman prose writer, whose chief work of HISTORY, the *Parallel Lives*, was translated from LATIN into English by Sir Thomas North as *The Lives of the Noble Grecians and Romans Compared Together*. As both forms of title suggest, Plutarch was more concerned to derive by ANALOGY cautionary truths from the lives of great men — 46 Greeks and Romans being grouped into comparable pairs for this purpose — than with historical accuracy in the modern sense. His consequent view of CHARACTER as exemplifying universal vices and virtues, and of great men as subject to the effects of the WHEEL OF FORTUNE, was strongly sympathetic to the orthodox Elizabethan mind. Indeed, Shakespeare's Greek and Roman plays follow Plutarch more closely than his English history plays do the CHRONICLES of HALL or HOLINSHED. Plutarch's collection of essays on miscellaneous subjects, the *Moralia*, was also influential in our period, notably on the establishment of the ESSAY form by MONTAIGNE.

Poet. In our period, this term denoted any creative writer, as had its Latin original *poeta,* not (as today) exclusively one who uses verse — as in the designation ORDINARY POET. 'Author' is often preferred to 'poet' in INDUCTIONS, EPILOGUES, and the like, and the *Oxford English Dictionary* contains no examples of the term 'dramatist' until 1678 or of 'play-wright' (for some time still hyphenated thus) until 1687.

Poetaster. A hack POET, or writer of indifferent plays or verse. The word was formed by the addition of the suffix '-aster', signifying incompleteness, rather than by the frequently-assumed ellision of 'poet' and 'taster': no element of plagiarism was therefore implied, but rather inadequacy or pretension in ART. Thus, when, in Jonson's play of 1601, the EPONYMOUS *Poetaster* Crispinus (supposedly a caricature of John Marston) is mocked for his 'crudities' — which he vomits up in a scene of splendid verbal purgation — he is actually advised to *study* the great poets with a view to their IMITATION in order to advance his cure.

Poetic Justice. Term coined in 1678 by the NEOCLASSICAL critic Thomas Rymer, to signify the supposed requirement that a play should have a morally appropriate ending, and so reward the virtuous and punish the wicked. Various of Shakespeare's plays were rewritten to secure 'poetic justice', which in critical usage thus has a much more specific sense than today's rather vague implication of 'getting one's just deserts'.

Poetics. See ARISTOTLE.

Poetomachia. See WAR OF THE THEATRES.

Policy. Although the present neutral sense of the term, signifying the pursuit of a conscious purpose in public affairs, was in use in our period, the discussion of 'policy' by MACHIAVELLI had led to the word also being taken to imply cunning and dissimulation in the unscrupulous advancement of political strategy or financial advantage — or, in the case of Marlowe's Barabas in *The Jew of Malta*, both. This ambiguity of senses is to be found as early as Nicholas Udall's MORAL INTERLUDE, *Respublica* (1553), in which one of the VICE figures disguises himself under the 'virtuous' name of 'Policy'.

Polis. Specifically, one of the city-states of Ancient Greece, and by extension the civic attributes and responsibilities thereof.

Poor Laws. Collective term for various statutes enacted during the sixteenth century, and amalgamated into the Poor Law Act of 1601. This was designed to make provision for the care of the 'deserving poor' (and the punishment of the supposedly undeserving), and had been made necessary by the ending under the REFORMATION of monastic charity and the more general decline in HOSPITALITY. Each PARISH was made responsible for its own poor, for which purpose the JUSTICES OF THE PEACE appointed 'overseers' — hence the concern that VAGRANTS and 'masterless men' (or, worst of all, pregnant women) should not be allowed to settle in a parish through which they passed, lest they added to its financial burden.

Popular School. Term sometimes used in modern criticism of the drama of our period to distinguish those dramatists who generally wrote for the PUBLIC THEATRES from those who wrote for the COTERIE or elite audiences of the PRIVATE THEATRES. Thus, playwrights such as Heywood, Dekker, Munday, and, of course, Shakespeare are usually regarded as belonging to the 'popular school'. But 'popular' in this usage — as by Alfred Harbage in his study of the RIVAL TRADITIONS — implies performances for heterogeneous or mixed audiences rather than exclusively for 'the common people', if regarded as synonymous with the working class.

Pox. Various diseases are characterized by 'pocks' or eruptive pustules, but *the* pox (or the great pox, or the French pox) was syphilis, or venereal diseases generally, of which there was a virtual epidemic during the JACOBEAN period. The symptoms are frequently alluded to in plays — as in Shakespeare's *Timon of Athens*, when the misanthropic protagonist, cursing harlots, mentions three of the commonest: aching bones, decay of the nose, and loss of hair. Like many sexually-related terms, the word 'pox' was also common as an imprecation — in plays, especially so after religious oaths had been forbidden as BLASPHEMY under the Act to Restrain ABUSES OF PLAYERS.

Predestination. The religious doctrine that all human beings are ordained from birth either to be saved (thus being among 'the elect') or damned for eternity. Although the doctrine had been formulated as early as the fourth century by St. Augustine, belief in predestination became a central tenet of CALVIN's form of PROTESTANT dogma, and of its English

PURITAN followers. Steadfast expression of one's belief might suggest a 'state of grace', as in JUSTIFICATION BY FAITH, but good works in themselves (or even sheer hard work, though it became a puritan characteristic) could not save a soul predestined for hell.

Prerogative. From the Latin, meaning a 'previous choice', and so, by extension, an 'established right' — but by our period usually indicative of the *royal* prerogative. This was later defined by the jurist Blackstone as 'the character and power which the sovereign hath over and above all other persons, in right of his regal dignity; and which, though part of the COMMON LAW of the country, is out of its ordinary course'. While such discretionary power, as employed by the Tudor monarchs, could work for the benefit of the ordinary people — for example, in curbing the excessive powers of the NOBILITY through enactments of the PRIVY COUNCIL and of 'prerogative courts' such as that of STAR CHAMBER — the early Stuarts used the royal prerogative to further their own absolutist ambitions, claiming the DIVINE RIGHT OF KINGS for its exercise. The royal prerogative, whose use was thus a factor in the events leading up to the civil wars, was severely limited (but not abolished, or even adequately defined) by the Bill of Rights of 1689 and the Act of Settlement of 1701.

Price Revolution. Term used by historians to describe the period of economic inflation throughout Europe during the sixteenth century. The causes of the inflation — felt at its worst in England, where prices rose by some 500 per cent — remains a matter of debate, some historians holding that the increase in the money-supply (largely through importations of gold and silver from South America) was responsible, others blaming an increase in population at a time when the supply of goods (especially foodstuffs) remained stable. Whatever the cause, it was indisputably the poorest who suffered most, as HOSPITALITY declined alongside the increase in prices, and faith in INTRINSIC VALUE became increasingly untenable.

Primogeniture. The right of inheritance, and of succession to the hereditary ranks of the NOBILITY, of the first-born legitimate son. One of the effects of this system was to produce a constant supply of impoverished younger brothers, whose frequent willingness in our period to trade their family name for the dowry of a MERCHANT's daughter contributed to some social mobility.

Primum Mobile. From the Latin, 'first mover', and so in the PTOLEMAIC SYSTEM of astronomy the furthermost of the heavenly SPHERES, which carried with it all the others.

Prince. Term used in our period to describe any sovereign ruler, whether of nation, dukedom, or principality, as in the titles of John Lydgate's *The Falls of Princes* (*c.* 1430) and, more crucially, in *Il principe* or *The Prince* by MACHIAVELLI. In England and FRANCE, in particular, a prince was increasingly held to rule by DIVINE RIGHT, as vice-regent to God, and although this was not the case in ITALY, many RENAISSANCE rulers there, such as the Medici, enjoyed a cultural and social influence out of all proportion to the extent of their political power.

Private Theatre.   Term used to distinguish one of the covered, indoor playhouses of our period (which thus required artificial LIGHTING) from the open-air PUBLIC THEATRES. Private theatres were at first the preserve of the CHILDREN'S COMPANIES, but the move of the King's Men to the Blackfriars as their winter quarters in 1609 anticipated other adult companies moving indoors. Although the supposedly COTERIE audiences of these theatres tended to be of a higher social class, this elitism was regulated by higher charges for admission rather than by any actual 'private' status, and the origin of the description is now uncertain. Possibly it derived from the end-on staging in such theatres, which resembled playing conditions in the private houses of wealthy citizens in which itinerant players had earlier performed. Other explanations include the wish of the managers of the boy companies to conceal their economic exploitation of their supposed pupils, or simply the hope that such a designation would permit them to claim the exemption from LICENSING restrictions allowed to 'private houses' in the domestic sense under the Act of 1572.

Privy Council.   Derived from the 'curia regis', or king's court, which had its origins in Norman times, the Privy Council by our period comprised an inner council of statesmen, officers of the royal household, and influential members of the COURT, numbering from twelve to fifteen during the reign of Elizabeth. It virtually constituted what would today be regarded as a form of 'cabinet GOVERNMENT', but without elected authority, although under Elizabeth most of its members were commoners. But whereas the Tudors were careful to provide an appearance of consultation with parliament, as with local interests, the Stuarts were (at best) untactful in their exercise of such PREROGATIVE power. The LORD CHAMBERLAIN was among the members of the Privy Council, in which capacity he was able both to exercise his legal control over the stage, and to defend it against the attacks of PURITANS and the CITY.

Problem Play.   A term coined in 1906 by F.S. Boas, to describe a group of Shakespeare's plays written in the early years of the seventeenth century, and now generally regarded as including *Troilus and Cressida*, *All's Well That Ends Well*, and *Measure for Measure*. Of these, the first defies any easy categorization by GENRE, while the last two, although

Profanity

apparently COMEDIES, seem to create unresolved moral ambiguities both of tone and in their 'resolutions'. Whether this is a 'problem' due to faulty workmanship, or reflects a deliberate wish by Shakespeare to 'break the form' of comedy, shifting the onus for judgement onto the audience by refusing the customary kind of CLOSURE, remains a matter of debate.

Profanity.   See ABUSES OF PLAYERS.

Progress.   A procession of the sovereign and his or her COURT to the houses of the NOBILITY or, on occasion, of suitably wealthy commoners, in various parts of the country. The royal progress originated in the medieval period as the only way (in the absence of modern forms of monetary dealing) of collecting the sovereign's feudal dues, in effect by consuming them in kind: but by the reign of Elizabeth the progress was also a way of impressing the royal *persona* upon her subjects, and of assessing their mood and grievances.

Prologue.   From the GREEK, meaning 'before speech', and in Ancient Greek drama indicating all that section of the play which preceded the first entrance of the CHORUS. Hence, an introductory section in any literary work, but during our period generally denoting the brief opening speech in a play of APOLOGY, EXPOSITION, or simple welcome. The responsible actor (in earlier times, sometimes the POET himself or his representative), who might assume the role of Chorus, would speak the prologue before the commencement of the play proper, though after the INDUCTION, if any. Shakespeare makes only intermittent use of the prologue, which went temporarily out of fashion during the JACOBEAN period in favour of the EPILOGUE — and so, like the DUMB-SHOW, is presented as somewhat old-fashioned in the play-within-the-play in *Hamlet* (*c*. 1601). The prologue to Gascoigne's *Supposes* (1566) is in prose, as are a number of others, and while the majority were in verse, the IAMBIC PENTAMETERS of the play proper were not always the chosen form. Bottom in *A Midsummer Night's Dream* thus ponders whether to have a prologue 'in eight and six' MEASURE or 'eight and eight'. A black velvet cloak was the usual COSTUME for the actor speaking the prologue.

Prompt-Book.   A transcript of the entire play, as approved for LICENSING by the MASTER OF THE REVELS. Plays sent for printing would sometimes be set from the prompt-book, which was entrusted to the safe keeping of the BOOK-KEEPER, who held it along with the PLOT of the play.

Prompter.   See BOOK-KEEPER.

Propriety.   See DECORUM.

Prosody.   General term for the craft and analysis of versification. Prosody describes and relates the various facets which together constitute poetic form: its MEASURE or meter (such as the PENTAMETER); its internal RHYTHM or pattern of STRESS (such as the IAMBIC); its RHYME-scheme (or in the case of BLANK VERSE the absence thereof); and its structure (whether in terms of stanza-pattern, the utilization of figures of RHETORIC, or, in the case of dramatic verse, such options as the alternating lines of DIALOGUE known as STICHOMYTHIA).

Protagonist.   From the GREEK, literally meaning 'first combatant', but used figuratively by ARISTOTLE to denote the 'chief actor'. In the dramatic festivals of Ancient Greece, this actor was as important in his own person (and for his right to choose the other two actors of the fully-developed form of Greek tragedy) as for the character he happened to be playing — rather like an actor-manager of the nineteenth or early-twentieth centuries. However, in NEOCLASSICAL and current usage, 'protagonist' denotes the chief character of a play, who may or may not be the 'hero'. Thus, in *The Merchant of Venice*, Antonio is given the EPONYMOUS role, but Shylock, while clearly not the 'hero' of the play, is arguably its true 'protagonist'. See also ANTAGONIST.

Protestant.   Term which originated in the description given to the followers of LUTHER who 'protested' against the decisions of the Diet of Speyer in 1529. It eventually came to embrace all those who supported the REFORMATION — in England, including both the supporters of the moderate settlement finalized in the Act of Supremacy of 1559, and the PURITANS who advocated more far-reaching reforms.

Ptolemaic System.   The belief derived from Ptolemy, the Ancient Alexandrian astronomer of the second century BC, that the earth was at the centre of the universe, encircled at ever-increasing distances by the heavenly SPHERES. Contrary to the conventional modern assumption, the placing of the earth at the centre of the universe, far from giving it primacy, put it — particularly in the context of the medieval belief in a CHAIN OF BEING — at the furthest distance from the PRIMUM MOBILE, thus making it, in the vivid image of the modern critic E.M.W. Tillyard, 'the cesspool of the universe, the repository of its grossest dregs'. In our period, the Ptolemaic system had not yet been displaced in the popular imagination by the Copernican system advanced in 1530.

Public Theatre.   Term used for the outdoor, galleried Elizabethan playhouses, distinguishing them from the indoor, covered, and artificially-lit PRIVATE THEATRES. Otherwise described as 'common playhouses', they were the preserve of the adult companies, who performed only in the public theatres until the King's Men took the 'private' house at Blackfriars for their winter seasons after 1609. The so-called POPULAR SCHOOL of dramatists wrote largely for the public theatres, whose supposedly more broadly-based audiences are also supposed by some scholars to have distinguished them from the COTERIE audiences of the private houses. Here, the cheapest part of the theatre (whose basic circular or hexagonal shape may have derived from that of the INN used by earlier itinerant players) was the uncovered YARD, where the GROUNDLINGS stood, while the galleries which surrounded the platform or APRON STAGE were provided, at a higher price, with seats as well as some protection from the weather. The single extant sketch from the period, by de Witt, brings into question the long-surviving belief of scholars in an INNER STAGE.

Punctuation.   Probably the most neglected aspect of the modern editing of plays of our period. While in most respects the tendency in critical editions is for greater faith to be placed in early authoritative texts, many editors still feel themselves free to 'modernize' the original punctuation, a practice they sometimes justify by the claim that it was imposed casually by printing-house compositors and so did not follow the FOUL-PAPERS, PROMPT-BOOK, or other authoritative copy. It is true that the punctuation of surviving original manuscripts is so light as to suggest that few printed texts could have real authority in this respect (Jonson's being the most notable exception), and that professional scribes making 'fair copies' seem to have followed their own inclinations. However, it should be remembered that even instinctively-imposed punctuation would probably have heeded the habits of spoken RHETORIC rather than of strict grammar, and so may be helpful in suggesting the units of speech and pauses customary in Elizabethan usage. The most frequent differences from modern practice are a more extensive use of colons, and of commas to indicate pauses where modern custom would require a full stop.

Purgatory.   The realm, intermediate between heaven and hell, in which the souls of the dead were supposed, in Catholic theology, to purge themselves of their earthly sins. Originating in the Jewish faith, and supposedly supported by certain references in the New Testament of the BIBLE, the 'Romish doctrine concerning purgatory' was condemned as 'repugnant to the Word of God' in the Articles of the Church of England (1562). Accordingly, a true PROTESTANT could only believe that GHOSTS emanated from hell, making doubts over the veracity of the claims of the Ghost in *Hamlet* a matter of real theological as well as dramatic importance.

Puritan.   A term, originally derogatory, first adopted in the 1560s to describe the extreme English PROTESTANTS who rejected the forms of worship established for the Church of England following the REFORMATION. While some puritans remained within the Anglican church, though still believing it to be over-dependent on ritual, others, such as the INDEPEN-DENTS, became 'dissenters', preferring to establish their own forms of worship, and also rejecting the leadership of bishops. Largely following the theological principles of John CALVIN, the English puritans became subject to persecution in the 1580s, and increasingly suspect to the authorities after the Martin MARPRELATE controversy. The acceptance by James I (as James VI of SCOTLAND) of the presbyterian church as established by John KNOX in Scotland gave the English puritans hopes of greater reforms when he came to the English throne in 1603, but the 'millenary petition' they presented to him was successful only in initiating the translation of the BIBLE which became known as the Authorised Version. Despite the exceptions claimed by the modern scholar Margot Heinemann, most puritans were strongly opposed to the theatre, which accordingly tended to be strongly opposed to puritans, who are frequently targets for its SATIRE — perhaps most memorably in Jonson's Zeal-of-the-Land Busy in *Bartholomew Fair*. In reality, most puritans were not such hypocrites as Jonson portrayed, but hard-working, upright CITIZENS, some of whom were wealthy MERCHANTS in the CITY of LONDON. The puritans were eventually (if temporarily) triumphant over the theatre, in securing their closure from 1642 until the Restoration in 1660.

Pyrrhic Foot. A verse FOOT of two unstressed syllables within the normal MEASURE of the line, also known as a *dibrach*. A 'pyrrhic foot' within the IAMBIC measure of the BLANK VERSE characteristic of our period would often be balanced by an adjacent foot of two stressed syllables (or SPONDEE).

Q

Quadrivium. The more advanced of the two medieval divisions of educational studies. The subjects of the supposedly more elementary TRIVIUM were regarded by traditionalists as the concern of the GRAMMAR SCHOOLS, while those of the *quadrivium* — arithmetic, geometry, astronomy, and music, all perceived as having to do with numbers — were the province of the UNIVERSITIES. However, during the RENAISSANCE there was dissatisfaction among HUMANIST scholars with this apparent emphasis on factual, 'real knowledge' as opposed to the forms of expression and evaluation which characterized the LITERAE HUMANIORES.

Quality. A term of various meanings during our period, including those still current today: but 'the quality' also signified the members of a profession or fraternity, especially the profession of PLAYING or ACTING.

Quarter Sessions. See JUSTICE OF THE PEACE.

Quarto. Not, strictly speaking, a particular size of book, but one made up of larger sheets folded twice, to form (from the Latin *quartus*) four leaves, and so eight pages. According to the dimensions of the original sheet, the actual size of a quarto volume was variable — from around eight to twelve inches in height, and from seven to ten inches in width. Since this was the format in which most individual editions of the plays of our period were published, the term 'quarto' is thus used generically to describe such editions — in Shakespeare's case, also to distinguish them from the collected edition of his works, in the larger-size format known as FOLIO.

Quatrain. Any verse stanza of four lines.

Quintessence. See ELEMENT.

Quorum. Literally, from the Latin, 'of whom', an abbreviation of the full phrase *quorum vos unum esse volumus*, 'of whom we wish that you be one'. Hence, the term indicated a person (or persons) whose presence was essential to make a meeting legal — in particular, during our period, for the more important cases to be tried before JUSTICES OF THE PEACE.

R

Realism. A term even more difficult to use with precision than NATURALISM, with which (just to add to the difficulty) it is sometimes used interchangeably. Historically, it has two almost opposite meanings, which, indeed, reflect opposing perceptions of 'reality' itself — first, in describing PLATO's belief, as reflected in the NEOPLATONISM of the RENAISSANCE, in the superior reality of ideal forms; and secondly, in asserting the objective and separate existence of the physical world, as distinct from any governing spiritual presence. In more general usage, the 'real' during our period signified something tangible and solid, a sense which persists in such a term as 'real estate' — but, again, this sense becomes confused by subjective differences over what *was* tangible, as, for example (in the matter of transubstantiation), whether the communion wafer and wine represented the 'real presence' of Christ. By the nineteenth century, 'realism' had taken on both its present more general sense, in opposition to 'idealism', and also its signification of certain forms of art (generally in opposition to the ROMANTIC) which sought accurately to reflect the human condition, often thereby (necessarily, in view of that condition during the nineteenth century) stressing its harsh and even 'sordid' elements. The essential difference between 'realism' in this usage and the closely-contemporary movement of naturalism lay in its less overtly 'scientific' approach, and so in its much reduced element of DETERMINISM. In the most general sense of the term, there is much 'realism' in Elizabethan and Jacobean drama and literature, though it is generally an incidental rather than essential quality, since no writer or critic of the time would have perceived the IMITATION of NATURE as involving a search for a precise mirror-image. Thus, in critical discussions relating to our period, 'realism' is probably a term best avoided: while acceptable descriptively and relatively (perhaps as the quality of a particular scene or nuance of characterization), it should never be sought prescriptively, as the criterion of a 'credibility' no writer at the time would have intended or thought desirable.

Recusant. From the Latin *recusare*, 'to refuse', the term is thus used to describe those who refused to attend the forms of worship of the Church of England — generally Roman Catholics, though an increasing number of PURITANS, notably the INDEPENDENTS, became recusants during our period. Shakespeare's father was included in a list of Stratford recusants of 1592, apparently because he feared being served 'process for debt' if he ventured out, and not from any Catholic sympathies.

Reformation. The breaking-away from the Roman Catholic (or 'universal') church which began as a formal movement early in the sixteenth century, under the impetus of the preaching of Martin LUTHER. Luther was, however, in part voicing concerns over forms of corruption in the church, in the critical spirit which had become widespread since traditional medieval SCHOLASTICISM began to give way before the HUMANIST consciousness. There was, for example, anxiety concerning the increasing worldliness of the papacy, and over weaknesses within the priesthood, varying from absenteeism, SIMONY, and PLURALISM, to a pervasive lack of true vocation. Attempts to stifle heresy by church institutions such as the INQUISITION only helped to heighten the resulting, widespread mood of anti-clericalism — which in English theatrical terms may be found in much of the FARCE of the earlier sixteenth century, as is a more positive assertion of PROTESTANT values in certain of the MORAL INTERLUDES. Luther was also concerned to eliminate many of the trappings of ritual, to assert the doctrine of JUSTIFICATION BY FAITH rather than by good works, and to make religious observance more a matter for the individual conscience, which required that the teachings of the BIBLE should become generally accessible in the VERNACULAR. Luther, together with John CALVIN (who laid greater stress on the doctrine of PREDESTINATION, and was the formative influence on the reformed Church of Scotland, under the leadership of John KNOX) and the Swiss reformer Zwingli, largely shaped the nature of the reformed churches of GERMANY, Scandinavia, Switzerland, and the Netherlands: but in England the Reformation took a more pragmatic course, inspired as much by the earlier teachings of John Wyclif and the Lollard movement (plus a considerable element of the sheer chauvinism of a developing NATION-STATE) as by the English humanists (who were not by any means always of a protestant persuasion) and the continental reformers. The issue of Henry VIII's divorce and remarriage thus probably served as catalyst rather than cause for the break with Rome which was eventually formalized in 1533. Apart from the permanent and marked economic impact — especially through the consequent changes in LAND usage — of the dissolution of the monasteries (1536-39), and the recognition of the sovereign as the head of the church, the intervening periods of greater reforming zeal under Edward VI and of the brief return to Rome under Mary meant that the eventual Anglican settlement (embodied in the Act of Supremacy of 1559) bore the hallmarks less of Henrician energy than of Elizabethan compromise. Its aim was at once to reconcile the nation and avoid over-antagonizing foreign powers: in the event, the increasing disaffection of the PURITANS, the focus for Catholic opposition provided by Mary Queen of Scots, and the open hostilities with SPAIN which followed her execution, saw neither aim completely fulfilled. However, the Elizabethan settlement remained the basis on which the Church of England was established throughout our period, despite the increasing religious and political polarization during the reigns of the less equipoised James I and his intermittently authoritarian son.

Regiment. The function and exercise of ruling power, especially through the SOVEREIGNTY of a PRINCE, as in the use of the word in the title of *The Monstrous Regiment of Women* (1558), by John KNOX.

Rejet. See ENJAMBMENT.

Renaissance. This term derives from the French, and literally means 'rebirth': it was coined only during the nineteenth century, in an attempt to encapsulate the new movements in the arts and thinking supposed to have spread westwards from their 'origins' in ITALY during the fourteenth or fifteenth centuries — though recent historians have pushed its beginnings back as far as the twelfth. The dangers of any such retrospective labelling (or dating) of so vast a concept were in this case compounded by the prevailing 'evolutionary' historical approach of the nineteenth century, and the belief, therefore, that the Renaissance was in significant ways *better than* the medieval period. By way of over-correction, some modern scholars, stressing what they believe to have remained constant in European thought, have gone a long way towards suggesting that the Renaissance was in many respects not even *different from* the centuries before. The limitations of both these extreme views should be borne in mind: yet the concept of the Renaissance remains of value as a shorthand way of expressing the impact of HUMANIST thought on literary and political developments, the importance of the 'rediscovery' of the CLASSICAL writings of Ancient Greece and Rome (in which PETRARCH was a moving force), and the shift in artistic values from the collective expression of a communal consciousness — as in the great medieval cathedrals, or in theatrical terms the corporate creation of the MYSTERY PLAYS — towards the expression of individuality found in the work of the great Renaissance artists, in the plays of the ELIZABETHAN and JACOBEAN age, or, for that matter, in the prevailing economic imperative towards capitalism. In the UNIVERSITIES, the primacy of the medieval QUADRIVIUM of advanced studies was increasingly being challenged by those who regarded the humanities, or LITERAE HUMANIORES, as of greater significance: and to all these factors may be added the major scientific advances of the time, ranging from the effects of the invention of gunpowder on warfare to that of printing on the advancement and dissemination of knowledge, or of the marine compass on the possibilities for exploration, colonization, and trade. The challenge to the PTOLEMAIC SYSTEM of astronomy, though of less immediate importance, was to prove even more devastating in its challenge to received ways of thinking, such as expressed in the concept of the CHAIN OF BEING. From the point of view of an English writer of the late-Elizabethan or Jacobean period, the impact of the Renaissance had come relatively late, and at a time when the religious divisions caused by the English REFORMATION, together with the pressures of economic individualism and the effects of the PRICE REVOLUTION, were causing new stresses within society. The Renaissance, then, is neither a definable 'movement' nor a clearly-marked time-span, but a convenient, retrospective label for a highly diverse set of events and shifting of moods, which together made the year 1400 (say) as clearly of the medieval period in England as the year 1600 (say) had become 'early-modern'.

Reported Text. In the BIBLIOGRAPHICAL CRITICISM of Shakespeare's plays, this term denotes one of up to six BAD QUARTO texts thought to have been derived from 'memorial reconstruction' of the plays by actors who had performed in them. The resulting texts, when compared with the FOLIO, or with 'good' quartos, may do less than proper justice to their author, but are often of interest for those differences which suggest how actors actually handled and spoke the works in performance, and for STAGE DIRECTIONS which may provide clues to contemporary production practice.

Revels, Master of the.   First appointed on a permanent basis in 1547, the Master of the Revels was the officer of the royal household who was directly responsible under the LORD CHAMBERLAIN for the staging of plays and other entertainments at COURT. These included actual 'revels', held traditionally from All Saints' Day (1 November) to the beginning of LENT (though generally restricted to the Christmas period during the reign of Elizabeth). Plays at court during this time included both MASQUES and works brought in by the professional companies. The powers of LICENSING plays for performance, given to the Master of the Revels in 1581, were extended during our period to include CENSORSHIP over the printing of their texts.

Revenge Play. A type of TRAGEDY, particularly popular during the earlier part of our period, in which a murder is avenged by a surviving father, son, or lover, often as much from an instinct of HONOUR as from a feeling of love or family piety. Although also found in the theatres of FRANCE and SPAIN, revenge plays in England were originally modelled on those of the Roman dramatist SENECA. The CONVENTIONS of the type were established as early as Kyd's *The Spanish Tragedy* (*c.* 1587) — a Ghost urging on the vengeance, a pretence of madness as DISGUISE for the revenger, and a long-delayed but bloody climax under cover of a MASQUE or DUMB-SHOW. Unlike Kyd, however, many later dramatists set revenge plays in ITALY, influenced by the popular TYPOLOGY of the Italian as prone to intrigues and long-hatched vendettas. The moral question of how far a revenger became tainted by his own action had become prominent by the JACOBEAN period, reflecting a wider moral debate on the conflict between the Mosaic code urging 'an eye for an eye' and the Christian injunction to leave vengeance to God. Marston's *The Malcontent* (*c*. 1603) is an example of what some critics have called a 'revenge comedy', conspicuous for universal forgiveness rather than all-round slaughter, while in the work of Webster the 'revenger' ceases to be the PROTAGONIST, and revenge itself becomes a yet more equivocal concept — a moral dilemma rather than a moral imperative. The blood still eventually shed in *Hamlet* may thus be contrasted with the warmed-over milk of human kindness which flowed as Beaumont and Fletcher responded to the new taste for TRAGI-COMEDY.

Reversal.   See PERIPETEIA.

Rhetoric.   From the Greek *rhetor*, a 'speaker in the assembly', and so a term used to describe the art of persuasion, both in the written word and the spoken (where it may be distinguished as 'oratory'). ARISTOTLE wrote his *Rhetoric* conscious from the first of the moral conflict between persuasion regarded as necessarily advancing the truth, and as an end in itself, in which deceptive techniques might be used to advance a good cause or a bad. Following the authority of such others among the ANCIENTS as Quintilian, Cicero, and Longinus, the subject became, together with LOGIC and grammar, part of the medieval TRIVIUM, while, as a linguistic art, rhetoric was no less a central concern for the HUMANISTS, as of the impulse to develop literatures in the VERNACULAR. Widespread illiteracy seems to have had the paradoxical effect of making audiences far more responsive than today's to the nuances of the spoken word: thus, in our period both SERMONS and DISPUTATIONS, as well as legal arguments, were enjoyed as much for their rhetorical qualities as their content. It is in this context that one should judge the so-called 'rhetorical' style of such plays as Kyd's *The Spanish Tragedy* or Marlowe's *Tamburlaine*, or the dramatic CONVENTION of the SET SPEECH — not for any lack of reciprocity (still less of REALISM) in the DIALOGUE, but for their quality of presenting well-developed and persuasive arguments. Although the terms used in rhetoric are often unfamiliar, the 'figures' or devices they describe can still be found in everyday speech or political debate.

Rhyme.   In its general sense, signifying a similarity of terminal sounds at the ends of verse lines — and present in the television jingle or the bawdy limerick as much as in poetry of a 'literary' kind — the meaning of 'rhyme' is clear enough. Defining why its use provides aesthetic satisfactions of so many different kinds is less so. Rhymes achieve quite distinct sorts of CLOSURE depending on their scheme: thus, the aa-bb-cc couplet-form is often self-contained (or purposefully almost disruptive if a run-on line or ENJAMBMENT is included), while the a-b-a-b form of many QUATRAINS is appropriate to a different kind of poetic development and expectation. In the drama of our period, the distinctive BLANK VERSE is, of course, unrhymed, making the occasional use of rhyme all the more noticeable — whether for emphatic purposes in SENTENTIAE, or climactic purposes as a TAG to a SCENE, or more organically, as (for example) in the frequent incidence of rhyming couplets in Shakespeare's *Richard II*. Here, examining the difference in dramatic purpose and effect between what has been called the 'sonances' of the HEROIC COUPLETS as opposed to the BLANK VERSE is a critical exercise surprisingly seldom undertaken.

Rhythm. The patterns of variation in syllabic STRESS, pitch, and resonance which occur in all dramatic (indeed, all spoken) language, whether in prose or verse. However, rhythm becomes more distinct and structured in dramatic poetry, being governed by its MEASURE, such as the IAMBIC pattern of syllabic stress, which, in the five-FOOT unit of line-length known as the PENTAMETER, constituted the BLANK VERSE which became the distinctive verse medium of the drama of our period.

Rival Traditions, The. Originating in the title of a book by Alfred Harbage, *Shakespeare and the Rival Traditions* (1952), this term has become a shorthand way of summing up Harbage's argument that writers like Shakespeare, Dekker, and Thomas Heywood were working as an essentially POPULAR SCHOOL of dramatists, in touch with the interests and needs of the ordinary people who comprised, however, only one part of the socially-mixed audience at the PUBLIC THEATRES, as opposed to the 'rival tradition' represented by writers like Middleton, Marston, Jonson, and Chapman, who largely (though not exclusively) wrote for the COTERIE audiences of the PRIVATE THEATRES — and whose plays more fully expressed the sense of dislocation prevalent in JACOBEAN society.

Romance. Deriving form the Old French *romanice*, meaning 'in the Romance language', and so used linguistically to distinguish work in the VERNACULAR rather than in LATIN. As a specific GENRE, 'romance' was a fictional narrative often concerned with themes of CHIVALRY and COURTLY LOVE — the three main 'matters' with which it dealt being classical legend, the Arthurian myth, and the age of Charlemagne. At first written largely in verse, by our period romances were often in prose, and had come to signify any tale of heroic or amorous adventures — normally among the higher ranks of society, as distinct from the FABLIAUX and

PICARESQUE tales of lower life. All, however, now found audiences among ordinary people, romances being especially popular in SPAIN until challenged by the BURLESQUE romance of Cervantes' *Don Quixote* (1605-12). As a 'tone of voice' rather than a genre, romance has been aptly described by the modern critic Frank Kermode as 'a mode of exhibiting the action of magical and moral laws in a version of human life so selective . . . as to obscure . . . the fact that in reality their force is intermittent'. In the drama of our period, 'romance' in this sense could describe plays of various kinds, from the anonymous COMEDY of 1598, *Mucedorus* (once ascribed to Shakespeare, but now consigned to the APOCRYPHA), many TRAGI-COMEDIES, and also the 'late plays' of Shakespeare. Beaumont's *The Knight of the Burning Pestle* (*c.* 1607) satirizes the conventions of romance, which by our period had, for the intelligentsia, derogatory connotations of the fanciful or absurd. Compare ROMANTIC, below.

Romantic. Although in one sense simply the adjectival form of ROMANCE, in the senses discussed above, this term came subsequently to be applied to the school of English poets of the late-eighteenth and early-nineteenth centuries, and to the literary approaches and attitudes of mind associated therewith. In this sense, the 'romantic' is to be distinguished from the CLASSICAL (more properly, NEOCLASSICAL) style of the earlier eighteenth century, and later from the more 'scientific' concerns of the movements known as REALISM and NATURALISM which arose to challenge it. Despite the illogicality of applying to Elizabethan and Jacobean writers a term concerned with a movement largely of nineteenth-century importance, the adjective 'romantic' is nonetheless sometimes to be found in critical terminology concerning our period: it may simply suggest a motif of 'love triumphant' in COMEDY, or (confusingly) be used in opposition to 'classic' as a (rather unsatisfactory) way of sub-dividing Shakespeare's work (notably his COMEDIES) by its supposed structure and SOURCES. It may (even more unsatisfactorily) also be used to distinguish spontaneous or 'inspirational' writing, such as Shakespeare's is often held to be, from that of writers such as Ben Jonson whose craft is ostensibly neoclassical, thus suggesting a 'romantic' freedom from the constraints of 'rules' or IMITATION in art. It may indicate a concern with the individual as opposed to his social context, or with NATURE and the 'noble savage' (not yet so elevated), as opposed to the 'urbane' values of the CITY and the COURT. 'Romantic' love may be opposed to physical or sexual, as in PLATONIC LOVE. Or 'romantic' may simply mean 'wildly extravagant' or 'impractical' — in which case, depending on the context, a landscape might be acceptably 'romantic', a political project only derisively so.

Round, Roundelay. Choral SONG, so designed that lines are taken up in succession by the singers, to form a kind of overlapping narrative. A version of 'Three Blind Mice', probably the best-known surviving 'round', was first published in 1609. The VICES in the MORALITY PLAY of *Mankind* (*c.* 1475) tempt the play's audience into singing a blasphemous CATCH , or comic 'round'.

Run-on Line.   See ENJAMBMENT.

S

Sackbut. Elizabethan name for the trombone. The sackbut was often used in combination with SHAWMS and cornets to form a small band.

St. James's Palace. This was built by Henry VIII on the northern side of St. James's Park, which the same monarch created as a nursery for his DEER. It was not until the reign of James I that formal gardens were laid out here. Although the COURT was on occasion held in the palace, and some MASQUES performed there, it did not become the principal royal residence in LONDON until after the destruction of WHITEHALL by fire in 1698, nor had the surrounding area been developed during our period into the fashionable district it was to become following the Restoration.

Satire, Satyr. Although these two terms are etymologically quite distinct, the Elizabethans wrongly believed that 'satire' derived from the GREEK 'satyr'. But this latter term signifies the mythological man-goat creature from which the 'satyr plays' of Ancient Greece derived their name, whereas the word 'satire' originated in the LATIN *satura*, a 'mixture' or 'medley' (like the herbal mix used to stuff a roast). It was thus applied in Ancient Rome to discursive poetic commentaries on contemporary manners and affairs, which later developed into a distinctive GENRE. The poet HORACE wrote satires that were relatively genial in attitude towards the life they described, whereas those of Juvenal were harshly critical of society: and this distinction between 'laughing' and 'lashing' satire has persisted. During the 1590s, satire had been largely a matter of poetic IMITATION of CLASSICAL models, but following the banning of such verse in 1599 satire became increasingly a dramatic mode, perhaps most notably in CITIZEN COMEDY. Even here, however, satire tended to be less topical and specific than in most of its present-day manifestations, and its writers were often recognizably in the conservative, COMPLAINT tradition of opposition to innovative social and economic trends. The modern critic G.K. Hunter thus aptly describes 'the standard satirist's vision of traditional good subverted to restless and baseless innovation'. Hunter was there referring to *The Malcontent* of Marston, which would have been regarded as a satire by contemporary audiences, although it is characterized more by sustained moral criticism than by wit — whereas in the plays of Jonson the comic tone prevails.

Scansion. In PROSODY, the description and analysis of the MEASURE,

RHYTHM, and RHYME-scheme of verse, according to its organization in syllables, metrical feet, and verse lines. Musical notation as well as the more familiar marks of accent such as the ICTUS can be useful when attempting to notate the scansion of dramatic BLANK VERSE, with 'rests' thus marking the relative lengths of the CAESURA.

Scene. Not only a unit of action within a play, as discussed under ACTS AND SCENES, but also a term sometimes used in our period to indicate either the TIRING-HOUSE, or the location of a particular play or episode thereof. The word was first used to describe the physical background to a play when the wings-and-shutters system facilitated such stage decoration during the Restoration period.

Schism. Term denoting a breakdown in the unity of the Catholic church, generally due to a political cause rather than on theological grounds. The 'great schism' — when rival political groupings elected their own popes in Rome and Avignon — lasted from 1378 to 1417, during which time a popular belief arose that no one would enter Paradise until the breach was healed. The term is not generally used to describe the fundamental, doctrinal divisions which occurred during the REFORMATION.

Scholasticism. A term used to describe the teaching of the SEVEN LIBERAL ARTS by the 'schoolmen' (*doctores scholastici*) of the medieval period, and so by extension often used to distinguish the thinking and methodology characteristic of the Middle Ages from the attitudes and approaches of the HUMANISTS during the RENAISSANCE. 'Scholasticism' derived from the teachings of the Christian fathers and the attempt to integrate into these the teachings of ARISTOTLE. In its attempts to systematize an unchanging world according to prediscovered rules, its debates were often limited to disputes over minute details of fact, interpretation, or method.

School Drama. Plays written for or performed by the boys of the GRAMMAR SCHOOLS, especially during the earlier part of our period, and so to be usefully distinguished (though not by all scholars) from the ACADEMIC DRAMA of the UNIVERSITIES. Originally played in LATIN, school drama was increasingly written in the VERNACULAR, and extant examples include the COMEDY *Ralph Roister Doister* (*c.* 1553), written by Nicholas Udall for the boys of Westminster School during his headmastership.

School of Night. Term, employed in Shakespeare's *Love's Labour's Lost*, supposedly describing a 'little Academe' of scholars and intellectuals led by Sir Walter Raleigh. Its members were said to include the dramatists Marlowe and Chapman. 'Night' referred to the hidden or obscure nature of the 'new PHILOSOPHY' they sought to uncover in the fields of science and religion.

Scotland. During the earlier part of our period a traditional enemy of England, but united with it following the accession of James VI of Scotland to the English throne, as James I, in 1603. Often in alliance with France against England, Scotland suffered a series of defeats during the fifteenth century, but became neutral following the final implementation of the REFORMATION in Scotland under John KNOX in 1560. The infant James VI came to the Scottish throne in 1567 following the abdication of his Catholic mother, Mary Queen of Scots, who then began her long and unhappy exile in England. English feelings towards the Scots remained equivocal, especially when James, at first welcomed to England when it became clear that his succession to Elizabeth would be undisputed, appeared to favour the followers he brought with him from Scotland (a joking reference to this was one of the causes of the imprisonment in 1605 of the collaborating dramatists in *Eastward Ho!*).

Scourge of God. A translation of the Latin *flagellum dei*, the attribution was apparently first given to Attila the Hun in the fifth century, and so by extension to any strong person who wreaks havoc upon those who have offended their maker. It is important that, as merely the instrument of divine displeasure, the 'scourge' need not himself be virtuous or, indeed, Christian: such, for example, was the popular view of Tamburlaine, as presented in Whetstone's *The English Mirror* (1586) and subsequently in Marlowe's play.

Semiology, Semiotics. Strictly, 'semeiology' (from the Greek, meaning 'knowledge of signs'), this term denotes the analytical study of SIGNS and sign-systems. The study of *processes* of signification and communication is sometimes distinguished as 'semiotics', though the two terms now tend to be used interchangeably. As an approach to theatrical performance (first attempted by the so-called 'Prague school' in the 1930s), semiology does not exclude a concern with language, recognized as one of the most important of sign-systems; but it emphasizes that as soon as words are *spoken*, especially within the conventionalized context of stage performance, so-called 'deictic' signifiers — such as 'this' or 'here' or 'now' — take on a weight quite absent from any they may carry on the printed page, while further systems of 'paralinguistic' signs (of pitch, volume, inflection, intonation) also and inescapably come into operation. No less, however, do other, *non-linguistic* codes of signification have their effects within the context of a theatrical performance — some familiar, such as the *scenographic* impact of the set and LIGHTING, some less often investigated, such as the *kinesic* (or gestural) and the *proxemic* (concerning the use of space and interactions between characters). A critical approach which takes into account such semiotic elements is not new — after all, ARISTOTLE was the first to acknowledge that music and spectacle were among the ingredients of TRAGEDY, while the DECORUM of NEOCLASSICAL dramatic theory insisted on appropriate forms of COSTUME, and eighteenth-century manuals of acting even tried to formulate precise rules for signifying emotions by means of facial expressions. However, in relation to the theatre of our period, semiotic analysis has largely to be limited to an investigation of what Umberto Eco has called the 'global semantic field' — that is, the way in which a play's language 'signifies' a model of its world — since there is little available evidence for a proper study of non-linguistic codes. Shakespeare's audiences, less fixated with the written word than we are today, would, however, almost certainly have been particularly responsive to signifiers with EMBLEMATIC associations, some of which, even when we are still able to recognize them, may now be difficult to convey (such as the importance and significance of coats of ARMS). In terms of the study of Elizabethan and Jacobean plays in present-day revivals, semiotic analysis certainly serves as a corrective to traditional 'literary' critical approaches: but its value is as servant rather than master, and no less than in STRUCTURALISM (with which it has common origins) can the misuse of its sometimes top-heavy terminology result in the mystification of what it purports to clarify. It is perhaps useful to bear in mind that semiology and semiotics are as much products of their cultural and historical moment as any other critical approaches, and should be utilized, warily but not ungratefully, in that light.

Seneca (4 BC–AD 65).   Roman playwright, who met his end — a suicide ordained by his former pupil Nero — with the STOICISM advocated in his own philosophical writings, and whose nine known works of TRAGEDY were probably not intended for performance. Of these, three were translated into English around 1560, and the remainder by 1581, but Seneca's work was also studied in the original LATIN, and used as a model for IMITATION in the SCHOOL and ACADEMIC DRAMA. Since relatively little was known about GREEK tragedy by the Elizabethans, Seneca's was the dominant CLASSICAL influence upon the drama of our period, particularly during its earlier years from *Gorboduc* (1561) to Kyd's *The Spanish Tragedy* (c. 1587) and Shakespeare's *Titus Andronicus* (c. 1592), and especially in the development of REVENGE tragedy (including the role of its GHOST). In general, the debt of the dramatists of our period to Seneca was felt more in such atmospheric matters as the emphasis upon bloodshed and violence, and in the use of devices of RHETORIC, including STICHOMYTHIA and the importance given to the SET SPEECH, rather than in matters of structure such as observance of the UNITIES and the formal division of plays into five ACTS.

Sennet. A fanfare of trumpet MUSIC often called for in the STAGE DIRECTIONS to the plays of our period, usually to mark the entrance of a royal personage.

Sententia (plural, *sententiae*). From the Latin, literally meaning an 'opinion' or 'judgement', as, indeed, in the continuing English usage of 'sentence' as a judicial decision. However, in literary usage a *sententia* or 'sentence' denotes a short moral maxim, appropriate for exemplary or illustrative use. Collections of such *sententiae* appeared as early as the twelfth century, when Peter Lombard compiled his *Four Books of Sentences*. By our period *sententiae* and similar EPIGRAMS were the stuff of COMMONPLACE BOOKS rather than of theological DISPUTATIONS. They are frequently to be found in plays in the form of proverbs, CLASSICAL quotations, or rhyming COUPLETS, often placed at the end of lengthy or SET SPEECHES, or as TAGS to an ACT or scene. In printed texts they are sometimes distinguished by italic type or by being enclosed in inverted commas — and were probably spoken by the actors also in a distinctive style, to denote that they served as a philosophical or moral comment upon the action rather than as an aspect of CHARACTER.

Sermon. An address on a divine subject given from the pulpit, market-cross, or other customary place. Since sermons, as an aspect of the Christian tradition, lacked CLASSICAL precedent, by the medieval period they had evolved their own rules and techniques — the *ars predicandi*, much advanced as a branch of the craft of RHETORIC by the 'preaching orders' of Dominicans and Franciscans. During our period they still had much popular appeal as well as value in EDUCATION — children at GRAMMAR SCHOOLS often being required to take notes on sermons, to be tested later on their subject matter. They were enjoyed, alongside DISPUTATIONS and plays, as much for their style as their content, and the poet and preacher John Donne, for example, was able to hold an audience at St. Paul's for two hours or more. With the development of printing, sermons were often collected into book form, and regularly dominated the output of published books as recorded in the STATIONERS' REGISTER.

Set Speech. Although this term is often loosely assigned to any dramatic speech which has a certain measure of self-containment, and seems to require an actor to depart from the reciprocity of DIALOGUE, the 'set speech' in the drama of our period (as also in its non-dramatic ROMANCES) had clear precedents in RHETORIC, and its importance was further emphasized by the use of the plays of SENECA as models for IMITATION. A 'set speech' might take the form of a retrospective report of past or offstage actions, a deliberation upon future plans, an APOSTROPHE to an absent or deceased person, or a reflection upon the speaker's own situation or state of mind. One of the major theatrical developments, according to the modern scholar Wolfgang Clemen, between the later ELIZABETHAN period on the one hand, and the mature Shakespearean and JACOBEAN periods on the other, was the way in which 'the formal set speech gradually becomes possessed of dramatic life', but was never displaced as a reflection of the audience's readiness to respond to the stylized and heightened definition of thought and feeling.

Seven Liberal Arts. Following ARISTOTLE, medieval scholars divided kinds of ART into the 'mechanical' and the 'liberal', the latter being concerned with brainwork rather than manual labour. The liberal arts were further divided into the elementary (hence 'trivial') TRIVIUM and the more advanced QUADRIVIUM. This division survived into our period, though HUMANISTS argued that greater understanding was to be derived from the 'humanities', or LITERAE HUMANIORES.

Severalty. Term used during our period for the supposedly progressive method of farming by means of ENCLOSURE.

Shadow. Term sometimes found to describe the roof over the projecting stage of the PUBLIC THEATRES. It was more commonly known as the HEAVENS. Figuratively, Shakespeare also refers to actors as 'shadows'.

Sharer. A member of one of the adult theatre companies of our period who was also a part-owner, and thus entitled to his 'share' of the profits. In Shakespeare's company, the King's Men, the sharers were also HOUSEKEEPERS, owning the theatre itself, but this was not the invariable practice. Compare HENSLOWE'S DIARY.

Shawm. Elizabethan form of oboe. Sometimes the name is used to distinguish the upper instruments, or HAUTBOYS, but it is also commonly used for the whole family.

Short Line. A line in BLANK VERSE of fewer than the normal five feet.

Shrovetide. The traditional period of CARNIVAL preceding LENT. See also HOLIDAY and APPRENTICE.

Sic. Latin term meaning 'so' or 'thus'. Usually italicized within square brackets [*sic*], it is used when a spelling, word, or phrase in a quoted extract might otherwise be thought to have been incorrectly transcribed.

Sign. Because of the relatively high rate of illiteracy in our period, shops and other businesses or trades normally declared themselves to their public by means of pictorial rather than written signboards — a custom of which the inn sign is the sole widespread reminder today. Title-pages of plays, sometimes reproduced in facsimile in modern editions, will thus often identify their publishers as to be found 'at the Angel in Paul's Churchyard' or the like. In Webster's INDUCTION to *The Malcontent* of Marston, one of the characters boasts that he can 'walk but once down by the Goldsmiths' Row in Cheap, take notice of the signs, and tell you them with a breath instantly', and while most Elizabethan audiences might not have been capable of quite such total recall, they would certainly have been accustomed to 'taking in', consciously or unconsciously, the barrage of visual signs, much as we do the mass of written information which confronts us everywhere today. This 'visual literacy' should be borne in mind when considering the audience response to such elements of the drama of our period as the DUMB-SHOW, the MASQUE, and even the very limited (and so all the more significant) stage furniture. This simple and recognizable sense of 'sign' connects with (and perhaps may help to demystify) its sense in SEMIOLOGY, where a 'sign' is, in Kier Elam's definition, 'a two-faced entity linking a material *vehicle* or *signifier* with a mental *concept* or *signified*'. To define that definition: a sign *stands for* something with a material existence, but by its intrinsic nature or qualities mediates our mental understanding of that object. On a stage, a throne thus becomes a *sign* rather than a *signifier*, since what is 'signified' is a whole range of ideas to do with sovereignty and hierarchy. The concept becomes more complex when one considers, for example, the multiplicity of what *could* be signified with extraordinary economy of means on the Elizabethan stage — a STAGE-POST thus a 'sign' which might represent 'itself', or the whole class of 'pillars', or a palisade, or a box-tree, or a wall to lean against, and so on.

Signature. The printed sheet which, when folded and cut, makes (for example) a section of four pages in a FOLIO or of eight pages in a QUARTO. To ensure the correct collation, or 'gathering', each page thus had its own 'signature', usually a combination of letters and numerals printed at its foot. Since these tended to be more accurate than the consecutive pagination (if any), page references to original editions of plays of our period (which usually lack ACT AND SCENE divisions) are often made according to their 'signature'. Contrast SIGNATURES, below.

Signatures, Doctrine of. The belief that the distinguishing features of a plant (its colouring, shape, etc.) indicated its appropriate use in herbal medicine. Thus, the yellow saffron was used for bilious attacks, while canterbury bells, being long-necked, were supposedly good for sore throats.

Similitude. Although today used in the general sense of a 'likeness' or

157

'simile', for the Elizabethans this was a term also synonymous with ALLEGORY, or parable, or any other exemplary kind of comparison.

Simony. Promotion to an ecclesiastical office in return for a financial reward. Simony was one of the abuses in church administration which led to the REFORMATION.

Slander. It is a generally-observed CONVENTION of the drama of our period that slander, no matter how improbable or unsubstantiated, is instantly believed — as Claudio is at once ready to think the worst of Hero in *Much Ado about Nothing*. Iago's slower-working insinuations in *Othello* thus reveal Othello as less rather than more gullible than would have been the audience's normal expectation.

Soliloquy. A speech by a character alone on stage (or an extended ASIDE in the presence of others) in which he expresses, often apparently taking the audience into his confidence, his private feelings, motives, or intentions. The soliloquy is rarely found in CLASSICAL drama, and the playwrights of our period were the first to establish it as an accepted CONVENTION: but its use by villains as well as by 'sympathetic' characters probably derives from the complicity with the audience of the VICE in the late-medieval MORALITY PLAYS, as much in the case of Richard III as in those of Marlowe's Barabas in *The Jew of Malta* or of Webster's Flamineo in *The White Devil*. In a play of heightened RHETORIC such as Marlowe's *Doctor Faustus*, the style of the soliloquies is less self-contained than are the clearly differentiated instances in, say, *Hamlet* or *Macbeth*. Soliloquies are to be found in COMEDY as well as in TRAGEDY, and perhaps the best-known occurrence in the HISTORY plays is the occasion in the First Part of *Henry IV* when Prince Hal declares his true feelings and intentions toward Falstaff and his Eastcheap cronies.

Song. An important element in the MUSIC of our period, songs were written either for unaccompanied performance, as in the case of the MADRIGAL, or (increasingly) for accompaniment by LUTE, as were the AIRS of John Dowland published in 1597. Much of the best poetry of the period was written for (or adaptable to) musical interpretation, and song formed a regular (though extraneous) element of the INTERVAL entertainment between the ACTS at the PRIVATE THEATRES. The use of song in the PUBLIC THEATRES seems to have depended as much upon the presence of a suitable performer in the company as upon its dramatic function. In Shakespeare's earlier work, the songs are largely confined to COMEDY, and often incidental, although later they are to be found used more consistently to organic effect, as in the case of Ophelia's songs in *Hamlet* (song often being used as a CONVENTION to signify madness) and those of the Fool in

King Lear (whose player, the CLOWN Robert Armin, was a noted musician). Some of Shakespeare's songs are original, while others are popular BALLADS or comic CATCHES, as found in *Twelfth Night*. Later, with the development of the MASQUE, song became an integral part of that entertainment. See also JIG.

Song School.   See PETTY SCHOOL.

Sonnet.   From the Italian *sonneto*, or 'little song', the sonnet was a short lyrical poem generally of fourteen lines in rhymed IAMBIC PENTAMETERS. Developed in Italy as early as the thirteenth century, the first great exponent of the sonnet was PETRARCH, who gave his name to one of its three basic forms, the others being the Spenserian and the Shakespearean. The sonnet was introduced into England by Wyatt and Surrey early in the sixteenth century, but became especially popular during the 1590s, when Shakespeare's sonnets (which generally took the form of three QUATRAINS and a closing COUPLET) are thought to have been written, though they were not published in full until 1609. The 'sonnet sequence' was extremely fashionable, and Numbers 1 to 126 of Shakespeare's thus form an apparently consecutive cycle addressed to (or about) a young man, while Numbers 127 to 152 concern the so-called 'Dark Lady'. Though often considered autobiographical, they need not necessarily have been so, such sequences often being written purely as literary exercises. With the JACOBEAN period, the sonnet form went out of fashion.

Soundings.   The trumpet-calls probably delivered from the hut above the TIRING-HOUSE in the PUBLIC THEATRES of our period. There were three 'soundings' at intervals of a few minutes before each performance.

Source.   The original material from which a play derives its plot, entirely invented plots being uncommon in the TRAGEDY of our period, though less so in COMEDY. Among Shakespeare's plays, only *Love's Labour's Lost*, *A Midsummer Night's Dream*, and *The Tempest* have no known sources, others of his works deriving variously from the CHRONICLE writings of PLUTARCH (for the Roman plays) and of HALL and HOLINSHED (for the English HISTORY plays), from FABLIAUX and Italian NOVELLE, from older plays, and from various originals in CLASSICAL literature, Chaucer, or contemporary writings. While elaborate studies have been made of Shakespeare's sources, they remain chiefly interesting for providing one of our few means of access to the dramatist's creative process — enabling us, for example, to consider whether he simplified his original or elaborated it, and how far he used the language as well as the raw material of his source.

Sovereignty.   The exercise of unrestrained power within the NATION

159

Spain

STATE. The term developed this specific and limited sense, as defined by Jean Bodin (1530-96), largely in response to the need felt in FRANCE for a power above the law which followed the period of disorder during the religious wars. Although the Stuart monarchs were attracted by this absolutist concept of sovereignty, and pushed their royal PREROGATIVE to its limits, it never successfully prevailed in England.

Spain. At the height of its political power and artistic achievement during the sixteenth century, Spain entered a period of slow decline in the seventeenth. To the English, Spain came to supplant France as the nation's 'natural' enemy following the death of Queen Mary in 1558, thanks not only to Spanish support for plots to restore England to the Catholic faith (mainly through the Jesuits), but also to the threat posed by her seafaring strength (and the wealth this had enabled her to win from her many conquests in the New World). Military conflict was precipitated by the revolt against Spanish rule in the Netherlands, which was both political in nature and a consequence of the PROTESTANT aspirations of the northern provinces under William of Orange, who declared their independence in 1587. Open war between England and Spain began in 1585, and was not formally concluded until 1605, although the defeat of the Spanish Armada by the English in 1588 reduced the immediate dangers, incidentally adding a sense of superiority (however accidentally created) to existing English chauvinism. Plays from Kyd's *The Spanish Tragedy* (*c.* 1587) to Middleton and Rowley's *The Changeling* (1622) reveal an impressionistic view of Spain, which seems to have been regarded as almost as suitable a setting for REVENGE tragedy as ITALY.

Spheres, Heavenly. The nine concentric divisions of the universe revolving around the earth in the medieval version still current during our period of the PTOLEMAIC SYSTEM of astronomy. These 'heavenly spheres' were the Moon, Mercury, Venus, the Sun, Mars, Jupiter, Saturn, the fixed stars, and, according to medieval theology, the PRIMUM MOBILE (beyond which some astronomers postulated a 'crystalline sphere', which was said to regulate the equinoxes). Medieval theology (and love of CORRE-SPONDENCES) held that each sphere was governed by one of the nine orders of angels. The 'music' or 'harmony' of the spheres was the theory formulated by the Ancient Greek scientist Pythagoras that, just as the pitch of notes depends on the rapidity of their vibration, so the differing velocities of the heavenly spheres must cause these to make sounds in their movement, in a harmony unheard by human ears.

Split Line. Term for a line of BLANK VERSE distributed between two or more characters, or interrupted by a pause for action, exit, or entrance, as specified in the STAGE DIRECTIONS.

Spondee. A verse MEASURE of two stressed syllables, derived from the Greek word for 'libation', since it was commonly used in the celebrations which accompanied such offerings to the gods. The occasional spondee found in BLANK VERSE has a slowing effect upon the delivery of the line.

Sprezzatura. A combination of cultivated nonchalance and easy contempt for vulgar opinion, supposedly affected by the ideal Elizabethan COURTIER. Shakespeare's description in *Coriolanus* of his EPONYMOUS character's 'noble carelessness' usefully evokes the quality.

Squire. See ESQUIRE.

Stage Directions. The instructions included in (or added to) the text of a play which specify ENTRANCES AND EXITS, and any other actions, sound effects, or MUSIC required. Today, dramatists often follow Bernard Shaw in composing very full stage directions by way of background, providing in the process almost novelistic descriptions of characters: but the printed texts of the plays of our period — even those of Ben Jonson, who was unusual in his personal oversight of his published plays — generally include only functional directions, and some of these may have been inserted by the BOOK-KEEPER rather than by the author. Shakespeare's stage directions tend to be fuller in such early plays as *Titus Andronicus* (*c.* 1592), written before he was working closely with a regular company, and again towards the end of his career, when he was probably sending his scripts from Stratford. Some directions, such as the frequent AS FROM (in 'as from hunting' or 'as from bed') raise questions as to CONVENTIONS of COSTUME or behaviour, others ('distracted', 'ravished') as to acting style, and yet others (WITHIN, 'above', 'thrust out', PASSING OVER) as to the structure of the playhouse. Good modern editions generally distinguish typographically between original stage directions and any clarificatory matter added by the editor: earlier editors were less scrupulous and often needlessly specific in providing such 'assistance', particularly in trying to deduce the whereabouts of SCENES which should remain unlocalized.

Stage-Keeper. The member of the staff or HIRELING of a theatre company whose job appears to have been that of general cleaning and maintenance.

Stage-Posts. The pillars at each side of the projecting stage of the PUBLIC THEATRES which supported the overhanging roof, or HEAVENS.

Star Chamber. Legally, the PRIVY COUNCIL sitting as a court of LAW, which became an important instrument of GOVERNMENT during the reign of Elizabeth. As a PREROGATIVE court, it was often supported by the common people as their only means of redress against over-mighty lords, but the early Stuarts were less tactful than Elizabeth in utilizing its powers to override the CIVIL and COMMON LAW (which it exercised, for example, in punishing the PURITAN William Prynne for a supposed slight in his HISTRIO-MASTIX against Queen Henrietta Maria for appearing in a MASQUE). The abolition of the Star Chamber was among the first acts of the Long Parliament in 1641.

State. Amongst a multiplicity of meanings, including that most common today as a synonym for the BODY POLITIC, this term for the Elizabethans would have signified in general usage a 'state of mind' or a person's social position (as in ESTATE) — and also, in specifically theatrical contexts, the throne used for royal characters (and indeed by the king's own person in MASQUES). It is now thought likely that this property was trundled or carried onto the stage, and was not always lowered from the HEAVENS, like the presumably more lightweight 'throne' in Marlowe's *Doctor Faustus*. The dais or 'scaffold' on which it is thought to have rested could also have been used alone when a simple variation of levels was required.

Stationers' Register. Under a decree of the STAR CHAMBER of 1586, any play (or other book) had to be entered in the register kept by the Stationers' Company (following its LICENSING by officials deputizing for the Archbishop of Canterbury or the Bishop of London). On payment of a small fee, copyright in the work was supposedly secured. The Stationers' Company enjoyed a MONOPOLY over printing and publishing, and, provided that a 'bookseller' was a member, the Company was not concerned how his copy of a play was secured — hence the relative lack of control over the PIRACY of popular texts, including the so-called BAD QUARTOS of Shakespeare. Some scholars believe that certain plays were entered as 'staying entries' — that is, by a sympathetic printer on behalf of a theatre company with no immediate plans for publication, but wishing to block a pirated edition. An entry in the register is thus no sure indication of a play's publication, or even of the date of plays which were eventually printed (*Troilus and Cressida*, for example, was entered in 1603 but not published until 1609), though an entry can sometimes give at least a terminal date when the year of composition is in doubt.

Stichomythia. From the GREEK term meaning 'talk by lines', and thus used to denote dramatic DIALOGUE rapidly alternating between characters. Often used by SENECA, it is marked by interrogations, antithesis, and repetition. Stichomythia is common in Shakespeare's earlier plays, notably *Love's Labour's Lost*, but is also to be found in later works, as for example in the opening of the interview with Gertrude in her chamber in *Hamlet*.

Stoicism. Originally a school of Ancient Greek PHILOSOPHY, which sought harmony with the divine will by abstention from human desires and the concerns of the outside world. In opposition to the stress of Epicurianism on the pleasures of the senses (pleasure being, however, defined as freedom from pain, not simply self-indulgence), stoicism was much in tune with the Roman sensibility, and is the underlying philosophy behind the plays of SENECA, whence its influence may be felt particularly in the REVENGE plays of our period.

Stress. The relative emphasis given to a word in a sentence or line of BLANK VERSE, where the IAMBIC combination (or 'stress-unit') of a short (or 'slack') syllable followed by a long 'stressed' (or accented) syllable is the norm. Patterns of stress in blank verse are, of course, often more complex than this, and the tension between the 'normal' stress implied by the MEASURE, the emphasis suggested by the meaning and context, and (especially for modern actors) the apparent 'grammatical' requirements, contributes to the interest and flexibility of blank verse as a mode of dramatic speech.

Structuralism. At its simplest, a 'structural' approach to a play or other work would imply the descriptive analysis of all those elements which contribute to the structure of a work, and their relationship to each other. Elaborating this procedure into the quasi-scientific pursuit of 'structuralism' implies, as Raymond Williams puts it, 'the sense not of a procedure or set of procedures but of an explanatory *system*'. Structuralism thus tends to shift the emphasis from the exploration of 'structure' as one of several ways through which a work may be examined, and towards 'structure' perceived as a self-sufficient area of enquiry, which may (indeed, must) properly exclude the processes of creation and reception. It thus diminishes the importance of what would traditionally be described as 'content' in favour of the complex internal relations within a work ('deep structure') which constitute its FORM — thus suggesting the attainment of an objectivity on the part of the 'structuralist' investigator which critics of few other predilections would dare claim. With roots similar to those of SEMIOLOGY, structuralism shares with it a deep mistrust of the connection between words and what they express: the words of a play are thus perceived as constituting not a unique and self-sufficient wholeness, a rhetorical version of a social reality, or the attempted simulation of emotional relationships, but a self-referring *structure*. Such an approach may on occasions be healthily corrective — for example, of the Bradleyan assumption that Shakespeare's plays give access to his mind, or, indeed, of any 'literary' critical approach which attempts to adduce a 'fixed' meaning or interpretation, since plays (of all literary works) are most demonstrably 'incomplete' outside the ever-changing circumstances of production.

Symbol

However, a structuralist approach, so far from accepting that a stage production seeks to render one among a multiplicity of meanings, logically denies 'meaning' to *any* production, perceiving it only as a set of internal relationships: in this respect, the acceptance by semioticians that words are only one among many modes of signification appears more positive and 'open' than the closed circle of structuralist analysis. It is perhaps worth stressing that structuralism is no less a product of its historical moment than such earlier critical emphases as the NEOCLASSICAL concern with PLOT and *outward* 'structure', or the romantic preoccupation with CHARACTER and inspired formlessness — which under the influence of Darwin and Freud led to the more 'scientific' movements of NATURALISM and REALISM, and subsequently to that quasi-psychoanalytic approach which is to be found in so much criticism of the earlier twentieth century. No less does structuralism reflect the tendency in sociology and technology to exclude (again in Raymond Williams's words) 'both producers and substantial products' in favour of 'their analytic reduction to the determining general relations'. The danger, as Williams continues, is of an analytical tool being mistaken for an objective test of 'truth' — which is, however, verifiable only on its own terms. The later developments of structuralism into DECONSTRUCTION and 'post-structuralism' go further in confronting the consequences of rejecting 'logocentric' (word-oriented) perspectives. The drudging lexicographer is ill-equipped to delve into the realms of indefinability thus opened up, beyond noting that they call into question not merely any and every literary, dramaturgical, or historical approach to a play, but the working premises of western civilization itself.

Symbol.   An object (or, in ALLEGORY, a quality), represented or described, which 'stands for' something other than itself. In literature, it may take the form of an IMAGE whose associations, in a particular context, suggest a parallel meaning — 'blood', for example, variously signifying sexual desire, ancestral connections, or violence, while diseases suggest various kinds of decay, or food different kinds of appetite. A symbol may draw on a traditional or folkloric 'language' — as in the DANCE OF DEATH, for example, or the use of the sun as suggestive of a god or godlike attributes — or, more rarely, it may be the original product of an individual sensibility. In an influential essay on *Macbeth*, the modern critic Cleanth Brooks envisaged Shakespeare as a 'symbolist poet': but such an approach typically assumes the leisurely *reading* of a play, rather than conditions of stage performance. Words themselves, of course, are 'symbols' for what they are intended to represent or express: but where no change in levels of reality is perceived in their use, they are preferably to be regarded as SIGNS in the sense used by practitioners of SEMIOLOGY. Visual 'signs', whether semiotic or hanging outside pubs, may be no less symbolic than verbal, in which case they are, properly, EMBLEMATIC.

T

Table-Book. Not a book 'for the table', but originally one made up of *tablets*, stiff sheets of ivory or waxed card, on which memoranda could be written. It was usually carried in the pocket, and so by our period 'table-book' was more or less synonymous with COMMONPLACE BOOK, as used by POETS and other collectors of 'commonplaces', EPIGRAMS, and SENTENTIAE.

Tabor. A small drum, usually played together with the three-holed pipe by a single performer — traditionally the CLOWN in the theatre companies of our period.

Tag, Tag Line. A term common in theatrical use since the eighteenth century to denote the last line, or concluding rhymed COUPLET, of an episode, SCENE, ACT, or completed play, employed both to effect the CLOSURE of that part of the action and to sum up its consequences or suggest a useful moral, often in the form of a SENTENTIA. It is used in this sense in modern critical writing on the plays of our period, and can also denote any pithy moral or proverbial saying, or the refrain to a set of verses.

Tarras. See UPPER STAGE.

Tavern. Aptly, in view of its descent from the Roman *taberna*, the tavern at first dealt mainly in wine, and even in our period its landlord continued to belong to the Company of Vintners. By contrast with the INN, the tavern was legally limited to supplying food and drink rather than accommodation, and was subject to various other restrictions. Thus, gaming and other forms of recreation and amusement were not allowed on the premises, and even 'tippling' was theoretically forbidden, as the prerogative of the lowlier ALEHOUSE — of which there were estimated to be over a thousand in LONDON in 1613, whereas an act of 1553 had limited the number of taverns to forty.

Tetralogy. From the GREEK, meaning a 'group of four', and so first applied to the TRILOGY of TRAGEDIES plus a SATYR play which constituted each playwright's submission for the prize awarded at the Ancient Greek festivals. In discussion of our period, the term is most familiarly applied to the two groups of Shakespeare's HISTORY plays — the three parts of

Henry VI plus *Richard III*; and *Richard II* plus the two parts of *Henry IV* and *Henry V*. These are usually known from their dates of composition as respectively the 'first' and 'second' tetralogies, although the chronological sequence of the events they portray is the reverse of this. Other 'tetralogies' exist from our period, notably that on CLASSICAL themes by Thomas Heywood, *The Golden Age*, *The Silver Age*, *The Brazen Age*, and *The Iron Age*.

Theatrum Mundi.   Literally, from the Latin, 'the theatre of the world', a familiar concept during the RENAISSANCE, suggesting that the world is a kind of theatrical representation in the mind of God. The theatre itself thus becomes microcosmic of this greater MACROCOSM, with God variously conceived as its 'playwright' or its 'audience', or both. The term was later applied to an even more microcosmic theatre, in describing the finale of travelling puppet-shows.

Theme.   This term, although often used loosely as synonymous with 'plot', more usefully distinguishes a guiding or underlying concern in a play, of which the plot may only be illustrative or exemplary.

Theophany.   Theological term for the appearance of a god, or the celebration thereof. It is sometimes found in critical usage to describe such an occurrence in a play.

Thirty-Nine Articles.   The set of religious doctrines which formed the basis of accepted belief in the Church of England. The Thirty-Nine Articles were formulated as such during the reign of Elizabeth I in 1571, following an earlier set of 'Forty-Two Articles' adopted in 1553. Although the articles finally rejected the sacrament of transubstantiation, certain tenets of PROTESTANT faith, such as PREDESTINATION, were dealt with more ambiguously. All clerics were required to affirm by oath their acceptance of the articles.

Throne.   See STATE.

Tireman.   A HIRELING of a theatrical company, whose duties included the supervision of COSTUMES and properties, and in the PRIVATE THEATRES the arrangement and renewal of the LIGHTING.

Tiring-House.   The actors' dressing and retiring room, now generally agreed to have been behind the stage. The stage may either have led directly off the tiring-house, or been accessed through an intervening corridor, off which the doors to the stage opened — so possibly constituting the much-debated INNER STAGE.

Tournament.   A form of single COMBAT on horseback, during which the opponents attempted to unseat or disarm each other by riding along opposite sides of a central barrier known as a 'tilt' —hence the phrase 'at full tilt'. A relic of CHIVALRY, the tournament — perhaps most famously celebrated on the FIELD OF THE CLOTH OF GOLD — enjoyed a revival under Elizabeth, though reduced largely to the form of an ALLEGORY in which the protagonists became Love, Honour, Albion, or somesuch, whose function was to defend the honour of the Queen, or GLORIANA. Two teams were usually opposed, as when Sir Philip Sidney played one of the Four Foster Children of Desire who attacked the Fortress of Perfect Beauty at the tournament of 1581 — held in the often-used setting of the open space before the Banqueting House in the COURT at WHITEHALL. Although James I preferred hunting DEER, his first-born son Prince Henry (d. 1612) developed the tournament as an elaborate form of spectacle, with Inigo Jones designing costumes and sets.

Town, The.   See WESTMINSTER.

Trade.   See MERCHANT.

Tragedy.   A dramatic GENRE which probably had its origins in a form of ritual sacrifice to the god Dionysus, and the accompanying celebratory hymn or *dithyramb,* but which by the fifth century BC had become formalized into a constituent part of the religio-theatrical festivities of Ancient Greece. ARISTOTLE spent much of the extant *Poetics* describing the nature, ingredients, plot, and qualities of the hero of tragedy, while NEOCLASSICAL critics, influenced by the stricter precepts of HORACE, tried to confine the form within narrow limits, particularly in regard to the adherence they stipulated to the so-called UNITIES. Sidney in the APOLOGY FOR POETRY advocated the observance of such rules by contemporary POETS: but most Elizabethan and Jacobean dramatists — influenced, though not prescriptively so, by SENECA — observed a more basic definition of the form, as concerned with the downfall of a PROTAGONIST, who might be good or bad or 'intermediate', and might or might not manifest a 'tragic flaw' or HAMARTIA. An early and distinctive sub-genre was the REVENGE PLAY, with its eventual bloodbath — but most tragedies of our period tended towards multiple climactic deaths, with some rightful inheritor or princeling left to anticipate an imminent restoration of order. (Whether or not there is potential for CATHARSIS in such climaxes is probably of more concern to present-day critics than it would here been to a contemporary audience eagerly anticipating the JIG.) Some critics have suggested that great tragedy is the product of a society in a state of painful transition: and it is certainly true that the medieval period, with its official certainty of Christian redemption, had little perception of what 'tragedy' might mean, while the eighteenth and nineteenth centuries — each certain in its own way of the security of the social order — produced little of interest in the form (although the 'bourgeois' or 'domestic' tragedy of the eighteenth century exerted an influence upon both melodrama and NATURALISM). Tragedy, as demonstrably 'serious' — despite the freedom with which dramatists of our period introduced elements of COMEDY or ROMANCE — has always attracted a greater share of critical attention than comedy, and it is therefore worth stressing the modern critic Muriel Bradbrook's calculation that comedies in our period actually outnumbered tragedies by around three to one. The extraordinary diversity of those that were produced — to consider only the best-remembered, the difference between the tragedies of Marlowe, Tourneur, Webster, and Middleton, not to mention the differences between *each* of the tragedies of Shakespeare — makes it very difficult to generalize about Elizabethan or Jacobean expectations of the form; and even its ostensible didactic function, as a theatrical version of the MIRROR FOR MAGISTRATES, was only perfunctorily fulfilled. There is little contemporary critical theory: Sidney's *Apology* was written too early to consider any but the most primitive attempts at the form, while Jonson's scattered remarks on tragedy are overshadowed by his failures as a practitioner. Perhaps we may only safely say that if comedy in part has to do with the problems of living and of perpetuating the species, tragedy deals with ways of understanding and so of accommodating death.

Tragi-Comedy. Although Sidney had inveighed in the APOLOGY FOR POETRY against the mixing of COMEDY with TRAGEDY into the 'mongrel' tragi-comedy, there were critically respectable precedents for this mixed or 'bastard' GENRE. The *Amphitryon* was described as a tragi-comedy by its author PLAUTUS, and more recently the Italian poet Guarini had defined tragi-comedy (in relation to his own *Il pastor fido* of *c.* 1585) as the blending of the PASTORAL tradition with the traditional BURLESQUE tone of the SATYR plays. Fletcher produced an English version of *Il pastor fido* as *The Faithful Shepherdess* (*c.* 1608), for which he offered the simple though tongue-in-cheek defence that a tragi-comedy 'is not so called in respect of mirth and killing, but in respect it wants deaths, which is enough to make it no tragedy, yet brings some near it, which is enough to make it no comedy'. Although this play marked the beginning of the vogue for tragi-comedy or ROMANCE, Fletcher's description would as aptly fit Marston's *The Malcontent* (1603) — but not so adequately the PROBLEM PLAYS of Shakespeare which have sometimes been so-described, although his later *The Winter's Tale* (*c.* 1610) is indeed tragi-comic in form. Scenes in otherwise 'pure' tragedy which nonetheless provoke laughter, often involving low-life characters, arguably offered a greater offence to the NEOCLASSICAL sense of DECORUM than does 'tragi-comedy', whose authors were, indeed, concerned to defend its distinctive generic 'rules' and precedents, rather than to assert 'artistic freedom' from formal constraints.

Tragic Flaw. See HAMARTIA.

Trap. Usually a trap-door was set towards the front of the projecting or APRON STAGE in the PUBLIC THEATRES, permitting access to the area beneath the stage — which was known as HELL by contrast with the HEAVENS above. An inventory in HENSLOWE'S DIARY contains a 'hell's mouth' presumably placed above the trap as an appropriately fearsome entrance to hell. Traps were also utilized in the PRIVATE THEATRES. The modern scholar T.J. King has calculated that of 276 plays examined between 1599 and 1642, 42 required a trap. A frequent function of the trap was to serve as an open grave, such as Ophelia's in *Hamlet*, into which at least Laertes was required to leap.

Traverse. Term used in STAGE DIRECTIONS to the plays of our period to denote a curtain. Whether this was a drawable stage curtain is not known, though this seems likely since the designation 'traverse' was also given to the painted curtains used in MASQUES.

Trilogy. Originally, the group of three TRAGEDIES entered for the dramatic festivals of Ancient Greece, which with the addition of a SATYR play completed each competitor's TETRALOGY. Only Aeschylus among the extant Greek tragic dramatists attempted to give a connecting THEME to his trilogies, but in criticism of the plays of our period some common element or continuity is usually denoted by the use of the term, the best-known trilogy being the three-part sequence of Shakespeare's *Henry VI* (which, however, becomes a 'tetralogy' if the historically-consecutive *Richard III* is included).

Trivium. The three supposedly more elementary (hence 'trivial') subjects — grammar, LOGIC, and RHETORIC — among the SEVEN LIBERAL ARTS of which the traditional educational syllabus was comprised. The 'trivium' was thus the basis of the GRAMMAR SCHOOL curriculum, while the subjects of the more advanced QUADRIVIUM were the concern of the UNIVERSITIES.

Trochee. A verse FOOT of two syllables, the first stressed and the second unstressed (*dum-di*). The trochee is thus the opposite of the normal IAMBIC foot (*di-dum*) of BLANK VERSE, with which, however, it was often combined, usually at the start of a line or immediately following the CAESURA. Perhaps Shakespeare's most daring line, from *King Lear*, is fully trochaic: 'Never, never, never, never, never' — the 'falling' effect here contrasting strongly with the 'rising' effect of the preceding, iambic STRESS of 'Thou'lt come no more'.

Tucket.   A FLOURISH or fanfare of trumpets, often required in the STAGE DIRECTIONS to plays of our period, and generally anticipating the entrance of royalty.

Tudor Myth.   Modern critical term denoting the interpretation during our period of recent English HISTORY, as in contemporary CHRONICLES, according to which the rise and eventual triumph of the House of Tudor was presented as redeeming England from centuries of conflict and civil war, thus healing the wounds caused by the usurpation and murder of Richard II. The two TETRALOGIES of Shakespeare's history plays cover this period in its entirety.

Typology.   Strictly, this term denotes the study of the symbolic representation of CHARACTER, and hence, in literary-critical usage, is often employed to describe the tendency for generalized attributes to be attached to certain kinds of fictional characters. DECORUM not only permitted but expected characters to be 'true to type' in the plays of our period — as when Bottom feels it sufficient definition of his role in the play-within-the-play in *A Midsummer Night's Dream* to enquire, 'What is Pyramus? A lover or a tyrant?' WOMEN were perhaps most subject to this kind of simplified presentation.

U

Ubi Sunt?   Latin expression, literally meaning 'where are they?', a proverbial reminder of the transitoriness of life and fame, and thus, allusively, a MEMENTO MORI. Critically, used to describe a literary or dramatic lamentation upon human MUTABILITY, of which early examples began with these words.

Unities.   It was a requirement of NEOCLASSICAL critics, largely following Castelvetro, that in the interests of VERISIMILITUDE drama should observe the 'three unities' of time, place, and ACTION. Of these, ARISTOTLE had mentioned that TRAGEDY normally confined itself to 'one revolution of the sun' merely by way of contrast with the duration of EPIC, while virtually ignoring place, and stipulating only unity of action. But the 'three unities' were widely observed by dramatists of the RENAISSANCE in ITALY and FRANCE — and largely ignored by the Spanish and English playwrights of our period. Thus, Shakespeare came close to observing them only in one of his earliest works, *The Comedy of Errors*, based on a plot from PLAUTUS, and again in one of his last, *The Tempest*. The 'three unities' should be distinguished from the broader concept of artistic unity, first defined by PLATO as the need for a work to have a coherent internal structure, free of EPISODIC distractions.

University.   Derived from the Latin *universitas,* meaning a GUILD or corporation, by our period a university had come to denote a formal association of scholars. Oxford and Cambridge, both dating from the twelfth century, were, after Salerno, Bologna, and Paris, among the earliest such foundations in Europe. Each of their constituent colleges (of which in both universities the number increased from ten to sixteen between 1500 and 1600) was governed by a Master (or Provost, Rector, etc.) and a council of Fellows. These colleges were loosely confederated into the degree-conferring body of the university itself, which had a politically-influential Chancellor at its head, and a Vice-Chancellor who dealt with day-to-day affairs. Students might enter the university as early as the age of fifteen to pursue the undergraduate course leading to the Bachelor of Arts: this was still based on the medieval TRIVIUM and, especially, the more advanced QUADRIVIUM, so that students supposedly progressed from a practical understanding of language (often completed at the GRAMMAR SCHOOLS) to the study of its uses as a medium of thought

(LOGIC) and of formal discourse (RHETORIC, of which poetry was considered one branch). An understanding of elements of PHILOSOPHY, based on the *Metaphysics, Ethics,* and *Politics* of ARISTOTLE, completed the course of studies, which also required participation in DISPUTATIONS both within the student's own college and in the university lecture halls, or 'schools'. To proceed to one of the higher faculties (LAW, Medicine, Music, and Theology), a graduate had first to obtain his MASTER's Degree, requiring a further three years of resident study and disputation. Thereafter, to obtain, for example, a Doctorate in Divinity could take nearly twenty years, though it was possible to obtain dispensations remitting part of the residency requirement. In Scotland, St. Andrews University was founded in 1411, Glasgow in 1453, Aberdeen in 1494, and Edinburgh in 1582, while Trinity College, Dublin, dates from 1591.

University Wits. Term used, at first somewhat disparagingly, by the professional players, to describe a group of dramatists writing in the late 1580s and early 1590s with the common attribute only of having attended one of the two UNIVERSITIES. The 'university wits' contributed in various ways to the final shift away from the older tradition of the INTERLUDES to the distinctive structures and forms of the later Elizabethan drama: among them, Nashe and Greene contributed to the development of Elizabethan COMEDY, while Marlowe and to a lesser extent Peele were (with the non-university man Kyd) instrumental in establishing BLANK VERSE as the distinctive medium of the drama. Though both men were also playwrights, Lyly had a strong but short-lived linguistic influence as creator of the fashion for EUPHUISM, while Lodge wrote the prose ROMANCE from which Shakespeare derived *As You Like It.* All were either dead or theatrically inactive by the time of the major regrouping of the companies which followed the PLAGUE closure of 1592-94.

Upper Stage. Either a purpose-built room above the main stage of the PUBLIC THEATRES of our period, or, more probably, a continuation of the first tier of the surrounding gallery, which might be used by the audience when the action of a play did not require an upper level. Contemporary STAGE DIRECTIONS require its use in various ways in some half of the surviving plays, and of the 28 such instances in Shakespeare, Andrew Gurr notes that upper-stage scenes average only 37 lines in length, and utilize a maximum of three characters, suggesting that only a limited area was available. It remains conjectural whether this 'upper stage' served also as a MUSIC room, or could be converted from a LORD'S ROOM, and there were doubtless variations between one theatre and another.

Usher. The assistant or vice-master in a GRAMMAR SCHOOL, who would also teach, as *abecedarius*, in any PETTY SCHOOL that was attached.

Usury. Still the term in use during our period for the loaning of money at interest, a practice long prohibited by the church as offensive to Christ's injunction to 'lend, hoping for nothing again', and frowned on by medieval SCHOLASTICISM as also outraging the dictum of ARISTOTLE that money, being a dead thing, could not breed. However, by the fourteenth century various expedients to circumvent the ban were already being practised by the increasingly influential European banking houses such as the Fuggers, based in Augsburg, to meet the requirements of MERCHANTS and others for capital. Thus, while 'usury' was still commonly associated with the communities of JEWS who had earlier been made dependent upon it for a livelihood, in practice Christian bankers proved altogether more usurious in their demands. During the REFORMATION, LUTHER continued to condemn usury, but it was justified by CALVIN. In England, a law of 1571 permitted interest of up to ten per cent, although this still left the lender liable to censure by the church. Both Marlowe's *The Jew of Malta* and Shakespeare's *The Merchant of Venice* deal with the consequent religious, social, and economic tensions, as do many other plays of our period, including the sub-GENRE of CITIZEN COMEDY.

Utopia. Although today taken to denote any ideal society or state, the term derives from the name given to one such specific state — Sir Thomas More's *Utopia* (1516), whose title was derived from the Greek *ou*, 'not' plus *topos*, 'place'. PLATO had created his own ideal state very much earlier in the *Republic*, and More's scheme was only the first of those formulated by early-modern writers. It proposed the abolition of private property, free education and medical care for all, religious tolerance, and limited labour, but its penal code was notably less in line with such 'liberal' thinking. It was not, however, altogether serious: utopian chamberpots were made of gold.

V

Vagrant. The legal description for any supposedly able-bodied vaga-
bond or wayfarer. Vagrants were grouped with 'rogues' and 'sturdy
beggars' to distinguish them from the more 'deserving' poor, who were
unable to work by reason of illness or age. While 'professional' vagrants
who preferred the hazardous lifestyle of the CONY-CATCHER and the BAWDY
BASKET undoubtedly existed, the prevailing official assumption that any fit
person might find employment if he chose drove many of the genuinely
unemployed into vagrancy as their only alternative to starvation. An act of
1547 enabled informants to enslave for two years any vagrants they turned
over to the JUSTICES, while any person willing to teach their children a
trade could seize such offspring without parental permission. Although
this act was repealed in 1550, a further statute of 1572 prescribed
whipping and piercing through the ear for a first offence, condemnation as
a felon for a second, and death for a third. This act also defined as
vagrants 'masterless men' without LAND, as also peddlers, tinkers,
jugglers, and minstrels. However, in also requiring that strolling players
must obtain noble PATRONAGE to avoid being viewed as vagrants, this act
contributed to the regularization of the theatrical profession by providing a
measure of security for those who did obtain such patronage. The
Elizabethan POOR LAWS, consolidated in 1598 and 1601, at last recognized
genuine unemployment, and placed responsibility for the care of the
'impotent poor' upon the PARISH: but those still condemned as vagrants
were subject to being whipped until bloody before being returned to their
places of birth.

Verisimilitude. Literally, 'likeness to truth'. Not to be confused with
later artistic attempts to achieve REALISM or NATURALISM, 'verisimilitude'
was rather more pedantically conceived during our period by the NEO-
CLASSICAL critics. Thus, Castelvetro advocated observance of the UNITY of
time because of the necessity for an audience to exercise its 'bodily
needs', while in his APOLOGY FOR POETRY Sidney ridiculed those plays in
which widely-dispersed geographical events all took place on the same
stage, because 'the player, when he cometh in, must ever begin with
telling where he is'. Such literal-minded (and entirely structural) insistence
on the 'unities' in pursuit of 'verisimilitude' shows, in fact, both a basic
failure to comprehend stage CONVENTIONS, and a quite unwarranted lack
of faith by educated men in the imaginative powers of a popular audience.

Vernacular.   From the LATIN, meaning 'native' or 'indigenous', this term is usually employed in describing the preferential use of one's own language in matters of education, literary creation, and scholarly debate, where traditionally LATIN had been used for such purposes — or, in England after the Conquest, the Norman French spoken at COURT and by all English kings down to Henry IV. A vernacular literature was well-established in Europe by the late-medieval period — perhaps most strongly in England, with its distinctive national tradition shaped by Chaucer, the Langland of *Piers Plowman*, and the poet of *The Pearl* — but it required the 'fixing' of linguistic usage to which the advent of printing in the second half of the fifteenth century gave impetus to make the writing of one generation assured of comprehension a few centuries later. The availability of the BIBLE in the vernacular was also a central demand of the PROTESTANT supporters of the REFORMATION.

Verse Measure.   See MEASURE.

Vice.   A perversely popular character, often a minor imp or devil, in the MORALITY PLAYS and INTERLUDES of the late-fifteenth and sixteenth centuries. He often accompanied the Devil himself, and specialized in 'tempting' the audience, with whom he often interacted directly. The three Vices in *Mankind* thus induce the audience into singing a CATCH which turns out to be obscene, and also into giving their money to see the Devil — situations full of interesting dramatic as well as moral ambiguity. The dramaturgical complexity associated with the Vice is carried over into our period in, for example, the complicity with the audience achieved through his SOLILOQUIES by Gloucester in *Richard III*.

Viol.   A type of stringed instrument popular in the Elizabethan period. Predecessors to the viola group, the instruments of the viol family were distinguished by their flat backs, greater number of strings (usually six), outward-curving bow, and other minor characteristics. A 'chest of viols' contained the complete set which constituted a CONSORT — two trebles, two tenors, and one or two basses. The bass viol, or viola da gamba, proved the longest surviving.

Virginal(s).   An early form of spinet or harpsichord, rectangular in shape, whose strings were plucked with a quill or plectrum. Its great popularity in our period was in part due to Queen Elizabeth's own skill as a performer, but the instrument was too muted in tone for theatrical use.

Virtù.   This quality might be defined as a combination of personal charisma or dynamic energy with a capacity for acquired learning, and was supposed to distinguish the true PRINCE who possessed it from his uneducated subjects, enabling him to take appropriate and effective political action. A quality distinctive to the HUMANIST sensibility, and turned to his own purposes by MACHIAVELLI, it had, however, also been honoured 'above all other virtues' in Ancient Rome, according to PLUTARCH: but it is by no means equivalent in meaning to 'virtue' in its present-day sense. Thus, Henry VIII undoubtedly exhibited *virtù*, but lacked many of the cardinal VIRTUES — notably fortitude, conceived as 'magnificence' or magnanimity. In the drama, the same might be said of Marlowe's Tamburlaine or Faustus.

Virtues, The Seven. Since the medieval relish for CORRESPONDENCES required seven virtues to set against the 'seven deadly sins', the Christian virtues of Faith, Hope, and Charity were added to the 'cardinal virtues' proposed by PLATO — Prudence, Justice, Fortitude, and Temperance.

Vulgaria. Schoolbooks containing English words and phrases, with LATIN translations appended, for use in GRAMMAR SCHOOLS. Hence, English is the 'vulgar tongue'.

W

Waits. Originally the watchmen of a town or city, who were traditionally skilled in MUSIC, especially the HAUTBOY.

War of the Theatres. A confusing and misleadingly-named affair, more aptly called the 'poetomachia' at the time, since it primarily concerned a dispute between POETS — that is, dramatists — rather than between playhouses (although the fact that it was conducted mainly in the PRIVATE THEATRES highlights the popularity of the CHILDREN'S COMPANIES around the beginning of the seventeenth century). Allegedly, a representation of Jonson by Marston in his *Histriomastix* began the affair, Jonson responding to this with an attack on Marston in his *Every Man out of His Humour* in 1599, and Marston returning to the fray with his *Jack Drum's Entertainment* of 1600. Jonson then added Dekker to his satirical targets in *Cynthia's Revels* and POETASTER, provoking Dekker to retaliate with his *Satiromastix*, all performed in 1601. It remains uncertain how far the grievances were genuine, and how far the 'war' was an experiment in the dramatic possibilities of SATIRE or even a worked-up publicity stunt to sustain interest in the private theatres and their playwrights: whatever the case, by 1604 Jonson and Marston were collaborating with Chapman on *Eastward Ho!* and Marston had fulsomely dedicated *The Malcontent* to his old 'enemy'.

Wardship. The power of the king or other guardian, descended from the feudal right of *custodia*, over the affairs of heirs who came into their inheritance as minors. The related right of *maritagium*, the disposal of royal wards in marriage (usually to the highest bidder, so long as he was of equal rank), was a particular abuse during our period, and was attacked by Jonson in *Bartholomew Fair* (1614).

Weak Ending. The use of a final unstressed syllable, or word not normally accented (a conjunction such as 'and' or 'but', or a preposition such as 'to' or 'of'), where the normal emphasis of an IAMBIC PENTAMETER would require a stress at the end of a line. Such a 'weak ending' almost invariably requires a running-on (or ENJAMBMENT) to the following line.

Westminster. District to the west of the CITY OF LONDON, deriving its name from the abbey church, as rebuilt there by Edward the Confessor, and from the nearby Palace of Westminster, the sovereign's original main residence in the capital. By our period, the Palace of Westminster had become the centre of GOVERNMENT and the adjacent (still surviving) Westminster Hall the seat of the LAW courts, while the nearby WHITEHALL PALACE was now the focus of COURT activity. Although often described as a city by virtue of these associations, Westminster did not in fact receive a charter and elect its own mayor until 1900, and during our period those areas of the present City of Westminster beyond the immediate precincts of the abbey and palace were subject to their own PARISH administration. While the consequent distinction between 'city' (the 'square mile' of the City of London itself) and 'town' (signifying the fashionable area of Westminster) was not common until the Restoration period, it may usefully be borne in mind, since the spread of the town houses of the NOBILITY westwards of the City along the Strand towards Whitehall, and the association of the City more exclusively with the trading and MERCHANT classes resident there, was already markedly apparent.

Wheel of Fortune. See FORTUNE.

Whitehall Palace. Largely laid out under Henry VIII, this rambling mixture of buildings, gardens, and sporting facilities spread from the northern end of the present Whitehall towards Charing Cross (the present Trafalgar Square), extending eastwards to the Thames and westwards towards ST. JAMES'S PALACE. Including in all some 2,000 rooms, Whitehall replaced WESTMINSTER as the main royal residence in the capital, and was thus the centre of COURT activity during our period, performances of plays being given in the Great Hall (on the site of the present Horse Guards Avenue). Plans for the elaborate rebuilding of Whitehall Palace were drawn up under James I, but only Inigo Jones's surviving Banqueting House — a setting for many MASQUES — was ever completed. The palace was largely destroyed by fire in 1697, when the court moved to ST. JAMES'S.

Wit. This is as difficult a word to define as it is to understand during our period, the more so since in modern critical usage its later, essentially comic associations are difficult to avoid, even if unintended. The word 'wit' is derived from the Old English *witan*, 'to know', and especially in the earlier Elizabethan period in some usages 'wit' continued to denote simply 'knowledge' — or, more particularly, the appropriate application or use of knowledge, through intelligence and a lively mind. By the later seventeenth century, 'wit' had come to have specific poetic associations, suggesting the dexterity of thought, or nice balance of imagination and sound judgement, needed for the turning of a CONCEIT. The term was thus undergoing a transition in meaning during our period: 'on the one hand', in L.G. Salingar's helpful summary, 'it came to signify high, inventive talent (*ingenium*), especially in literature', while on the other 'it was attached to mere displays of verbal ingenuity, with an intonation of jesting — or, in modern slang, one-upmanship': hence the WIT-COMBAT. Generally, 'wit' employed as an abstract concept was perhaps more likely to signify the first of these senses, while a *person* described as 'a wit' — as, for example, one of the UNIVERSITY WITS — was more likely to display 'wit' of the ingenious variety.

Wit-Combat. Term used to describe a conventionalized debate or argument in which facility with language or the employment of skill in RHETORIC was the predominant requirement. In real life, this might take the form of a DISPUTATION (a fairly informal scholarly exercise in the GRAMMAR SCHOOLS, but part of the requirement for a degree in the UNIVERSITIES), or simply those mock-disputes for superiority in WIT anecdotally attributed to the POETS who drank in the Mermaid Tavern, or to the 'Sons of Ben' (Jonson's group of disciples) at the Devil. Such 'wit-combats' are also to be found in the plays of our period, as in 'disputes' between the FOOL and other characters in various of Shakespeare's plays, or in such 'love-hate' relationships as that between Beatrice and Benedick in *Much Ado about Nothing*.

Witchcraft. This may usefully be distinguished from the practice of MAGIC by necromancers, whether fraudulent or self-deceiving, since witchcraft in most alleged cases was probably no more than the application of folkloric wisdom by 'cunning' (or knowledgeable) men and women of the countryside, whose largely herbal remedies almost certainly did far less harm than the 'cures' attempted by orthodox physicians. However, the attribution of blame for natural disasters as well as praise for natural (or naturally-assisted) cures led to such people being regarded as followers of BLACK rather than white magic, and consequently to their persecution. Such 'witch-hunting' increased greatly during the reign of James I (though it never reached the extremes found in some continental countries), as did the penalties for conviction. Elderly widows or spinsters guilty of nothing worse than the eccentricities of old age or loneliness also became suspect, especially if they enjoyed the companionship of a cat, dog, or other creature who might be suspected of being a 'familiar' sent by the devil — while those who needed to beg for their subsistence might even have found it useful to encourage speculation about their powers. Some actual devil-worship, or adherence to the 'old religion', may have survived, but evidence of covens, black sabbaths, and suchlike is conspicuously rare. The witches in *Macbeth* are in this respect less representative than the lonely, muddled old Mother Sawyer in *The Witch of Edmonton*, itself based on a witchcraft trial of 1621. See also DEMONOLOGY.

Within.   A STAGE DIRECTION, usually simply calling for MUSIC or some other aural effect to be heard, as from a distance or at least unseen.

Women.   In the theatre of our period the roles of younger women were always taken by BOY PLAYERS, though adult males may have played the more elderly or 'character' female roles. Mature women in their prime of life are relatively seldom to be found as prominent dramatic characters (Cleopatra and the Duchess of Malfi being among the notable exceptions), partly because of the greater difficulty of their being adequately impersonated by male actors, but also because the prevailing TYPOLOGY tended to present women as either young, desirable, and unmarried— or married, shrewish, and discontented. Again, these expectations are not invariably satisfied — Shakespeare, for example, giving us both an unmarried 'shrew' in *The Taming of the Shrew*, and a highly reasonable married woman in *The Comedy of Errors*. The role of women during the RENAISSANCE in general, and in English society during our period in particular, has been the subject of much recent exploration, and the proper subject of rigorous examination by feminist critics. That women were sexually, economically, and indeed in virtually every respect subordinate and subject to male domination cannot seriously be disputed — indeed, in many respects, their independence was even more restricted than during the later medieval period, when certain trades, such as brewing, had traditionally been respected as women's. Now, the female in WARDSHIP was perhaps the most completely enslaved, while only the widow of means could enjoy a relative degree of independence, especially if protected by the privileges of her late husband's GUILD. And while the PURITANS advocated a greater degree of equality in MARRIAGE, their leaders would have confined women to wifely duties: Martin LUTHER thus declared, 'let them bear children till they die of it; that is what they are for' — while for John KNOX all women were 'weak, frail, impatient, feeble, and foolish'. But if proper sympathy for such subordination, and for the related operation of the 'double standard', is not to be distorted into an unhistorical expectation that dramatists should have differed from the rest of the population by being more 'modern' in their attitudes, it becomes all the more noteworthy that, within the bounds of permitted expectation and CONVENTION, women as portrayed in the drama of the period often assert a considerable independence of spirit and of action. The major TRAGEDIES of two of the greatest JACOBEAN practitioners of the form, Webster and Middleton, are mainly concerned with female PROTAGONISTS, while from the early *Love's Labour's Lost* to the late TRAGI-COMEDY *The Winter's Tale*, Shakespeare often makes his women characters not only more sensible than the males, but chiefly instrumental in shaping the action.

Woodcut.   A term which describes both the usual form of illustration in an Elizabethan BROADSIDE, EMBLEM BOOK, or other piece of popular literature, and the technique whereby it was produced — literally, of cutting the design in reverse into a block of wood. Published plays were not generally illustrated in this way, except occasionally on their title-pages, in which case the woodcut becomes one of the rare pieces of ICONOGRAPHIC evidence concerning the theatre of our period. However, such evidence has to be treated with caution, since the artist may have been more concerned with an imaginative view of the 'story' than a representation of the play as performed.

Y

Yard. The area surrounding the raised platform stage of the PUBLIC THEATRES of our period, in which the GROUNDLINGS stood. Certain parts of the yard may on occasion have been reserved for the actors' use, as is suggested for example by the STAGE DIRECTION discussed under PASSING OVER.

Yeoman. Legally, a farmer who held LAND by FREEHOLD with a value of at least forty shillings a year. Often, such smallholdings had originated in the late medieval period, when a villein had been able to purchase for cash the commutation of his feudal services. By our period, however, the inflation of the PRICE REVOLUTION in combination with other factors made the yeoman's status less precisely definable. Overbury's CHARACTER of 'A Yeoman' in 1615 — which stresses his honesty and sturdy independence, pride in plain-living, and simple dressing — continues: 'though he be master, he says not to his servants, "go to the field", but "let us go".' However, John Earle's 'character' of 1628 emphasizes rather the yeoman's simplicity and lack of sophistication. In the drama, he is usually portrayed as content with his lot and fiercely proud of it, as is the blunt character of Old Carter in *The Witch of Edmonton*: but in reality the more successful yeoman would often aspire to GENTRY status (by 1703, he is being described simply as 'half farmer and half gentleman'), while the less fortunate declined to a new kind of servility as farm labourers.